The *Essential* Horticultural Business Handbook

Proven techniques, forms, and resources to make your small business more focused, organized ...and profitable!

Frank H. Crandall III

Frank H. Crandall III Horticultural Services

Published by Frank H. Crandall III Horticultural Services
P.O. Box 132, Wood River Junction, RI 02894

Crandall, Frank H. III.
    The Essential Horticultural Handbook: Proven Techniques, Forms, and Resources to Make Your Small Business More Focused, Organized...and Profitable!: Frank H. Crandall III – Wood River Junction, RI: Frank H. Crandall III Horticultural Services

        ISBN-13: 978-1456346850
        ISBN-10: 1456346857
        LC Control Number: 2010919516

1. Business planning. 2. Success in business. 3. Horticulture I. Title.

Cover and book design by Frank H. Crandall III and Elise A. Torello

Picture credits: Roland Gutierrez, Shane Photography, Warwick, RI, back cover and title page
                    Cover photo: University of Rhode Island Botanical Garden: The Kathy
                            Mallon Perennial Garden and Chet Clayton Rose Garden;
                            photo by Frank H. Crandall III

Printed in the United States of America by CreateSpace.

Acknowledgements

Writing, completing, and publishing a book takes a team effort; this book was no exception. Several individuals need to be recognized for their support, contributions, and guidance through this two-year process.

Ken Mazur, my good friend and confidante, gave me the confidence to proceed with my second book after he had performed numerous roles assisting with my first book.

My daughter, Heather Crandall, for typing my handwritten manuscript into the first draft of this book.

Sheryl Ellal, my former marketing director and bookkeeper, for creating and modifying some of the forms contained in this book.

Also, many thanks to those experts who contributed articles about their specialties: John Tickner, CPCU, Steve Brusini, Esq., Dave Nichols, Lynda Martel, Dr. Kimberly Stoner, and Terry Malaghan, C.P.A.

Lastly, I want to thank my fiancée, Elise Torello, for her tireless efforts to format, re-format, create charts and tables, type in changes, edit, and bring this handbook to reality. Her talents with various computer programs were essential to getting the book completed in a form that the printer could use. I am deeply indebted to Elise for her contributions and support.

Disclaimer

- Sample landscape companies used in this handbook are fictional, with no reference to companies which may have the same name.
- I have made every attempt to be accurate with figures, charts, calculations, and website information contained within this book. If there are errors, please contact Frank Crandall at FrankCrandall3@gmail.com.
- In adopting some of the estimate techniques, realize that you have to calculate your own expenses, overhead, and profit margins. The examples used are samples, not figures you should use for your own company.

<u>Dedication</u>

Because of her tremendous support and assistance in making this handbook possible and her unwavering love, I dedicate this book to Elise Ann Torello, my fiancée and life partner.

The Essential Horticultural Business Handbook
Table of Contents

List of Tables 5

List of Figures 6

Chapter 1: INTRODUCTION 9

Small Business Challenges 9

Resources to Help Organize Your Business 10

Wood River Evergreen's Experiences and Lessons Learned 10

Chapter 2: ESTABLISH A MISSION 13

Conceive a Purpose 13

Determine Strategies Needed to Implement the Mission 13

Seasonal vs. Year Round 15

Distribute the Mission 16

WRE Experience 17

Chapter 3: BUILD A BUSINESS PLAN 19

Why Create a Business Plan? 19

Components of a Business Plan 20

Safe Green LLC Business Plan 22

Uses for the Completed Plan 25

WRE Experience 26

Chapter 4: CREATE A STRONG BRAND 27

What is a Brand? 27

Elements of a Brand 28

Importance of Your Brand 29

WRE Experience 31

Chapter 5: BUSINESS MARKETING AND PROMOTION 33

Developing a Marketing Plan 33

Marketing Techniques 35

Classical Radio Ad Program 35

Invest in Public Relations 36

The Evans Mobil Phenomenon 38

WRE Experience 39

Chapter 6: COMPANY FINANCES 41

The Profit and Loss Statement 43

The Balance Sheet 44

Cash Flow Analysis 46

Accounts Receivable and Accounts Payable 48

WRE Experience 50

Chapter 7: BUDGET, CASH FLOW, AND RELATIONSHIPS WITH FINANICAL ADVISORS 51

Budget 51

Steps for Formulating a Budget 53

Seasonal Business Cash Flow 58

Relationships with Financial Advisors 59

WRE Experience 62

Chapter 8: COMPANY STRUCTURE, ORGANIZATION, AND LEGAL ENTITIES 63

Company Structure 63

Company Organization 65

Legal Entities 69

WRE Experience 74

Chapter 9: ATTRACTING, HIRING, RETAINING…AND FIRING EMPLOYEES 75

Ten Steps to Building a Winning Team 75

Firing Employees and Eliminating Negativity from your Team 89

WRE Experience 90

Chapter 10: EVALUATIONS FOR EMPLOYEES AND YOUR COMPANY 93

Components of the WRE Evaluation Program 93

Employee Evaluation Summary 100

Employee and Customer Evaluation of your Company 101

WRE Experience 103

Chapter 11: ESTIMATING FUNDAMENTALS 105

Estimating Preliminaries 105

WRE Experience 117

Chapter 12: IMPLEMENTING THE ESTIMATING FORMULA 119

The Overhead and Profit Method 119

The Retail Method 121

The Effect of Discounting on Profit Margins 125

Estimating Applications 126

WRE Experience 135

Chapter 13: THE WRE ESTIMATING PROGRAM AND JOB COSTING TO MEASURE PROFITABILITY 137

The WRE Estimating Program 137

Job Costing Program 148

WRE Experience 156

Chapter 14: INCREASE SALES TO IMPROVE PROFITABILITY 157

Ten Steps to Better Sales 157

Written Estimates, Contracts, and Change Orders 161

Sales Tips 163

WRE Experience 164

Chapter 15: LEADERSHIP WITH INTEGRITY 167

Definitions of Leadership 167

Leadership Qualities 168

Styles of Leadership 169

The Serving Leader 171

Integrity: A Leader's Compass 172

WRE Experience 173

Chapter 16: EMBRACING TECHNOLOGY TO IMPROVE EFFICIENCY AND PROFITABILITY 175

Benefits of Computerizing 175

Identify Tasks to Computerize 177

Change the Way You Work 179

Kinds of Software and Fundamental Applications 180

Five-Step Plan for Computerizing 182

Choosing Computer Hardware 183

WRE Experience 184

Chapter 17: MANAGEMENT TIPS FOR SUCCESS 187

Frank's Fifteen Management Tips for Success 188

Chapter 18: THE FUTURE OF SMALL HORTICULTURE BUSINESSES 199

Landscape Project Scenario: The year 2025 207

Future Horticultural Plans...208

In Conclusion 208

Chapter 19: EPILOGUE 211

Bibliography 215

Appendix A: Websites with Additional Information...221

Appendix B: Measurement, Conversion, and Equivalent Tables for Horticulturalists 227

Endnotes..235

List of Tables

Table 1: Twelve Possible Horticultural Business Niches 14

Table 2: Five Valuable Techniques for Using Public Relations Opportunities 36

Table 3: Safe Green, LLC Sample Job Levels 67

Table 4: Code of Behavior 86

Table 5: Sample Vehicle/Equipment Costs 110

Table 6: Sample Vehicle/Equipment Budget Form 112

Table 7: Safe Green, LLC Overhead Allocation Table 115

Table 8: Comparison of Overhead and Profit Method and Retail Method 122

Table 9: Sample Lawns Mowed on a Typical Day 126

Table 10: Compost Tea Applications Typical Billing Day 129

Table 11: Material Coverage Table 229

Table 12: Weight Conversion Table 230

Table 13: Materials Weight Table 230

Table 14: Volume Conversion Table 231

Table 15: Liquid Equivalent Table 232

Table 16: Markup vs. Gross Profit Margin 233

List of Figures

Figure 1: Sample Mission Statement 13

Figure 2: Safe Green, LLC Example Sales Graph 15

Figure 3: Wood River Evergreens, Inc. Mission Statement 17

Figure 4: Importance of Branding: Lynda C. Martel 30

Figure 5: Wood River Evergreens, Inc. Logo 32

Figure 6: Sample Press Release 37

Figure 7: Safe Green, LLC Profit & Loss January 1, 2008 through December 31, 2008 42

Figure 8: Safe Green, LLC Balance Sheet as of December 31, 2008 45

Figure 9: Cash Flow Analysis, Safe Green, LLC, January 1, 2008 - December 31, 2008 47

Figure 10: Sample Accounts Receivable 48

Figure 11: Sample Accounts Payable 49

Figure 12: Safe Green, LLC Budget: January 1, 2009 through December 31, 2009 52

Figure 13: Safe Green, LLC Gross Sales (Actual Sales 2008, Projections 2009) 55

Figure 14: Safe Green, LLC Combined 2008 Profit & Loss and 2009 Budget 56

Figure 15: Expert Advice on Loans and Financing 60

Figure 16: Expert Advice from a Certified Public Accountant 61

Figure 17: Safe Green, LLC Organizational Chart 65

Figure 18: Sample Job Description 68

Figure 19: Sample Landscape Services Contract 70

Figure 20: Legal Advice: Stephen M. Brusini, Esq. 71

Figure 21: Business Insurance Tips: John C. Tickner 73

Figure 22: Sample Application for Employment 78

Figure 23: Employee Handbooks: David Nichols, Human Resources Consultant 85

Figure 24: Job Performance Evaluation Score Sheet 95

Figure 25: Employee Self-Evaluation Form 97

Figure 26: Employer Evaluation Form 99

Figure 27: Job Satisfaction Survey Card 102

Figure 28: Sample Employee Labor Budget Form 106

Figure 29: Examples of Materials Cost Markup.. 109

Figure 30: Sample Formulas Calculating Overhead Recovery Percentage, Profit, and Gross Sales to Achieve Desired Profit.. 116

Figure 31: Overhead and Profit Method.. 120

Figure 32: The Retail Method.. 121

Figure 33: Sample Landscape Proposal.. 123

Figure 34: Sample Safe Green, LLC Estimates Using the Overhead & Profit Method and the Retail Method.. 124

Figure 35: The Effect of Discounting on Profit Margin.. 125

Figure 36: Lawn Mowing Estimate.. 126

Figure 37: Estimating Mulch and Costs for Landscape Beds.. 127

Figure 38: Compost Tea Application Estimate.. 128

Figure 39: Small Tree Pricing Example.. 130

Figure 40: Sample Landscape Maintenance Services Estimate Form..132

Figure 41: Customer Contact Information Sheet.. 139

Figure 42: Job Estimate Input Sheet.. 141

Figure 43: Sample Equipment, Trucking, Subcontractor, and Labor Rates.. 145

Figure 44: Financial Summary Sheet.. 146

Figure 45: Plant Picking Ticket.. 147

Figure 46: Construction Services Job Report.. 149

Figure 47: Maintenance Services Job Report.. 151

Figure 48: Estimated Job Cost Spreadsheet.. 153

Figure 49: Actual Job Cost Spreadsheet.. 154

Figure 50: Job Costing Summary Sheet.. 155

Figure 51: WRE's Guarantee.. 162

Figure 52: Traditional and "Serving Leader" Organizational Models.. 172

Chapter 1: INTRODUCTION

Since I began my landscape business over 38 years ago I have experienced the joys and heartaches of owning my own company. In my first book, "Lessons from the Landscape: My Path to Business Success and Personal Fulfillment," I traced the successes and shortcomings my landscape design, construction, and maintenance firm faced along with my personal challenges, growth, and experiences. Running a business can be difficult, and even more so without an effective plan, helpful resources, and specific forms, formulas, and features to organize your business for success. Throughout the years I have certainly made my share of mistakes while incorporating the lessons I've learned to make my company stronger, efficient, and more profitable.

One resource that would have been extremely valuable to me throughout the life of my business is a detailed horticultural business handbook. Ideally, this handbook would have contained information about business planning, marketing tips, branding, company finances, hiring and firing employees, evaluating employees, estimating and job costing, sales techniques, computerizing, management tips, and experiences from an actual landscape company.

Therein lies the purpose of this book: a horticultural business handbook that new and established companies can use to plan, grow, transition, and improve their firm's success, profit margin, and organization. I don't pretend to have all the answers, but with many years of experiences I can provide insights that could be valuable for new, established, or struggling horticultural businesses.

Besides providing specific resources, charts, proven forms, and formulas, the horticultural handbook will feature my business's (Wood River Evergreens, Inc. (WRE)) experiences and lessons learned at the end of each chapter. Hopefully, horticultural companies can identify with a landscape firm that has faced many of the challenges they have experienced, and benefit from specific recommendations for implementation of possible solutions.

Ours is an exciting, rewarding, and at times precarious profession with new challenges appearing all the time. This horticultural handbook's main purpose is to share resources, forms, and experiences with horticultural firms looking to improve their operations, better organize their company, and increase their profit margins.

Small Business Challenges

I could fill several chapters listing all the challenges small businesses are experiencing, but will settle for listing some of the major ones facing each of us today:

1. A stagnant economy

2. Increased cost of liability and vehicle insurance, health insurance, and taxes
3. Rising prices of supplies, new equipment, and vehicles
4. Volatility of fuel costs
5. Local, state, and federal regulations: environment, pesticides, zoning, wages, Occupational Safety and Health Administration (OSHA), highway inspections, horticultural licenses and certifications
6. Difficulty finding sources of motivated, dependable and skilled labor
7. Reduced access to financing: loans, credit lines, and credit cards
8. Effects of weather on our nursery crops, garden center sales, and maintenance schedules
9. The difficulty of running a seasonal business with limited income in the winter months
10. Maintaining profitability and year round cash flow

Resources to Help Organize Your Business

One of the main features of this handbook is to include information on numerous small-business topics in one publication. A wide range of topics including business planning, marketing, estimating and job costing, business finances, employee hiring and firing, and computerizing your company are included in this book. Additionally, the appendix contains many state, local, and university websites and departments to gain additional information. The bibliography includes sources of specific in-depth business advice and suggestions. Each chapter will contain proven horticultural business forms, including daily work sheets, employee evaluation forms, and detailed estimating forms–ready for implementation in your business.

The main goal of this book is to provide you with up-to-date, valuable information, which you can immediately adapt to your business to solve problems, better organize your company and chart a path for increased productivity and profit.

Wood River Evergreen's Experiences and Lessons Learned

Over the last 38 years I have developed, borrowed, and improved on numerous business organization ideas, methods, forms, techniques, and formulas, most of which are included in this handbook. Feel free to use, change, or adapt any of these that will work for you. I have been in business for years, but continue to revise my forms each year to better serve my organization.

One of the key lessons I have learned is that operating a small business is an organic process. Processes that worked 15 years ago need to be revamped now. Markets that served me well for many years now have dwindled with new markets emerging. Change is the one constant I can report to you! Learn to anticipate change, embrace it, and make plans for an evolving future in the horticultural field. In each chapter I will explain my business experiences with the specific topic covered and highlight my lessons learned. Hopefully this practical feature will make the topic more real and ultimately save you from making the same mistakes I did.

Essential Points:

1. New and established companies can use this horticultural business handbook to improve their firm's success, profit margin, and organization.

2. Small businesses are facing numerous challenges including a stagnant economy, rising prices, volatile fuel costs, difficulty in finding skilled labor, reduced access to financing, weather effects, and maintaining year-round cash flow.

3. Operating a small business is an organic process. Change is the one constant!

Chapter 2: ESTABLISH A MISSION

Conceive a Purpose

The most important first step in creating (or refining) a business is to clearly state your company's purpose or vision. What are your objectives, expectations, and aspirations? Writing down the components of your business vision into a mission statement will set the tone for all the strategies needed to implement this vision. Without a clear purpose, how will you (and your employees, customers, and banker) know where you are going and how to devise a plan to get there? Having passion, talent, and confidence are essential characteristics for a horticultural business owner but they are not enough. Writing down your vision and sharing it with employees, clients, and a professional support team is necessary for your success.

I knew from the first day I began my full-time landscape business in 1985 (after operating WRE part-time since 1972) that I wanted a full-service company offering clients in southern Rhode Island and southeastern Connecticut landscape design, construction, and maintenance services including masonry, carpentry, and landscape lighting. However, it wasn't until I actually wrote down my vision in 1995 and shared it with my employees that my mission was fully understood, embraced, and implemented. Having a vision for you and your business is critical, but the sooner you write down your intentions, goals, and aspirations the sooner they will become reality.

Throughout this handbook, I will illustrate points using a model company I call "Safe Green LLC." Figure 1 shows Safe Green LLC's mission statement.

Safe Green LLC Mission Statement

Safe Green LLC is a 5-year old landscape company specializing in lawn care and property maintenance. The company is dedicated to providing earth-friendly products and services to consumers living in coastal Rhode Island communities. Our customers are seeking to improve the quality and health of their landscapes through the use of 100% organic products and services with low or no impact on their watershed properties.

Figure 1: Sample Mission Statement

Determine Strategies Needed to Implement the Mission

In today's business climate it is essential to have strategies that will accent your unique selling proposition. What are the special services, products, or talents your business has which no one else does? From the beginning of my landscape career I have worked on coastal properties in southern Rhode Island and southeastern Connecticut. Over the years our company has become expert with the special conditions of coastal landscapes: salt-, wind-, and drought-tolerant plants; coastal lawn seed mixes; protective maintenance for exposed plants; Coastal Resources Management Council (CRMC) coastal regulations; recently developed organic techniques; and products to minimize fertilizer and pesticide runoff. This coastal landscape niche strategy has worked well matching our strengths and expertise with coastal property owners who appreciate knowledgeable personnel working on their valuable properties.

After you survey the market and analyze the competition for your horticultural business, you can determine which niche will work best for you (Table 1).

Table 1: Twelve Possible Horticultural Business Niches

• Residential or commercial maintenance	• Raising organic annuals, perennials, or trees and shrubs
• Landscape design or landscape architecture	• Landscape construction (residential or commercial)
• Arborist/tree work	• Landscape lighting
• Wholesale or retail nursery	• Masonry and hardscapes
• Garden center	• Plant health care
• Ponds and water features	• Lawn care (organic or traditional)

Part of your strategy should be to objectively look at your strengths, passions, talents…and weaknesses. Try to match your interests with the major focus of your business. If you really enjoy building walls and patios, make hardscapes a specialty niche of your company. Inevitably you will be asked to plant beds around the patio and possibly install landscape lighting or a small water feature. Find qualified companies that can serve as subcontractors to help expand your service offerings, which will go a long ways toward creating satisfied clients.

Remember that when you first start your company, and even years later when your business has grown, you are the face of the company. Your style, personality, and communication skills are helpful to market your business and to keep your team motivated and focused.

In developing your strategy to implement your mission, carefully choose a demographic group that has a need for your services and will be willing to pay for those services. For us, the coastal communities fit our profile for needing coastal landscape services and are in a position to afford them–even in difficult economic times.

Your geographic service region should include areas that are a reasonable travel distance from your business location. When I first began WRE, I serviced a much wider area than I do today. With satisfied clients in a particular area, referrals will be your lifeblood. Although 90% of our work is along the southern New England coast, I have found that from year to year the number of projects changes from community to community, depending on how much building and renovating is occurring.

Once you have a geographic area that works for you, treat it like gold! Referrals will allow you to grow, but unsatisfied clients will soon have you searching for other new areas in which to work.

Seasonal vs. Year Round

No aspect of running a business has provided more consternation to me than the seasonal nature of our landscape design, construction, and maintenance firm. Like most horticultural businesses, the vast majority of income is earned between April and December, with the winter months showing minimal cash flow. I find that the work running the landscape business is year-round, but the income is seasonal (Figure 2)! Tips to help manage seasonal cash flow are covered in Chapter 7.

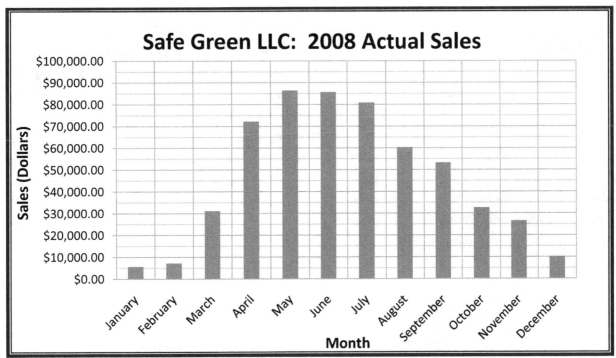

Figure 2: Safe Green, LLC Example Sales Graph

Many maintenance and landscape firms supplement their off-season income with snow plowing and sanding services. From year to year it is impossible to predict how much snow there will be, which is why not all landscape firms offer this service. The winter months are a great time to finalize landscape designs and other projects for the spring. One huge advantage of having slower winter months is that it gives horticultural businesses an opportunity to review the past year, evaluate their operation, and make changes to improve their company. As the economy fluctuates, competition increases, and industry conditions evolve, it is even more important to identify change, make adjustments, and move into the future with revisions that will work for your firm. The off-season is a great time to review your mission, make any adjustments, and plan strategies for the upcoming year.

Distribute the Mission

If you have a clear vision of what type of company you want but it is "all in your head," you need to write it down. Once on paper the next step is to share it with your employees (who will help implement it) your clients (who will purchase your services) and your financial advisors (who will help finance your vision). Everyone likes to know where they are headed, and will work diligently to get there if the goals are clear and well known.

Besides being posted in your place of business for employees and clients to see, the mission statement should be in your company handbook and in your business plan (discussed in Chapter 3). As your business grows, an employee handbook will become necessary. Employment issues, status and records, benefit programs, payroll, work conditions, leaves of absence, employee conduct, disciplinary action, and termination, as well as non-competition, non-solicitation, and confidentiality agreements are important for the employees, the employer, and other interested parties like insurance companies, bankers, and potentially lawyers.

In 2004 we hired a human resources consultant, Dave Nichols, to help revise our handbook and to make sure it met the latest legal requirements. The money we spent on revising the handbook was well worth it. Insurance companies and bankers have been impressed with the completeness of the handbook. Several potential legal situations involving employees have been avoided because of the handbook, which each employee signs every year (see Chapter 9 for more information about employee handbooks).

<u>Wood River Evergreens, Inc. Mission Statement</u>

Wood River Evergreens, Inc. is dedicated to providing award-winning landscape design, installation, lighting, and maintenance solutions to customers in Rhode Island and southeastern Connecticut who wish to enhance the beauty, value, safety, and health of their seaside and coastal landscapes.
Eco-friendly techniques will be our primary methods of landscaping.

Our customers will always come first. We know that their satisfaction is directly connected to our long-term success. We will treat each client with respect and courtesy, perform each job with integrity, and deliver the utmost in quality--consistently.

Figure 3: Wood River Evergreens, Inc. Mission Statement

WRE Experience

Our current mission statement, which was created in 1995 and revised in 2004 and 2008, has served us well (Figure 3). The mission, besides identifying the major services, also describes the philosophy and values of our company. A good, effective mission statement will evolve over time along with your business and as conditions change in your industry.

Our mission statement sets the tone for direction of our company. Every team member is reminded of our mission with postings in our office and at orientation day each March when the new season begins. Time spent concerning your company's purpose will pay real dividends as your employees recognize the vision, direction, and expectations of the company.

<u>Essential Points:</u>

4. Define your purpose with a written mission statement.

5. Share your vision with employees, customers, and business contacts.

6. Periodically review your mission and adjust as needed.

Chapter 3: BUILD A BUSINESS PLAN

Why Create a Business Plan?

Ben Franklin was quoted as saying "By failing to prepare, you are preparing to fail." No truer words have been spoken. My failure to write a business plan in 1985, when I entered the field full time, nearly cost me my business and my home.

From 1985 to 1989, my landscape business grew from $50,000 in sales to over $900,000. I was riding an economic expansion which I fully expected to continue indefinitely. Then, unfortunately, a recession hit in 1990 resulting in $450,000 in gross sales–a 50% drop! The next year was equally dismal, with $460,000 in sales. I was caught totally unprepared. I laid-off workers, sold equipment and vehicles, and if not for a generous loan from an aunt I would have gone out of business.

My banker at the time refused to loan me any more money and bluntly suggested that I declare bankruptcy, which I refused to do. The solution came to me when I saw a business plan seminar being offered at the Washington Trust Co. bank. I signed up for the course, determined to create a plan that would set a course for my business: where it was going, and how I intended to get it there.

The seminar was enormously helpful. It guided me through the process of setting goals and listing strategies to reach them. I developed a marketing plan, made financial projections, did a cash flow analysis, and outlined my equipment, vehicle, and labor needs. Equally important: I created a contingency plan in case my primary plan didn't materialize.

At the conclusion of the course I had compiled a comprehensive business plan which I presented to my banker. After reviewing it along with my financial request, he agreed to restructure my debt, establish a credit line for my business, and give our company the financial backing it needed to stay afloat and prepare for the future.

What changed the bank's point of view? The detailed business plan did. It clearly showed the direction in which we were headed, described how we would meet our financial obligations, and laid out a contingency plan in case we did not make our sales projections. It demonstrated that we were organized and gave the banker a sense of security, knowing we had a plan for growth with the means to achieve it. Within 60 days of submitting our plan and financial request, our debt was reorganized and a credit line was in place. Since that time, we have always had an evolving business plan in place.

Whether you are beginning a business, looking to expand an existing company, or seeking re-organization of existing finances, a sound business plan is essential. In addition to its role for financial matters the plan serves as a benchmark for you to track success and shortcomings as your company implements the plan. Sharing the vision and goals with your employees will entice them to help achieve the plan's goals. The plan serves as a road map to the future.

Components of a Business Plan

Once your mission statement and strategies are completed (Chapter 2), work on your business plan can take place. Although there are variations in business plan components, I have chosen the major aspects which are useful to horticultural and many other small businesses. There are several excellent resources for assisting in completion of your business plan; these are referenced in Appendix A, Section VI.

The executive summary may be the most important section of your business plan. It will be a clear depiction of your business: its vision, strategies, and vital information about your company. Successfully completing the components of the executive summary will put you well on your way to completing a basic business plan.

Components of the executive summary which should be included are:

1. Company Summary – Include the business name, its location, a brief history of the business, its ownership details, its legal status (sole proprietorship, partnership, Subchapter S Corporation, C Corporation, or Limited Liability Company (LLC)), whether it is a new or established business, its major products or services, the current state of your industry, and what the key financial needs are.

2. Market – What are the characteristics of your customers? Research specific demographic data, trends in the horticultural field, and location of your market.

3. Competition – List your major competitors and describe differences between your offerings and your competition's. What percent of the market does each possess, and what are your competitive advantages?

4. Product/Service Features and Benefits – Describe your product or service in detail: delineate your distinguishing benefits that customers will choose, and why your product is better than the competition's.

5. Marketing and Sales Strategies – What is your advertising and promotion plan? Which methods and media will you use (direct mail, newspaper, radio, T.V., cable, website, email, public relations, etc.)? Who will conduct sales, and what is your sales strategy?

6. Operations – Briefly summarize major business functions (raising plants, constructing landscapes, lawn care applications, creating landscape designs, selling products at a garden center, etc.). What challenges do you face (finding land, personnel, financing,

equipment), what competitive advantages do you have, and how do you plan to address challenges in the future?

7. <u>Management and Staffing</u> – Who makes up your management team, what are their qualifications and background, what are your current staffing and future employee needs, and how will you address future management and employee growth?

8. <u>Financials</u> – Include a profit and loss statement, balance sheet, cash flow projections, and source of funds including how they will be used.

9. <u>Contingency Plan</u> – Bankers like to see a "contingency plan" in place describing how you will pay back any loans if your sales projections fall short. Also have an exit plan in case the business doesn't make it, which would leave bills paid and assets sold.

The best way to complete the executive summary is to finalize the nine categories listed and then write a short (roughly two-page) summary identifying the key points in a clear, compelling fashion. Most individuals reading the executive summary want to know the significant information concisely before reading the backup information. Remember to cover the key points: Who, What, Where, How, and When.

I have included a sample business plan our model company, Safe Green LLC (next page). This plan can help provide you with ideas as you design your horticultural business plan. Several resources which will provide specific help and guidance with your business plan are listed in the appendix.

Safe Green LLC Business Plan

<u>Executive Summary</u>

<u>Mission Statement</u>

Safe Green LLC is a 5-year-old landscape company specializing in lawn care and property maintenance. The company is dedicated to providing earth-friendly products and services to consumers living in coastal RI communities. Our customers are seeking to improve the quality and health of their landscapes through the use of 100% organic products and services with little or no impact on the surrounding watershed.

1. <u>Company Summary</u> – Safe Green LLC, founded in 2005, specializes in lawn care and property maintenance for coastal properties in the RI towns of Westerly, Charlestown, Narragansett, South Kingstown, and Jamestown.

   Dedicated to using earth-friendly products, services, and techniques, the business has grown to service over 75 coastal customers generating over $500,000 in gross sales annually (including lawn care, lawn mowing, pruning, and landscape maintenance services).

   Since 2008, all products and services have been organic, following the NOFA (Northeast Organic Farming Association) Organic Land Care Standards. The owner, Bill Green, a 2002 URI horticulture program graduate, and his six-member staff are dedicated to providing the best, safest, truly organic programs.

   With the demand for earth-friendly products and services increasing at a 10-15% rate each year, the outlook for Safe Green's growth is very promising.

2. <u>Market</u> – Safe Green's customers are upscale, educated, and busy professionals. Most are between 45-65 years old, with yearly income of $100K and above, and own single-family residences in coastal RI valued at $500K and over.

   Cost is not as important to their clients as quality, reliability, and customer service. About 90% of Safe Green's customers live in Westerly, Charlestown, South Kingstown, Narragansett, and Jamestown, RI.

   With the trend toward more organic and eco-friendly landscape services, Safe Green's organic lawn care program and eco-friendly plant health care program are in increasing demand. With concerns about the effect of pesticides used in the landscape (and their effect on rivers, nearby ponds, and the ocean) customers are demanding pesticide-free, safe treatments on their properties. Safe Green is positioned to meet this challenge with their 100% organic lawn care program and NOFA approved land care techniques and products.

3. <u>Competition</u> – Safe Green LLC is the sole 100% organic landscape firm in southern RI. There are two other major competitors, Lawn Care Inc. and Coastal Landscape Co., who both offer an organic lawn care option but are primarily traditional, chemically-based lawn care and landscape firms. Lawn Care Inc. has approximately 15% of the organic market in coastal RI, and Coastal Landscape Co. has approximately a 10% share. Neither offers the complete program that Safe Green LLC does, which includes five NOFA-accredited staff members, extensive organic land care training, 100% organic products and services, and a mission to be completely organic in their approach.

   Safe Green LLC currently has approximately 7% of the organic lawn care market with a goal of expanding to 10% in 2010 and 15% by 2012.

4. <u>Product /Services Features and Benefits</u> – Safe Green LLC is the only local landscape firm offering a comprehensive organic lawn care program including chemical and biological soil tests, organic fertilizers, compost applications, compost tea sprays for lawns, trees, shrubs and gardens, over-seeding lawns with endophytic seed mixes, aerating, and culturally appropriate lawn mowing and watering recommendations.

   Customers like the idea of our coordinated, comprehensive, holistic approach based on testing, site analysis, and discussions with client. Our extensive list of satisfied customers provides our new clients a great measure of confidence that they will get the results they deserve and expect.

5. <u>Marketing and Sales Strategies</u> – Safe Green's marketing goal is to attain 10% market share of organic lawn care in coastal RI by 2010, and 15% share by 2012. Strategies to attain the increased share include:
   a) Stimulate customer demand for our organic lawn care services in the RI coastal communities through targeted advertising in local newspapers, scheduling talks with local environmental organizations, running ads on the local classical radio station, and establishing a rewards program for existing customers who refer new clients to Safe Green LLC.
   b) Increase sales efforts in the coastal community using our detailed, informative marketing packet. The packet features descriptions of our company and mission, our organic lawn care services, our eco-friendly landscape and plant health care services, our pricing and warranty, and our customer referral list.
   c) Expand our website to include details about our programs, sources for more information, contact information, and early sign-up options for our services, workshops, and special events.

6. <u>Operations</u> – Safe Green LLC operations work out of a 6-acre farm in Woodville, RI. The site allows for storage of equipment and vehicles, an area to make our own compost, and a plan to expand the brewing of our own compost tea. We raise perennials and small shrubs organically on several acres of pastureland using water from several wells on the property.

   The Woodville location is within 30 minutes of most all our customers. About 90% of our projects are located between Westerly and Narragansett, RI making coordinating and implementation easy. With a talented crew that has been together for five years, completing lawn care and maintenance services is professional, timely, and efficient.

   Our major challenges are to explore ways to expand our compost tea production, market our services, and seek financing to help fund these efforts.

   Completion of this business plan is intended to give us a roadmap for the future and provide information for the local bank to consider our financial requests.

7. <u>Management and Staffing</u> – Bill Green, a URI horticulture graduate, has always been passionate about plants, organic landscape techniques, and helping people solve their landscape problems in the most eco-friendly way possible. After attending the NOFA Organic Land Care Program in 2008, Safe Green has used only NOFA and Organic Materials Review Institute (OMRI) listed products. His staff, primarily NOFA accredited professionals, share Bill's organic passion and provide a very talented, dedicated crew to implement the company's organic mission. Two staff members are URI graduates, one is a UCONN graduate, and three have been landscaping for over 10 years. Two trusted staff members, Joe and Mary, have had supervisory experience and will play key roles in the expansion of Safe Green LLC. Each winter Bill sends his staff to horticulture and business seminars to help prepare them for new and greater responsibilities.

8. <u>Financials</u> – Please refer to the sample Profit and Loss Statement (Figure 7), Balance Sheet (Figure 8), and Cash Flow Analysis (Figure 9), discussed in detail in Chapter 6. The Actual and Projected Sales Chart (Figure 13), is described in Chapter 7.

9. <u>Safe Green LLC Source of Funds</u> – The company has been profitable for the last several years, with a $94,674 profit in 2008 and a projected profit of $122,647 in 2009. For 2009 there will be considerable investment in advertising, promotion, and printing as the marketing plan is implemented. In addition to the net profit as a source of investment for Safe Green LLC's expansion, new sources of funding in the form of an equipment loan will be needed to purchase a compost tea

extractor, storage tanks, pumps, cleaning units, and a tea sprayer to meet the increased demand of organic lawn care services ($38,000). The installation costs, building of a shed to house the tea equipment, and training expenses will be provided by Safe Green LLC (value $24,000), taken from profit and our savings account.

10. <u>Contingency Plan</u> – Safe Green LLC is in good financial condition, having had several profitable years, a projected $122,647 profit in 2009, and a $38,375 savings account. Based on projections and the history of increasing organic sales there should be no problem repaying the $38,000 loan; however, in case sales slow down or diminish, we have established a contingency plan to pay off the loan:

    a) In a worst case scenario funds in the savings account could be used to pay off the loan in full.

    b) Safe Green LLC has several vehicles and pieces of equipment that could be sold to pay for the new equipment.

    c) One of our competitors is interested in our compost tea services and would consider purchasing our compost tea operation if we decided to not continue with it.

Realistically, with the increased demand for our services, we plan to pay off the loan earlier than the 7-year term proposed making the contingency plan moot!

Uses for the Completed Plan

There are several uses for a completed business plan that will help your business grow and develop:

1. Raising money is often a primary reason for writing a business plan, and as I experienced, a well-thought out plan is an absolute requirement for getting funded by any professional banker or money manager. Although not one of my strengths, I have learned to understand the differences between, and the value of, financial statements, income statements, balance sheets, assets, liabilities, equity, the cash flow statement, cost ratio analysis, and cost accounting. The better one understands the role of their financial tools and how they relate to your business, the easier it is to make logical and realistic financial forecasts for the business. The financial component of the business plan is what bankers (and investors) focus on the most. You have to be able to demonstrate your total understanding of the numbers!

2. The business plan can serve as a benchmark to track success…and shortcomings. The plan can alert the company when certain areas of the business aren't working. When setting goals in the plan (sales increases, overhead reduction, new market penetration, new service offerings etc.), be sure to gauge your current situation and use it as a benchmark to track your progress (or lack of it). It is important to establish time and budget parameters at the outset of goal-setting and be willing to pull the plug on any investment of energy, money, or labor that does not generate the desired return before reaching the end of those parameters.

3. The business plan acts as a road map to the future: where we are now, where we are headed, how we will get there, what we will need along the way, when the process will begin, and how we will know when we have reached our destination. Because the plan is shared with the team and revised as needed with their input, the overall direction is clear and we all can work together to achieve the same goals.

WRE Experience

Several times during the past six years several divisions within our company were eliminated when they were no longer meeting our goals, particularly in the financial arena. Our Christmas tree operation, a mainstay for over 25 years, was eliminated in 2003 because of lagging sales and financial losses. Our foray into the sprinkler business was brief due to a shortfall when it came to meeting our high standards of customer service and satisfaction as well as our financial goals.

Currently, in 2010, we are revising our business plan again due to the economic downturn. We are examining all aspects of our business to see which services should be retained, eliminated or enhanced. Our 5 year plan to convert our business into an organic company has experienced some successes but progress has not met our initial projections. At our winter planning meetings, as a team, we will revise our plan and move forward with a comprehensive plan for the future, recognizing the changing conditions.

Essential Points:

1. A sound business plan is vital to start a new business, expand your business, or re-organize your company.

2. The business plan will serve as a guide for you, your employees, and the bankers needed to finance your plan.

3. As conditions change, revising your business plan will allow you to move into the future with confidence.

Chapter 4: CREATE A STRONG BRAND

The purpose of a business is to create a customer and satisfy the customer. Marketing is about creating relationships with your customers that cultivate an emotional preference for your brand.

What is a Brand?

A brand is a collection of many things: an expectation of performance, a mark of trust and integrity, a reputation, a consistent experience, and a collection of memories. Today's buying decisions are made on promises that transcend products or services. The promises are rooted in human emotions. It's not about what you do; it's about what customers want, what motivates them to buy, and why they want to buy from you. A brand is not part of your business. IT IS YOUR BUSINESS!

Strong brands are those that survive market shifts, economic downturns, and product setbacks. They are brands that have created an indelible mark in the minds of the customers without considerable effort.

Several examples of world known companies will illustrate strong brands: Harley Davidson (motorcycles), Nike (athletic shoes), Coca Cola (soda), Apple (iPods, iPhone, & iMac computers), and McDonalds (fast food). In the sports world the New England Patriots represent football excellence as do the Boston Red Sox and New York Yankees in baseball. All of these companies have extremely high brand recognition and have survived numerous economic challenges over the years.

Name the top three company names that come to mind when discussing your particular horticultural business. What characteristics do these companies have that contributed to their brand recognition? Survey the following list of company descriptors to see which ones fit their brand:

Top quality product or service	Responsive	Communicate well
Follow-through	Professional	On time delivery
Polite	Great to work with	Consistent product or service
Expensive	Fair price	Creative
Honest	Cheerful	Imaginative
Reliable	Successful	Ethical
Independent	Innovative	Warranty

How do customers feel about your brand? If you are a small company, you are your brand. Your values, communication skills, personality, project management, follow-through, and responsiveness all contribute to your brand identity. For all companies, surveying their customers about their respective brands is extremely important. What do they need? What problems are they trying to solve? What motivates them to buy? How willing are they to buy from someone else? What does your brand mean to them? How your customers feel about your brand isn't a casual question–it is the crucial question!

In addition to a customer survey, mailing an evaluation card after a project is completed can be very effective and eye-opening. After each landscape project is completed we send out an evaluation postcard (our report card) soliciting feedback on the design, installation, crew, communication, final results, and potential for referring our company in the future. The categories are rated (see sample evaluation card, Figure 27, in Chapter 10): 1 = did not meet expectations, 2 = met expectations, 3 = exceeded expectations, and 4 = far exceeded expectations. Based on the average of the ratings we get a score (for example, 3.2), which is added to all the other project scores. In the off season we calculate our overall average to set a higher standard for the next year. Individual evaluation card problems are addressed to improve customer satisfaction.

Elements of a Brand

How does your brand measure up? Consider your brand in terms of brand name awareness, brand loyalty, perceived quality, and brand associations:

1. Brand awareness – What is the strength of the brand's presence in the customer's mind? Measurement categories include: recognition (have you seen this brand before?), recall (what brand names do you recall?), top of mind (the first brand name recalled), and dominant (the only brand name recalled).

2. Brand loyalty – Loyalty is created by the customer and creates a barrier to entry by competition. This results in predictable sales and profit stream. It elevates you above price wars and positions your company for price premiums. A brand without loyal customers, however, is vulnerable.

3. Perceived quality – This contributes to profitability by enhancing prices and market share. Perceived quality and value drives financial performance of the company. Often this is the principal strategic thrust of the business (top quality of product and service vs. lowest price).

4. Brand associations – The customer makes associations with the brand that the product and service are reliable, top quality, and consistent. The company is the leading firm

in the industry. Customers associate the firm's logo with expectations of a reliable experience.

A brand is more than a symbol; a brand behaves like a guarantee. A brand is becoming more and more important across all product and service categories. During economic downturns a well perceived brand becomes even more important. Those clients looking to do landscape projects will be looking for brand recognition, quality, and value. Although some landscape firms will try to land jobs primarily on price, ultimately those representing quality, reputation, and value will be successful.

Those potential customers basing their decisions solely on price probably are not the customers you are seeking, particularly if you are looking for a long term relationship via a maintenance contract after the project is completed. Your brand can be short-lived if you don't support the brand, invest in it, and impress your employees with the significance of the brand.

Importance of Your Brand

A strong brand sets a company apart from the competition. In our market, our brand stands for an award-winning, full-service, coastal landscape design, construction, and maintenance firm dedicated to exceptional customer service. Since 1996 we have been fortunate to win 24 landscape awards recognizing our quality work, dedicated employees, and wonderful clients. Additionally, we offer an industry-leading 3-year warranty.

In a competitive situation, a strong brand can be effective in finalizing projects even when you are the high bidder. One client recently chose our company even though our estimate was 20% higher than the other bidder. She explained that WRE was chosen because of our professional presentation, the quality of the work we do, other projects and referrals, our reputation, and her feeling that we were the right company for the job.

With a strong brand you can leverage the offering of additional products or services for continued growth. Eight years ago, when we first offered masonry services, it was readily accepted by our clients. Since that time, the masonry division has served as a vital part of our brand, resulting in numerous referrals for our masons' exceptional work. During economic downturns your strong brand can provide a dependable revenue stream from loyal customers. That's why defining, developing, and defending your brand is so critical to your long-term survival. Striving to be the best horticultural company in your area will set you apart from your competition and provide a secure footing in challenging times.

Your brand is the most valuable asset your company owns. A brand that captures the mind gains actions. A brand that captures the heart gains commitment. Internalize it from the way you answer the phone to the way you answer your conscience.

Lynda C. Martel is Director of Marketing for DriveSavers Data Recovery. She is responsible for marketing DriveSavers professional data recovery services to consumers, corporations and government agencies worldwide.

Establishing a strong brand name is a critical marketing component in any business. Consumers connect to brands on an emotional level. If their perceptions of themselves (affluent, environmentally-conscious, discerning, sensible) resonate with certain brand qualities (highest-quality, organic, native, drought-tolerant), they will choose this brand over others in the market...even if the pricing is higher or the product is harder to acquire. If the brand continues to deliver on the vision of what the consumer believes the brand must be and do, they will remain loyal to the brand over time (for example, Apple and Nike)—sometimes for generations (Coca-Cola, Mercedes Benz).

How small business can strengthen their brand. Small businesses can strengthen their brand name in the same ways big businesses do. Brands are built on a promise (Hint: most strong brands consistently under promise and over deliver.) Take a look at your business. Observe these things:

1. What are you selling?
   a. Begin with the tangibles (shrubs, annuals, native plants)
   b. Consider the intangible (customer experience, service, location)
   c. How does the market perceive what you sell (too expensive, good value, high quality)

2. Who are your best customers?
   a. Consider the data (females, 50+, affluent, urban dwellers, etc.)
   b. Consider their profiles (experienced landscapers, beginners, city dwellers)
   c. Consider what they want, need and desire (native plants, hardy plants)

3. Who are your toughest competitors?
   a. What do they sell, how and to whom?
   b. What is the perception of their products/service?

Building a strong brand begins with appropriate market positioning: that is, knowing what the customer needs and wants in your market, and delivering it to them in a way that no one else can. In the horticultural business, this could mean creating a brand that promises to deliver only one type of very special plant (large specimen trees, hard to find plants) or a brand that promises a relaxing experience while they shop for everyday plants (well-landscaped garden atmosphere). When you are clear on who your target audience is, and what their desires are, you can begin to build your brand by broadcasting the brand "promise" to them in your advertising campaigns. Understanding your brand's promise will guide you when creating a brand experience for your customers, either in your store, online, or in their imaginations as they listen to your radio ads and read your monthly newsletter. By checking in on your customers periodically, making small adjustments designed to satisfy and delight them further, they will respond by remaining loyal to your brand over time. This simple formula is the root that has sprouted every strong brand name on the market today.

Figure 4: Importance of Branding: Lynda C. Martel

WRE Experience

When marketing director Lynda Martel joined our firm in1998, she helped my staff and I understand the full value of our own brand (Figure 4). She undertook the strengthening of our existing brand, increasing brand awareness in our markets, and creating relationships with customers that resulted in a preference for our brand. Her actions included:

- Refreshing the WRE logo to reflect where the company had been and where it was going. Ensuring that the logo is used consistently across all communications vehicles (uniforms, letterhead, invoices, thank you cards, customer evaluation cards, newsletters, advertising, signage, etc.)

- Defining the brand's core value as we had with the company's mission statement, promoting its meaning to all employees, and emphasizing employees' roles in supporting the brand in terms of product quality, customer service, and the promise of satisfaction.

- Developing a marketing plan to promote the brand message in existing and potential markets through the use of tactics such as radio ads, newsletters, customer brochures, television/cable exposure, garden club presentations, and speaking engagements at industry trade shows.

- Designing an employee recruitment program to attract hardworking, responsible, talented employees who embody the brand.

- Measuring all of our activities against the core values of the brand; promoting the idea that the brand is a living, dynamic entity that needs leadership, direction, and defending.

Our brand loyalty is strong enough to provoke a call to us from clients when they're approached by our competition. One client has had us landscape four different homes since 1996. Another client has had us landscape four homes, a horse farm, and a restaurant. We sincerely appreciate their customer loyalty, which has allowed our firm to grow and succeed.

Our logo has become well-recognized and respected throughout southern New England (Figure 5). But our brand is more than a symbol; it's a guarantee that a project will be top-quality, the team will be professional, courteous, and fun to work with, we will warranty the work we do, and if there be a problem it will be corrected.

Figure 5: Wood River Evergreens, Inc. Logo

<u>Essential Points:</u>

1. A strong brand will separate your business from the competition…especially in difficult economic times.

2. A brand is more than a symbol or logo, a brand behaves like a guarantee.

3. Your brand is the most valuable asset your company owns. Define, develop, and defend your brand…it is critical to your long term survival.

Chapter 5: BUSINESS MARKETING AND PROMOTION

Developing a Marketing Plan

Regardless of the size of your company, developing a marketing plan is critical to reaching your market and financial goals. The business plan (discussed in Chapter 3) defines your overall financial goals and is typically used to gain financial support. The marketing plan, as a component of your business plan, defines the company's market position and is used to reach your financial goals. This strategic planning–an intentional, calculated, deliberate plan of action–is essential for you to reach your business goal.

What is the role of the marketing plan? The plan will specify by product, service, market and region, how to accomplish the company's goals in the most efficient manner.

There are numerous benefits of the marketing plan:

1. The plan identifies the most promising business opportunities and explains how to take advantage of them.

2. It defines obstacles to achieving the business's goals and ways to overcome these obstacles.

3. Through setting short- and long-term goals for the company, a "plan-of-action" is developed for all members of the firm.

4. The plan works to keep the teams focused and unified in their work efforts.

5. Most importantly, the plan sets benchmarks, charts the activities, and analyzes the results as the plan is implemented.

Contents of the marketing plan can vary but most have: an executive summary, the company's mission, scope, and goals, a situation analysis, marketing objectives and programs, budgets, pro-forma Profit & Loss and balance sheets, and benchmarks and controls. Rhonda Abrams, in her book *Business Plan in a Day*, has a very clear and straight-forward method for making a marketing and sales plan[1].

Creating a strategic marketing plan can be summarized in five steps:

1. <u>Establish Your Mission Statement and Goals</u> – In Chapter 2 we described how you conceive a purpose and list strategies to achieve your stated mission and business goals. What do you wish to accomplish? List your sales, staffing, profit, and marketing goals. When do you want to accomplish these goals? Be specific and realistic in your time frame.

2. <u>Analyze your Current Situation</u> – Who are your customers? Where are they located? What are their problems and needs? How can you solve their problems? Describe your unique selling proposition (USP), which puts your company in a position to meet customer's needs. What is your position in the market now? Largest? Best quality? Cheapest? Cutting edge service? Where do you want to be in 3 years? 5 years? 10 years? What challenges do you face? Will your present situation allow you to reach your goals? Who are your major competitors? What are their strengths and weaknesses? Determine the market "gap" and position your product or service as the "best" solution to that need. Your "USP" could be, for example: the largest supplier or widest selection of locally grown plants; the only 100% organic lawn care company; the only one-stop landscape design, construction, maintenance firm in the area; etc.

3. <u>Set Marketing Objectives</u> – Marketing objectives define what you have to do to reach your goals, when you have to do it, and where you should focus your activities. Your objectives should be results –oriented, measurable, attainable, flexible, consistent and challenging. Sample objectives:
   - Increase net profit by 10% over 2008
   - Increase maintenance division sales by $50,000 in 2009
   - Increase tree selling price margin from 33% to 50%

4. <u>Select Your Strategies</u> – Once your objectives are identified, strategies to support attainment of the objectives need to be selected. How are you going to reach your objectives? Why are you going to reach them? Sample strategies:
   - Strategy to achieve profit objectives: raise prices or reduce overhead by 10%
   - Strategy to achieve revenue objectives: acquire ten new maintenance accounts worth $5,000 each
   - Strategy to achieve pricing objectives: increase retail tree price markup percentage from 50% to 100%.

   Strategies are chosen to reach your objectives based on your company's strengths, personnel, and expertise.

5. <u>Develop the Action Plans</u> – In order to achieve the objectives that have been set, specific action plans need to be developed so that everyone in your company understands the goals, strategies, and methods chosen to achieve success. Plans to support a profit increase will include detailed budgets, a purchase order system, and stocking program. Plans to support a revenue increase will include sales and marketing communication for the company and reviewing staffing needs to achieve the increase. To insure the success of the action plans, two-way communications with the staff early on are essential. Scheduled input sessions to discuss progress and

accomplishments, analyze the results, and update the plan will be necessary as the process moves forward.

The marketing plan keeps you moving towards your goals. The situation analysis defines who you are and where you are now. Objectives and strategies chart the course to where you want to be. Marketing programs are the action steps to get you there!

Marketing Techniques

I have always been fascinated with marketing techniques used by other businesses, and over the years I have been in business I think I have used most of them. Marketing needs and choices change as your business evolves. In the infancy of the business, exposure in newspapers, cable ads, radio ads, discount coupons, and direct mail promotions were prominent. As the business became more established and recognized, our advertising campaigns changed in technique, content, and target audience. Once we had a solid customer base we relied more on a WRE newsletter, targeted radio ads, public relation efforts, our website, and speaking engagements at local garden clubs.

Central to the change in our promotional efforts was the fact that over 90% of our new projects were from client and vendor referrals. Knowing also that 80% of our new business was from 20% of our customer base, we concentrated our efforts on our growing base of loyal customers. However, for any business to grow and survive new clients are necessary. To attract new business we have concentrated our marketing efforts in three areas: classical radio ads, public relations, and the Evan's Mobil landscape display in Pawcatuck, CT.

Classical Radio Ad Program

When my former marketing manager, Lynda Martel, recommended an advertising program on a classical radio station, I was less than enthusiastic. She assured me that the demographics for the classical radio audience matched our target audience: 45-65 year old professionals with incomes over $100,000 and who own very high-end homes. I reluctantly agreed to move ahead with the program. Mark Halliday, our sales representative at the radio station, set up recording sessions in which I answered questions about our business, services, and products. We had an easygoing conversation during which I spoke about WRE and, more importantly, I educated our potential customer base about landscaping in general.

The results were well beyond my expectations. To date the ads have generated more than 45 projects. Equally important, I receive frequent feedback from clients, friends, and new acquaintances on how much they enjoy listening to me discussing various landscape topics.

Classical radio advertising has turned into a primary promotional tool for our company. So, what started out as a lukewarm endorsement on my part I can now heartily say works!

Invest in Public Relations

An effective, low-cost (and perhaps more refined) method of marketing that has worked well for us is public relations (P.R.). Included in this marketing category are free press, becoming the expert in a particular horticultural area, and civic marketing. Although public relations techniques can be low cost in terms of dollars there is an investment of time, planning, and follow-up that is needed for your efforts to succeed. Table 2 lists five techniques to use in generating public relations exposure for your company.

Table 2: Five Valuable Techniques for Using Public Relations Opportunities

1.	Develop a contact list of local news, photo, business, and feature editors
2.	Create relationships with newspaper editors: call them, invite them to visit you, and provide them with the information they need to make their job easy!
3.	Write right! Use simple words and active verbs. Use words that form pictures of your ideas...and edit, edit, edit!
4.	A picture is worth a thousand words. Furnish well-composed, professional, glossy 8" x 10" or 5" x 7" photographs (or email a photo if requested). Show people in action using the product.
5.	Establish yourself as the "expert" in your field. Contact local garden clubs, environmental groups, and horticultural organizations to speak. Become a guest on local radio/TV talk shows. Submit articles to trade/consumer magazines. Ideas for stories: • Promotions and special events • Business anniversary • Profile of owner or business • Trends in the industry • Unique product or service addition • Establish a contest • Be creative!

Over the years, numerous articles have been printed about our business: its growth, new services, special events, and most recently about the publishing of my first book. This type of coverage is accomplished by developing relationships with local newspaper editors. We provide them with well-written information from which to develop a story, press releases about newsworthy awards, certifications or achievements (Figure 6), or press kits containing photos and background information about our company. Editors are constantly searching for unique, newsworthy events, which you can provide for them. We also invite editors to visit our WRE landscape design center showcase, which is always a source of good photo opportunities for seasonal horticultural and gardening information. We keep in touch regularly, and sincerely thank them for any coverage we receive. Over the years, the free publicity WRE has received has been extremely valuable to the company.

PRESS RELEASE

FOR IMMEDIATE RELEASE

WOOD RIVER EVERGREENS, INC.
ANNOUNCES ITS $1,000 "GREEN CAREERS"
SCHOLARSHIP FOR LOCAL HIGH SCHOOL SENIORS

Wood River Evergreens, Inc. has created a $1,000 "Green Careers" Scholarship for qualifying senior year high school students interested in pursuing a career in horticulture or education.

"Careers in the green industry are very rewarding at all levels," states the owner of Wood River Evergreens. "We want to stimulate new blood in our profession by rewarding and supporting those students that are interested in entering it." Because of Wood River Evergreen's owner's teaching background and his high regard for the teaching profession, the scholarship will also support students choosing education as a career.

Candidates will be asked to complete an application letter explaining why they are pursuing either of these vocations, and why they believe they deserve the scholarship. The student with the most compelling story will be chosen as the winner. The scholarship will be awarded in June.

Interested students should contact the Wood River Evergreens office in Woodville, RI, and ask for details about the scholarship.

Wood River Evergreens, Inc. is an award-winning, full-service landscape design, construction and maintenance firm specializing in coastal landscapes. Their office is located at 101 Woodville Road, Hope Valley, RI. For more information, call 401-364-3387.

Figure 6: Sample Press Release

Another effective P.R. technique is to become the "expert" on a specific topic. Topics like water conservation, organic methods of landscaping, new plants on the market, plant health care, or new advances in landscaping can all be effective for submitting articles to newspapers, appearing on local radio or T.V. programs, and speaking at local garden clubs, trade shows, and universities. Through a relationship with the University of Rhode Island, I frequently help teach a landscape management course and appear as a guest on the "Plant Pro", a regular feature on NBC's local television news program.

This type of publicity technique is one that I thoroughly enjoy. For years I have enjoyed speaking at green industry events all over New England. For the last six years I have spoken at NOFA's 5-day land care courses held in CT, MA, RI, and NY. Since I firmly believe in the organic movement and in converting our company into an organic firm, I find the opportunity to speak to the ever growing number of AOLCP's (accredited organic land care professionals) and to share my lessons from years in the horticultural profession extremely rewarding.

Civic marketing (helping others in the community) has been another main element of our public relations program. I feel strong obligations to give back to my local community. I have donated products and services to the Greater Westerly–Pawcatuck Chamber of Commerce to be used in their landscape; installed a memorial garden for the fallen firemen of the Ashaway Fire Department; donated time and materials to the McCourt Memorial Garden commemorating 9/11 victims from the New London, CT area; donated materials and equipment to the Angel Memorial Project at Westerly Hospital, Westerly, RI; and in memory of a deceased member of our team, Lianne Maher, we run an annual golf tournament that supports the Lianne Maher Memorial Scholarship Fund which supplies two $2500 scholarships to high school seniors intending to major in education or horticulture in college each year. I am happy to participate in these worthy causes and will continue to give so that others can have opportunities like those which I have had.

The Evans Mobil Phenomenon

Of all the marketing techniques I have used, the most successful is the landscape garden display we installed at Evans Mobil gas station in Pawcatuck, CT. I refer to this commercial garden as "The Evans Mobil Phenomenon." Incredibly, this landscape display has generated over 140 referrals to WRE, numerous landscape awards for Evans Mobil and WRE, and many newspaper articles bringing very favorable press to Evans Mobil and WRE.

Why has this display, on a 65'x12' corner island at Evans Mobil gas station, been so successful? When I first met the owner, Ellison Evans, at the gas station 14 years ago, he expressed his desire for a landscape that would attract attention, look professional, improve the appearance of this business property, have color and interest all year long, and "be the talk of the town!" The design my landscape designer Mary Jo Girard and I came up with met all of

Ellison's demands. The display garden featured graceful contours, vibrant perennials, evergreens, two small flowering crabapples, a small waterfall, and several turf areas.

The most unique features of the landscape, however, were the areas designated for seasonal plant changeovers. The changeover areas were teeming with crocus, tulips, and daffodils that brightened the landscape in the spring. Pots of pansies, which last until the summer changeover in June, were planted amongst the bulbs for a continuous display of color. For summer, we replaced the pansies with New Guinea impatiens, scaevola, and Proven Winner™ petunias in colors that matched Mobil's corporate colors of red, white, and blue. In September, the fall changeover design featured the gold and yellow hues of mums, with asters and kale interspersed for their interesting texture and long life span. Pumpkins and cornstalks add to the October festive decorations.

The Christmas display is the highlight of our seasonal changeover program. Each year we transform Ellison's island landscape into a special Christmas scene. In addition to replacing the mums with pots of evergreen boughs, the planting beds and gas station are decorated with wreaths and red bows and lights. Evergreen trees are placed throughout the island, also decorated with red bows and lights. A sleigh loaded with gifts and pulled by reindeer is placed in full view of the major roads and busy intersection.

No one could have predicted the incredible success of this small island planting. Ellison is frequently calling me to pass along compliments he receives from pedestrians who pass by and customers who drive into his station. Students from the local middle school wrote letters to Ellison commending him for improving the downtown area. The landscape has generated many published newspaper articles, photographs, and feature stories. Additionally, the local community was motivated to improve other downtown businesses with landscaping, including the planting of state-owned roadside islands.

A great deal of the success of this island garden display goes to Ellison Evans, who had the vision to invest in creating a landscape display for his gas station. As a result, he created a symbol of "green" landscaping for the whole community, those driving past his place on their way to Westerly, and his customers to enjoy. It certainly has been a win/win for Evan's Mobil, WRE, and the community.

The Evans Mobil phenomenon proves that marketing doesn't always have to involve an expensive advertising program or four-color-brochure; it can be one high-profile project done in a location frequented by a large number of potential customers.

WRE Experience

At the root of our marketing success is a marketing plan. The plan outlines our short- and long-term goals, our marketing objectives and strategies, and sets a course of action to follow with built-in benchmarks that help us measure the effectiveness of programs. The times when our company has experienced financial difficulties were when we failed to use, modify, or re-direct our marketing plan. Seasons change, people change, and market conditions change, requiring adjustments in your plan to reflect those changes. In our seasonal business, the winter is a great time to re-evaluate goals for the next season and set new strategies if needed.

In the winter of 2003 we evaluated one of our divisions, the Christmas tree and wreath business, which had failed to make a profit for three years. Although there was a great sense of loyalty to the Christmas business, its loyal customers, and festive atmosphere, the division was dropped because it could not meet our financial goals. As you analyze your own company, set goals for all aspects of your business and create benchmarks in your plan so that each year you can compare the sales results with your financial goals. Adjustments may be needed to achieve the results you want. We typically give a new division or service three years to be successful. Economic conditions may speed up that time frame, but using your marketing plan as a guide will help you navigate the choppy economic waters.

Another key part of the marketing plan is to understand your market: who and where your customers are. We know that over 90% of our clients are located on the coast between Mystic, CT (to the west) and Narragansett, RI (to the east). We know our clients' demographic: they are upscale, educated, and busy professionals. Although cost is a factor, other factors such as personal attention, attention to detail, quality, outstanding service, meeting deadlines, eye-pleasing results, and guaranteed satisfaction are also extremely important.

Knowing where our markets are, our clients' demographics, and our clients' expectations, we can develop our positioning statement: "An award-winning, full-service landscape design, construction, and maintenance firm specializing in coastal landscapes." Our entire marketing effort is directed to this clientele–to solicit new customers, maintain our existing client base, and foster relationships with area vendors who can help us with client referrals. By continually revisiting our marketing plan, we can adjust or refine our tactics so that only the most effective marketing techniques are used to achieve our goals.

Essential Points:

1. The marketing plan outlines short- and long-term goals, defines marketing objectives and strategies, and creates an action plan with benchmarks to measure the program's success or shortcomings.

2. Experiment with various marketing techniques to find those that work for your company.

3. Investing in public relations (free press, becoming an expert in a particular horticultural area, and civic marketing) will produce returns far beyond your expectations.

Chapter 6: COMPANY FINANCES

Anyone who has operated their own business knows that dealing with your company's finances is the most agonizing, stressful, frustrating, yet important responsibility an owner has. Many sleepless nights are spent wondering if there will be enough money in the checking account to meet payroll, or when a client will pay their over-due bill, or where and when the next landscape project will happen! Oh, the joys of running your own business! A friend of mine recently sold his turf business and shared with me that it took him over a year to fully relax, sleep at night and rid himself of the anxiety of meeting payroll and paying bills. He did admit, however, that he is now thrilled not having that responsibility anymore!

Although I know that the financial matters of my business are vital to its continued success, I freely admit that they are my least favorite activities. I would much rather visit with clients, assist in marketing efforts, speak at a local garden club, or visit a local nursery supplier than meet, discuss, and plan a budget, review financial updates, or plug in job-costing data. To make financial tasks more palatable, I have put into place people and processes that allow me to balance the more "enjoyable" aspects of my job with the tedious job of managing money.

 I have hired extremely talented and dedicated employees who perform the key financial tasks of estimating, billing, job costing, bookkeeping, and accounting. Over the years I have hired key people to assist with the financial needs of the company: a systems manager, accountant, financial advisor and consultants who have helped create systems for job costing, financial statements, corporate tax returns, detailed budget programs, and future planning for the financial health of the company. Not only do your trusted employees and advisors help systemize your current operation, they also provide the ground work for future expansion–without having to re-invent all of your working systems.

Keeping in mind that "profit" is not a dirty word, there are many ingredients to ensuring a profitable company: an accurate estimating program, accurate job costing (both of which will be discussed in detail in Chapter 12 and Chapter 13), great employees, an effective marketing plan, and a real understanding of your key financial statements. Understanding the value of your profit and loss (P & L) statements, balance sheet, cash flow statement, accounts receivable, and accounts payable will help guide your company to profitability and allow you to make the necessary corrections in direction when the numbers reveal issues. By analyzing your major financial reports you can determine the overall financial health of the company, its strong and weak areas, where the profit centers are, where potential cash flow problems may arise, and the overall net worth of the company. To fully understand these uses and others, let's take a detailed look at a sample P&L statement (Figure 7), balance sheet (Figure 8), cash flow statement (Figure 9), accounts receivable (Figure 10), and accounts payable (Figure 11).   These statements are based on our model landscape firm, Safe Green LLC.

Profit and Loss (P & L) Statement

Ordinary Income/Expense			
Income		**Expense**	
40000 · Plant Revenue	$60,720	60100 · Accounting Fees	$1,284
41000 · Material Revenue	$98,672	60200 · Advertising and Promotion	$3,720
42000 · Equipment Revenue	$68,908	60500 · Auto Exp.-Officer/Admin	$926
43000 · Labor Revenue	$291,100	61000 · Bank Service Charges	$252
44000 · Sub-Contract Revenue	$30,750	61200 · Business Consultants	$750
49000 · Other Misc. Income	$1,900	61400 · Contributions	$520
Total Income	*$552,050*	61500 · Dues and Subscriptions	$250
Cost of Goods Sold (COGS)		64300 · Equipment Rental/Office	$196
50000 · COGS-Plants	$31,575	64500 · Liability Insurance	$2,871
51000 · COGS-Materials	$57,345	65250 · Licenses and Permits	$250
55000 · COGS-Labor Costs		65350 · Meals and Entertainment	$340
55100 · Wages	$136,520	65750 · Merchant Fees	$922
55200 · Payroll Taxes	$19,724	65800 · Miscellaneous	$1,500
55300 · Medical Benefits	$5,751	65850 · Office Supplies/Expense	$1,803
55400 · Workers Comp	$5,351	66000 · Payroll G&A	
55500 · Uniforms	$450		
55600 · Simple IRA-Employer		66100 · Administrative	$29,186
Contribution	$630	66200 · Officer	$52,785
Total COGS-Labor Costs	*$168,426*	66400 · Officer Medical	$3,837
56000 · Supplies & Small Tools	$3,453	66600 · PR Tax expense	$9,771
57000 · Vehicle & Equipment Costs (includes accumulated depreciation)	$44,345	*Total 66000 · Payroll G&A*	*$95,579*
58000 · Subcontract COGS	$18,600	67200 · Postage and Delivery	$553
Total COGS	*$323,744*	67500 · Printing and Reproduction	$948
Gross Profit	**$228,306**	67700 · Rent	$10,400
		67800 · Repairs and Maintenance	$1,739
		68000 · Taxes-Property and Other	$523
		68500 · Telephone	$2,624
		68600 · Travel	$935
		69000 · Utilities	$2,727
		Total Expense	**$131,612**

Net Ordinary Income:	$228,306 − $131,612 =		**$96,694**
Other Income/Expense			
Other Income			
72000 · Other Income			$2,850
Total Other Income			*$2,850*
Other Expense			
82000 · Interest Expense			$4,870
Total Other Expense			*$4,870*
Net Other Income			($2,020)
Net Income (Profit)			**$94,674**

Figure 7: Safe Green, LLC Profit & Loss January 1, 2008 through December 31, 2008

The Profit and Loss Statement

A P&L (Profit and Loss) statement, sometimes called an income statement, tells you whether the company is making a profit. It will show a company's profitability over a specific time frame: monthly, quarterly, or yearly.

The P&L will begin by calculating income (revenue). In our sample landscape company (Figure 7), the P&L shows that total income from the sales of plants, materials, equipment, vehicles, subcontractors, and labor revenue is $552,050. From this total income is subtracted the cost of goods sold (plants, materials, equipment expenses like insurance, gas, oil, and repairs, labor expenses, and subcontractors costs), $323,744, to arrive at the gross profit of $228,306.

From the gross profit are subtracted other non-direct expenses called G&A (General and Administrative) or operating expenses. These would include many of your "overhead" expenses: contributions, dues and subscriptions, office expenses, legal fees, licenses, meals and entertainment, office supplies, payroll officer and administrative, postage and printing, rent, telephone, utilities, and bad debt expense. Subtracting the total expense ($131,612) from the gross profit ($228,306), we get the net ordinary income ($96,694). After subtracting interest expense, we arrive at net income or profit ($94,674). This is a very important number for you…and your banker!

What are some of the key points the P&L can tell you?

1. <u>The overall health of your company</u>. If the net profit is substantial you may have potential tax liabilities at the end of your fiscal year. If your net income is a loss it can alert you to review your income and expenses to see where you can make changes to push the numbers back into the black. Also, by comparing last year's P&L with the current statement you can see where changes have occurred altering your income and expenses.

2. <u>The profit margin of your products</u>. This can be analyzed and compared with the previous year's results. Looking at materials revenue and materials expense you can see the net difference is $41,327, which is a 42% margin. If the previous year's material margin was 35% the company has made significant progress in increasing its margin.

3. <u>A comparison of this year's gross profit percentage with the previous year</u>. The gross profit percentage is (Total Income – COGS) divided by total income, then multiplied by 100. This is a good measure of how your direct expenses have changed from year to year. Reducing your total COGS will increase your gross profit!

4. <u>What your non-direct expenses are</u>. Your non-direct expenses (G&A, or operating expenses, overhead) can be a major factor in the profitability of your company. Keeping G&A expenses under control are essential to ensuring a net profit.

Frequently reviewing the G&A categories will allow you to detect out of line expenses and make reductions before it is too late in your season. One of the values of establishing a budget at the beginning of the season is that you can set G&A benchmarks, which can be reviewed as the year progresses.

A P&L should be generated monthly so that you can examine the results, identify problem areas, and quickly take steps to correct them. Interim P&L statements can be useful in presenting your bank a snapshot of where you are financially at various times during the season. Bankers do not like surprises, so the more information you can provide about your profitability (or shortfall), the more helpful they can be in suggesting a course of action to take. For smaller companies, quarterly updates or mid-year P&Ls provided to your accountant and bank will help keep them up-to-date on your company's financial situation.

Our company uses QuickBooks® accounting software and can generate interim (monthly) P&Ls in a matter of minutes. The sooner the financial health of the company is understood, the more rapidly steps can be taken to improve profitability: reducing staff, cutting overhead, charging more for a product, etc.

The Balance Sheet

The balance sheet (Figure 8) will give you a clear picture of the financial strength of the company. The company's solvency can be determined by comparing the value of your current assets to your current liabilities. Also, the net worth (stock holder's equity) of your company can be seen as the last line item on the balance sheet. The actual value of your firm may be lower or higher depending on a number of factors. For example, equipment that has tangible value although fully depreciated, inventory that is obsolete yet still on the books, and intangible assets like substantial goodwill and brand recognition, can influence the true value of your company.

What are key points the balance sheet can tell you?

1. It will demonstrate your solvency as a company. You predict liquidity by comparing the value of your current assets to your current liabilities. If you have more assets than liabilities, your solvency may be acceptable as long as your cash flow is adequate (the Safe Green LLC example shows $286,833 assets - $93,998 liabilities = $192,835 equity). If assets equal liabilities, a problem could arise. For example, selling an out-of-date inventory will not generate enough money to retire your debt. If your liabilities exceed your assets, you will be facing imminent cash flow problems. This warning must be taken seriously, and immediate action should be taken to get more cash into the business.

2. Your company's net worth will be shown as the last line item (stockholder's equity). Your company's actual value may be substantially higher or lower as explained

previously. However, the net worth on the balance sheet is a starting point for determining the actual value of your business. Your business will be measured by its progress in increasing revenues and profits, and in building a strong balance sheet. By monitoring your balance sheet you can measure the company's health, net worth, and future profitability.

The Balance Sheet

ASSETS			LIABILITIES & EQUITY		
Current Assets			Liabilities		
Checking/Savings			Current Liabilities		
10000 · Checking		$35,920	Accounts Payable		
10100 · Payroll Checking		$8,143	20000 · Accounts Payable		$20,331
10250 · Savings		$38,375	Total Accounts Payable		$20,331
10500 · Cash on Hand		$780	Credit Cards		
Total Checking/Savings		$83,218	20200 · VISA		$6,860
Accounts Receivable			20300 · Master Card		$10,343
12000 · Accounts Receivable		$25,785	Total Credit Cards		$17,203
Total Accounts Receivable		$25,785	Other Current Liabilities		
Other Current Assets			21000 · 401K/IRA Withhold.		$3,524
15000 · Inventory Asset		$90,514	23000 · Payroll Tax Liabilities		$1,232
Total Other Current Assets		$90,514	24000 · Sales Tax Payable		$750
Total Current Assets		$199,517	25000 · Customer Deposits		$2,200
			Total Other Current Liabilities		$7,706
			Total Current Liabilities		$45,240
Fixed Assets			Long Term Liabilities		
18100 · Furniture & Fixtures		$32,905	28200 · KUBOTA Loan		$13,800
18300 · Leasehold Improvements		$40,032	28400 · Business Loan		$22,623
18500 · Machinery & Equipment		$177,839	28600 · Pickup Loan		$12,335
18700 · Office Equipment		$31,214	Total Long Term Liabilities		$48,758
18800 · Vehicles		$147,789	Total Liabilities		$93,998
18900 · Accumul. Depreciation		($342,463)	Equity		
Total Fixed Assets		$87,316	31000 · Capital Stock		$2,000
			35000 · Retained Earnings		$96,161
			Net Income		$94,674
			Total Equity		$192,835
TOTAL ASSETS		$286,833	TOTAL LIABILITIES & EQUITY		$286,833

Figure 8: Safe Green, LLC Balance Sheet as of December 31, 2008

Cash Flow Analysis

Predicting cash flow (Figure 9) through your business on a monthly and yearly basis is critical, especially for a seasonal business like landscaping. Much of the cash flow analysis is based on projections which can change from month to month. This analysis can tell you how growth will affect your cash flow or how a credit line will ease your cash shortage during off-season periods. Cash flow projections begin with your profit and loss statement. Your primary source of capital is the operating funds. Profits will support cash flow; losses will strap your cash reserves. Several points to remember when building a cash flow statement: depreciation is not deducted from a cash flow statement, principal payments are included in the cash flow, and revenue does not immediately turn into cash because of the time it takes for receivables to be paid by customers.

Even established companies experience cash flow problems. The need for a pool of cash reserves or line of credit to draw upon will depend on whether you sell for cash or on credit. Equally important is whether you purchase with cash or can charge items bought. Preparing for those times of cash flow shortages is critical to preventing financial disaster with your firm.

Although growth in revenues is a goal in any company, without sufficient working capital cash flow problems can choke off the expansion. Cash flow projections will be essential to predict increased revenue, profits, overhead, and expenses. This type of analysis will help ease the potential cash flow shortages as the growth uses up operating capital faster than it can be replaced. A working capital loan or credit line will be needed to keep the company's cash flow coming.

Key points about cash flow projections:

1. Cash flow statements help to predict when cash flow problems will appear and how much money will be needed to meet the shortfall.

2. Growth in a company, although desirable, can put a real pinch on cash flow without sufficient access to working capital. Credit lines or capital loans can be essential to adequately fund the company's expansion without creating serious cash flow shortages.

3. Good cash flow does not ensure profit. A company can have positive cash flow and still be losing money. It is important that the P&L statement and cash flow statement be used in concert, ensuring that profits and good cash flow are occurring with your business.

Cash Flow Analysis

	Income	Expenses			Differential
		Fixed	Variable	Total	(Profit/Loss)
January	$5,650	$15,831	$0	$15,831	-$10,181
February	$7,233	$15,831	$0	$15,831	-$8,598
March	$31,170	$15,831	$16,550	$32,381	-$1,211
April	$72,200	$15,831	$47,660	$63,491	$8,708
May	$86,350	$15,831	$59,376	$75,207	$11,142
June	$85,670	$15,831	$51,000	$66,831	$18,838
July	$80,777	$15,831	$36,620	$52,451	$28,325
August	$60,233	$15,831	$23,000	$38,831	$21,401
September	$53,299	$15,831	$21,000	$36,831	$16,467
October	$32,678	$15,831	$6,170	$22,001	$10,676
November	$26,590	$15,831	$4,000	$19,831	$6,758
December	$10,200	$15,831	$0	$15,831	-$5,631
Totals	$552,050	$189,980	$265,376	$455,356	$96,694

Figure 9: Cash Flow Analysis, Safe Green, LLC, January 1, 2008 - December 31, 2008

Accounts Receivable and Accounts Payable

Accounts receivable statements are used in projecting the amount and timing of customer payments to your company (Figure 10). Accounts payable statements are used to project how much and when you will have to pay your vendors (Figure 11). QuickBooks® (and most other accounting software) can generate an aging report showing each customer/vendor invoice, date due, and those that are 1-30 days, 30-60 days, and over 90 days old. It is important to review both of these account statements weekly so that you can plan your future cash flow needs, incoming as well as outgoing. These reports are very effective management tools to facilitate good cash flow.

With frequent reviews of the accounts receivable statement, you can spot particular customers who are falling behind in their monthly payments. Having a policy for handling past due accounts is very effective in bringing the receivables up to date. After several friendly

Accounts Receivable Statement

Customer	Current	1 - 30	31 - 60	61 - 90	TOTAL
A	0.00	142.50	0.00	0.00	142.50
B	909.20	0.00	0.00	0.00	909.20
C	1,927.88	0.00	0.00	0.00	1,927.88
D	0.00	676.30	0.00	0.00	676.30
E	0.00	630.00	0.00	0.00	630.00
F	632.50	0.00	0.00	0.00	632.50
G	0.00	431.60	0.00	0.00	431.60
H	450.00	365.40	0.00	0.00	815.40
I	1,200.00	0.00	0.00	0.00	1,200.00
J	271.10	1,535.60	0.00	0.00	1,806.70
K	763.20	0.00	0.00	0.00	763.20
L	480.45	0.00	0.00	0.00	480.45
M	1,410.00	4,060.27	0.00	0.00	5,470.27
N	0.00	374.10	605.00	0.00	979.10
O	610.00	0.00	0.00	0.00	610.00
P	0.00	0.00	311.37	0.00	311.37
Q	723.00	0.00	0.00	0.00	723.00
R	267.20	0.00	0.00	0.00	267.20
S	735.00	0.00	0.00	0.00	735.00
T	275.00	0.00	0.00	0.00	275.00
U	1,855.00	1,989.20	0.00	0.00	3,844.20
V	885.56	0.00	0.00	0.00	885.56
W	0.00	2,261.45	0.00	0.00	2,261.45
X	450.00	0.00	0.00	0.00	450.00
Y	995.00	0.00	0.00	0.00	995.00
Z	0.00	1,177.72	0.00	0.00	1,177.72
TOTAL	14,840.09	13,644.14	916.37	0.00	29,400.60

Figure 10: Sample Accounts Receivable

reminders on the monthly bill and accompanying statement have produced no results, a phone call should be made to determine the reasons for lack of payment and to make arrangements for future payments. However, the statement shows that most of the customers are paying within the first 30 days–an extremely positive cash flow sign.

Looking at the accounts payable total ($31,783.50), notice that it is $2,387.90 more than the accounts receivable total. Unless there are more projects nearing completion, you will be unable to pay all of your vendors when the receivables come in. Check to see if past monthly reports indicate the same shortfall. If so, you need to take steps to increase sales, speed up collections, or minimize purchases until there is sufficient cash flow to meet (and exceed) your monthly payables. Since some payable accounts are stretched out to 60 or 90 days, it would be advisable to pay these overdue accounts soon to minimize interest expenses and prevent vendors from suspending charging privileges. A phone call to each overdue vendor will go a long way toward maintaining a positive relationship.

Accounts Payable Statement

Vendor	Current	1 - 30	31 - 60	61 - 90	> 90
A	0.00	576.00	0.00	0.00	0.00
B	46.00	334.40	124.00	0.00	0.00
C	0.00	181.84	47.64	741.73	0.00
D	0.00	256.50	27.00	695.33	186.76
E	0.00	27.29	0.00	0.00	0.00
F	3,485.00	3,176.46	2,096.85	0.00	0.00
G	27.00	0.00	0.00	0.00	0.00
H	127.02	10.65	0.00	0.00	0.00
I	0.00	7.44	64.83	0.00	0.00
J	251.43	0.00	0.00	0.00	0.00
K	0.00	786.00	0.00	0.00	0.00
L	18.94	15.78	0.00	0.00	0.00
M	4,824.02	0.00	0.00	0.00	0.00
N	0.00	0.00	64.21	0.00	10.15
O	2,160.35	780.00	0.00	0.00	0.00
P	88.87	71.42	673.33	62.65	0.00
Q	0.00	0.00	60.69	0.00	0.00
R	571.57	574.65	169.50	0.00	0.00
S	2,000.00	0.00	0.00	0.00	0.00
T	0.00	0.00	35.00	70.00	0.00
U	0.00	0.00	74.90	0.00	0.00
V	535.50	3,259.00	0.00	0.00	0.00
W	0.00	0.00	40.76	0.00	0.00
X	1,742.97	0.00	0.00	0.00	0.00
Y	0.00	54.40	54.40	0.00	0.00
Z	493.27	0.00	0.00	0.00	0.00
TOTAL	**16,371.94**	**10,111.83**	**3,533.11**	**1,569.71**	**196.91**

Figure 11: Sample Accounts Payable (Total: $31,783.50)

WRE Experience

Dealing with financial matters has been one of the most frustrating aspects of running our business, yet is the most critical to our success as a company. I have learned a great deal about financial statements over the years and the value of having knowledgeable, experienced bookkeepers, accountants, and advisors at our disposal. Even with diligent financial planning, a seasonal landscaping business like ours can face yearly challenges with unpredictable sales, stock market fluctuations, and periodic recessions.

Critical to navigating the unpredictable financial waters is regular reviews of the P&L statements, balance sheet, and cash flow sheet with concrete adjustments to correct shortfalls and unexpected expenses. I have instituted a casual weekly lunch meeting with my bookkeeper to review our short-term (three week) cash needs, accounts payable, accounts receivable, upcoming major expenses, and a list of projects we are working on and their tentative completion dates. Monthly, we take a look at the P&L to determine our financial status. Since we have adopted this informal, relaxed setting for our financial meetings, I have viewed the finances in a different light. However, the announcement that I have a large check coming in soon always improves the mood of the meeting!

In addition to your bookkeeper, relationships with your accountant, banker, and financial advisors are very important. Planning a budget is critical for any horticultural business, especially a seasonal one like ours. These topics will be covered in Chapter 7.

Essential Points:

1. Learning about your P & L Statements, Balance Sheet, Accounts Receivable and Payable, and Cash Flow Sheet are critical to the financial health of your company.

2. Reviewing these statements frequently will help prepare you for corrections needed to keep your company profitable.

3. Relationships with your bookkeeper, accountant, financial advisor, and banker are important resources you need to make a priority.

Chapter 7: BUDGET, CASH FLOW, AND RELATIONSHIPS WITH FINANICAL ADVISORS

Your profitability as a company will depend, in good measure, upon how well you prepare and use a budget and ensure a steady cash flow (even in the slow off-season), and upon your relationships with bookkeepers, accountants, bankers, and financial advisors. My experience has shown that severe crises developed when I didn't have a comprehensive budget in place, forcing me to make unpopular and costly decisions about personnel, benefits, equipment, and vehicles. Without a budget in place there really are no benchmarks to gauge your financial situation until it is too late, requiring drastic steps to keep the company afloat. With a detailed budget in place you can track your progress weekly, monthly, or quarterly to see how you are doing. If gross sales do not meet projections, or employee expenses are too high, or overhead is climbing too much, you can make adjustments to bring the numbers in line. Waiting until the end of your fiscal year can be too late, then requiring draconian cuts that could affect the financial health of the company. Let's examine the three elements of profitability–budget, cash flow, and financial advisors–starting with preparing a budget.

Budget

What is a budget? A budget is a detailed plan to achieve specific company goals. The goals are derived from the overall company strategy (discussed in Chapter 2), which may be revised from year to year as economic, competitive, and employee conditions change. Keeping a pulse on the economic heartbeat nationally as well as in your geographical region is indispensable in developing your budget. You will budget differently during a recession (with decreasing sales, lower property values, and uncertainty) as in an era of expansion (with increasing sales, growth opportunities, and potentially higher pricing). Also, you need to be aware of industry trends which can influence your overall plan. What is the outlook for new housing starts? Are more customers asking for organic landscape services? Do communities you service have summer water bans? What are the most requested services and products?

Depending on your answers to these questions and more, your ultimate company goals, strategy, and budget will reflect your responses to these trends and issues. Ignoring trends or failing to adequately address them in your business planning will soon result in fewer sales, affecting the whole fabric of your company. Addressing trends, embracing change, and being innovative will put you at a competitive advantage with increased sales, customer loyalty, and company profitability–all this from a well planned budget (Figure 12)!

Ordinary Income/Expense

Income		Expense	
40000 · Plant Revenue	$69,828	60100 · Accounting Fees	$1,500
41000 · Material Revenue	$118,000	60200 · Advertising & Promotion	$5,000
42000 · Equipment Revenue	$75,798	60500 · Auto Exp.-Officer/Admin	$1,000
43000 · Labor Revenue	$334,764	61000 · Bank Service Charges	$300
44000 · Sub-Contract Revenue	$35,360	61200 · Business Consultants	$1,200
49000 · Other Misc. Income	$2,000	61400 · Contributions	$600
Total Income	**$635,750**	61500 · Dues and Subscriptions	$350
Cost of Goods Sold (COGS)		64300 · Equipment Rental/Office	$200
50000 · COGS-Plants	$36,627	64500 · Liability Insurance	$3,000
51000 · COGS-Materials	$68,814	65250 · Licenses and Permits	$350
55000 · COGS-Labor Costs		65350 · Meals and Entertainment	$750
55100 · Wages	$156,998	65750 · Merchant Fees	$900
55200 · Payroll Taxes	$22,682	65800 · Miscellaneous	$1,500
55300 · Medical Benefits	$6,786	65850 · Office Supplies/Expense	$2,500
55400 · Workers Comp	$6,207	66000 · Payroll G&A	
55500 · Uniforms	$500	66100 · Administrative	$30,000
55600 · Simple IRA-Employer Contribution	$750	66200 · Officer	$54,000
Total COGS-Labor Costs	**$193,923**	66400 · Officer Medical	$4,000
56000 · Supplies & Small Tools	$4,000	66600 · PR Tax expense	$10,000
57000 · Vehicle & Equipment Costs (includes accumulated depreciation)	$44,249	**Total 66000 · Payroll G&A**	**$98,000**
58000 · Subcontract COGS	$21,390	67200 · Postage and Delivery	$750
Total COGS	**$369,003**	67500 · Printing	$2,500
Gross Profit	**$266,747**	67700 · Rent	$11,500
		67800 · Repairs and Maintenance	$2,000
		68000 · Taxes-Property and Other	$600
		68500 · Telephone	$2,800
		68600 · Travel	$1,200
		69000 · Utilities	$3,000
		Total Expense	**$141,500**

Net Ordinary Income:	**$266,747 - $141,500 =**		**$125,247**
Other Income/Expense			
Other Income			
72000 · Other Income			$3,000
Total Other Income			*$3,000*
Other Expense			
82000 · Interest Expense			$5,600
Total Other Expense			*$5,600*
Net Other Income			*($2,600)*
Net Income			**$122,647**

Figure 12: Safe Green, LLC Budget: January 1, 2009 through December 31, 2009

Steps for Formulating a Budget

There are two ways to assemble your budget: top-down budgeting and bottom-up budgeting. In top-down budgeting the owner or management sets specific goals for sales, net income, profit margins, and expenses. Managers for divisions within the company will then plan their season around the budget target figure they are given. Bottom-up budgeting involves managers or supervisors putting together budgets for equipment, supplies, personnel, etc. they feel is needed to accomplish the goals of their department. After submission of the initial budget requests, management will make adjustments until a final budget is approved.

At WRE we use a combination approach to our budgeting, with team leaders submitting requests for equipment, tools, supplies, vehicles, and personnel. As the owner I take this information, along with several other critical financial documents, to plan our budget. The WRE budget process is as follows:

1. Solicit requests from team leaders in the masonry, construction, and maintenance divisions and from the office manager for supplies, equipment, tools, vehicles, and personnel for the upcoming year.

2. The bookkeeper generates a "Sales by Customer Summary" from QuickBooks® which lists sales by customer for the year. I use this form to write in next to their previous year sales what I predict each customer may provide for the upcoming year. Although an educated guess (based on, in some cases, 5 to 10 years of business with us), it is still a guess! I try to be realistic and conservative in my predictions; try not to be overly optimistic in your projections! Remember during the year that all of your corresponding goals, profit margins, and budget success are dependent on your gross sales projections.

3. All of our employee expenses are contained on an Excel™ spreadsheet (Figure 28 in Chapter 11) which includes all employees, wage rates, regular hours and overtime hours, gross pay, employee expenses (Federal Insurance Contributions Act (FICA), state unemployment insurance (SUI), federal unemployment insurance (FUI), health insurance, simple individual retirement account (IRA), worker's compensation, and uniforms), total employee expenses, holiday hours, unit hours, total hours worked, billable hours, billable hourly rates, and total revenue projected per employee. This valuable form tells us many significant items as we develop the budget:

   - The total expense for each employee (not just gross pay) and the corresponding revenue to be generated by the employee.

   - It identifies total direct labor and total non-direct labor (G&A), which is not generating revenue.

- By removing or adding several new employees in the form we can see the true savings or cost to the company of adjusting personnel instead of just assuming what the effect might be.

- When raises are considered, they can be entered in the form and instantly show the effect on employee costs–with no corresponding improvement in revenue generation unless billable rates are raised.

Most small horticultural companies are used to making employee additions or reductions based on their gut feeling. Now there is a way to base decisions on sound financial numbers, ensuring that your decisions won't adversely affect your budget goals.

4. Another key spreadsheet is the "Vehicle/Equipment Budget Form" (Table 6 in Chapter 11). This Excel™ form identifies all of our vehicles, trailers, tractors, and major equipment; the year they were purchased, and all expenses they incur during the year. There are rows for miles driven annually, miles per gallon, gallons used, total gasoline costs, maintenance and repairs, property tax, road tax, insurance, interest, annual registration, and depreciation cost. After entering the data we can determine total vehicle cost for the year and total fleet costs for our company. For those vehicles driven on the road we have converted their cost to a per mile figure. Equipment like tractors and Kubota backhoes have had the annual cost converted to a per hour figure. Knowing what each vehicle and piece of equipment costs is extremely important in budgeting how you will recoup the vehicle expenses. By adding replacement value to your vehicle and equipment charge rates, you can make sure that your vehicles actually make money for you. Since carefully calculating our vehicle and equipment costs and charging appropriately in our estimating program for all vehicles, we have exceeded our total vehicle costs by an average of 15%, adding an average of $35,000 towards our bottom line.

The equipment and vehicle sheet can identify pieces of equipment or vehicles that maybe too costly to keep, and therefore should be sold. It also identifies the exact cost per mile so that you can charge appropriately for trucking and delivery fees.

5. An actual sales table for each month during the previous year is helpful to plan the upcoming year's month to month sales (Figure 13). It also serves as an essential element to create monthly cash flow projections. In my budget planning I like to compare the previous two years' month-by-month deposit totals. Taking into account changes in the economic climate, trends in our industry, and our marketing outlook I will generate month-by-month sales projections. Typically I will generate three scenarios–low, mid (expected), and high projections–so I can have options ready in case my estimates do not materialize. This part of the budget process is critical to the success of the budget since all of your assumptions about expenses (net profit, etc.) are dependent on the total gross

sales. Years of experience have allowed me to be fairly close each year, but that doesn't ensure profitability unless the rest of the budget falls in line and is regularly monitored.

Gross Sales

	2008 (Actuals)	2009 (Projections)
January	$5,650	$8,500
February	$7,233	$10,500
March	$31,170	$38,000
Total 1st Quarter	$44,053	$57,000
April	$72,200	$78,000
May	$86,350	$90,000
June	$85,670	$98,000
Total 2nd Quarter	$244,220	$266,000
July	$80,777	$84,000
August	$60,233	$66,750
September	$53,299	$65,000
Total 3rd Quarter	$194,309	$215,750
October	$32,678	$46,000
November	$26,590	$36,000
December	$10,200	$15,000
Total 4th Quarter	$69,468	$97,000
2008 Year Total	$552,050	$635,750

Figure 13: Safe Green, LLC Gross Sales (Actual Sales 2008, Projections 2009)

Profit & Loss, Budget

Ordinary Income		
Income	**_2008 P & L_**	**_2009 Budget_**
40000 · Plant Revenue	$60,720	$69,828
41000 · Material Revenue	$98,672	$118,000.
42000 · Equipment Revenue	$68,908	$75,798
43000 · Labor Revenue	$291,100	$334,764
44000 · Sub-Contract Revenue	$30,750	$35,360
49000 · Other Misc. Income	$1,900	$2,000
Total Income	_$552,050_	_$635,750_
Cost of Goods Sold (COGS)		
50000 · COGS-Plants	$31,575	$36,627
51000 · COGS-Materials	$57,345	$68,814
55000 · COGS-Labor Costs		
55100 · Wages	$136,520	$156,998
55200 · Payroll Taxes	$19,724	$22,682
55300 · Medical Benefits	$5,751	$6,786
55400 · Workers Comp	$5,351	$6,207
55500 · Uniforms	$450	$500
55600 · Simple IRA-Employer Contribution	$630	$750
Total COGS-Labor Costs	_$168,426_	_$193,923_
56000 · Supplies & Small Tools	$3,453	$4,000
57000 · Vehicle & Equipment Costs (includes accumulated depreciation)	$44,345	$44,249
58000 · Subcontract COGS	$18,600	$21,390
Total COGS	_$323,744_	_$369,003_
Gross Profit	**_$228,306_**	**_$266,747_**

Figure 14: Safe Green, LLC Combined 2008 Profit & Loss and 2009 Budget

6. The last step is reviewing the last year's P&L statement and beginning to input your projected numbers for gross sales, net profit, expenses, employee costs, vehicles and equipment costs, etc. (Figure 14). Review each line of the budget, especially the G&A expenses, making assumptions for the next year. Will each line item go up or down? Once you have filled in the projected budget, run a copy of the planned P&L. Be prepared to re-think and adjust expenses and sales to achieve the results you want. It is much better to make hard decisions about the upcoming season during the budget formulation stage than during the season when you may be working 10-16 hours a day.

Although budgeting can be a science, there are nuances to putting all of the pieces together. Years ago I avoided the "budget" process like the plague; however, I now enjoy the challenge of assembling a budget that is complete, realistic, and works!

Profit & Loss, Budget (Continued)

Ordinary Expense		
Expense	**2008 P & L**	**2009 Budget**
60100 · Accounting Fees	$1,284	$1,500
60200 · Advertising and Promotion	$3,720	$5,000
60500 · Auto Exp.-Officer/Admin	$926	$1,000
61000 · Bank Service Charges	$252	$300
61200 · Business Consultants	$750	$1,200
61400 · Contributions	$520	$600
61500 · Dues and Subscriptions	$250	$350
64300 · Equipment Rental/Office	$196	$200
64500 · Liability Insurance	$2,871	$3,000
65250 · Licenses and Permits	$250	$350
65350 · Meals and Entertainment	$340	$750
65750 · Merchant Fees	$922	$900
65800 · Miscellaneous	$1,500	$1,500
65850 · Office Supplies/Expense	$1,803	$2,500
66000 · Payroll G&A		
66100 · Administrative	$30,000	$30,000
66200 · Officer	$54,000	$54,000
66400 · Officer Medical	$4,000	$4,000
66600 · PR Tax expense	$10,000	$10,000
Total 66000 · Payroll G&A	*$95,579*	*$98,000*
67200 · Postage and Delivery	$553	$750
67500 · Printing and Reproduction	$948	$2,500
67700 · Rent	$10,400	$11,500
67800 · Repairs and Maintenance	$1,739	$2,000
68000 · Taxes-Property and Other	$523	$600
68500 · Telephone	$2,624	$2,800
68600 · Travel	$935	$1,200
69000 · Utilities	$2,727	$3,000
Total Expense	**$131,612**	**$141,500**

Net Ordinary Income	***$96,694***	***$125,247***
Other Income/Expense		
Other Income		
72000 · Other Income	$2,850	$3,000
Total Other Income	*$2,850*	*$3,000*
Other Expense		
82000 · Interest Expense	$4,870	$5,600
Total Other Expense	*$4,870*	*$5,600*
Net Other Income	*($2,020)*	*($2,600)*
Net Income	**$94,674**	**$122,647**

Figure 14, continued.

Seasonal Business Cash Flow

Few responsibilities in running a horticultural business are more important than providing timely cash flow, especially with seasonal businesses. The primary role I play for my business is ensuring cash flow on a year-round basis, from the depths of our winter off-season to the times when the expected customer payment does not arrive. Eliminating this burden from running a small business would probably result in many more business owners! Over the years, I have used numerous methods to ensure cash flow which I will share with you here. Keep in mind that profitability will certainly help your positive cash flow, but not every year is guaranteed to be a profitable one. Some of the options available for providing cash flow:

1. Create a cash flow projection for your business for the upcoming year (discussed in previous budget section). Having owned a seasonal landscape firm for so many years, I can predict with certainty my best income months will be April through November. Cash flow analysis will show you the times that the business will need additional cash to meet your fixed expenses and carry you until income increases in the spring.

2. Look at your accounts receivable on a weekly basis. Are there customers that need a reminder phone call to speed up collections? Consider a discount for prompt payment (2%) which will help improve your cash flow at a minimal cost. For major landscape projects have clearly outlined payment terms on a signed contract. For projects under $20,000 we request a 50% deposit, balance when completed. Projects over $20,000, terms are 40% deposit, 40% mid payment, 20% when completed. Change orders are due in full when approved. Staying in communication with clients during a large project is essential to customer satisfaction and final payment!

3. Credit lines obtained at your local banks can be a source of off-season cash flow. Most banks require the line be paid off for at least 30 days each year. Recently, with the worsening economic situation, many banks have dropped their credit lines, making it more difficult for small businesses to survive the off season.

4. Credit cards can be used to help alleviate cash shortages and in some cases can be used similarly as credit lines. Be careful of the interest rates being charged. It is worth calling the credit card companies to request a lower rate, especially if you have been a long-term customer.

5. I have tried numerous incentive programs during the winter season to encourage the flow of money into my company at that time. Recently, we offered a 10% discount for the next year's maintenance services with a pre-payment of the average of the last two years' April and May maintenance bills. The response was very encouraging. Many of our clients who participated saw it as an opportunity to save money while helping our winter

cash flow. Another method was to offer Landscape Plant Discount Certificates valued at $100, $500, or $1,000. These certificates could be purchased for 33% off in exchange for full payment by March 1st. Customers could use the certificates any time during the season. Installation would be extra and charged at the time of planting.

6. Another source of money for your company is business loans. They can be used for new purchases, consolidation of debt, SBA-backed, or expansion capital. All of the information I have described so far–mission, objectives, business plan, marketing plan, P&L statements, balance sheet, budget, and cash flow projections–will be very important for the banker to see. I recently interviewed a local banker specializing in business loans to find out what she looks for in a new business loan request, and she shared some very useful advice (Figure 15).

7. Borrowing money from friends or family can be an option of last resort in a severe cash flow crunch. I was very fortunate in 1992 to have an aunt who loaned me enough money to survive an economic crisis, allowing our business to pay our bills and move ahead as a young landscape firm. Be aware that if you borrow from friends or loved ones, you risk alienating the lenders and damaging these relationships if you are unable to pay the money back. It is much better to plan ahead–have a business plan, cash flow analysis, and a detailed budget for securing a business loan–than have to seek out friends or relatives for survival!

Relationships with Financial Advisors

I cannot over-emphasize the importance of establishing and maintaining your relationships with financial advisors (accountants, bankers, bookkeepers, financial planners). They can be your lifeline in times of need. In your own company the bookkeeper plays critical roles for you and the company. When hiring for this position, look for someone who is experienced, focused, trustworthy, comfortable with financial programs, organized, and truly enjoys bookkeeping. You are depending on this person to provide accurate, up-to-date financial data and reports that influence your weekly, monthly, and yearly decisions about your firm…choose wisely!

Creating and maintaining a relationship with a local banker is necessary, especially if you have loans with the bank or anticipate expansion which may require additional funding. Keep your banker informed of your situation–both successes and shortcomings. Better that he/she is aware of your status than taken by surprise. Bankers like to be periodically updated with P&L's, balance sheets, and information about your businesses condition. Share with them any publicity, awards won, or special certifications your staff has achieved. Invite them to events, an open house, a memorial golf tournament, or an early morning breakfast get-together. Your openness with your banker will pay dividends in the long term.

Below is an interview with a local banker who oversees commercial lending and business development for a southern New England credit union. Her duties include structuring and managing the department as well as portfolio management. Business development includes having products that are competitive and useful, and serve as backup to the mortgage and consumer loan process. Additionally, she serves on the credit committee, which deals with policy compliance, portfolio risk, and exception loans.

What do you, as a local banker, look for from a small business applying for a loan?

Capital!! Companies need to have capital. Too many pull their capital out in some fashion and leave the company volatile, or they don't have any to invest in the beginning. Often they look to a bank to provide that capital, but again that makes for a weak foundation (and we don't lend startup capital in most cases). Also necessary is a good management team, which would involve their character. Résumés that speak to the ability to run the business are important. Of course, good credit still carries weight. Also collateral should be at 80% of the loan amount in most cases. And most importantly, the company must have the capacity to repay the loan--CASH FLOW.

What advice you would give a small horticultural business trying to grow their firm?

#1: Make sure they have capital of their own to put into the business. #2: Make sure to know how much money it takes to make money. Without that knowledge down to the penny, it is impossible to know if your business is making money based just on sales.

What resources do you recommend for advice about business loans, finances, and accounting?

Taking a course on small business accounting is very helpful. Having a frank, honest discussion with a trusted commercial loan officer as to your business plan is a great idea. They can tell you where you may have holes in your plan or ask you questions you may not have thought of.

Any other advice?

Know where you want to be in 5 years, 10 years, and 15 years. And I am not talking about sales. There are so many factors that need to be looked at in your business life and personal life. Time goes fast and we need to think more about the future than the right now.

This is a true story: someone came in for a loan to open a coffee house. When asked how many cups of coffee they needed to sell to make a profit, they said, "I don't know, but I know the place down the road is doing really well." Most likely the place down the road, if doing well, does not have a lot of overhead. Perhaps they only pay rent, have no loans to repay, and have a good system of accounts receivables/payables, and some form of capital. The person who came in for this loan is in no position to start a business and there is no way a bank would give them a loan.

Figure 15: Expert Advice on Loans and Financing

Terry Malaghan is a CPA and senior manager of the Westerly, RI branch of Sansiveri, Kimball & Co., LLP, a certified public accounting and business advisory firm. He works with clients on their corporate and individual income tax returns and provides tax planning for clients in a variety of industries.

What should a horticultural business look for when choosing an accounting firm?

The firm should have the necessary licenses and accreditations. The accountants should be state CPA's (Certified Public Accountants) in good standing. They should have a diversity of capabilities and years of experience. You want a good-sized company that can offer needed support with paralegal, financial, tax preparation, and estate planning services. The accountants should be a member of your team of advisors along with your lawyer, banker and insurance agent to help provide you with the necessary coordinated yet objective advice. Periodic meetings with this team can help you weather financial storms and assist with expansion. Most importantly, you should have a personal contact with an accountant who takes a critical look at your situation and feels free to offer objective (and sometimes unpopular) advice and guidance.

Describe several mistakes small horticultural companies should avoid.

One of the key mistakes is entering a new business with limited experience, especially in fields in which they are not formally trained. Gaining a good background in horticulture first is advisable before committing to a new venture. Completing a business plan with a budget and projections is essential when first starting out. Those companies anticipating expansion and growth need to have a plan for working capital. During growth is when there will be a need for extra money to sustain a positive cash flow. Completing a pro forma budget will help assure that money is there when cash flow crunches occur...and they will happen!

What are several lessons of which horticultural firms should be cognizant?

Foremost, individuals starting a business need to accept that BUSINESS=RISK. There are no guarantees in the world of business and you must be prepared to fail and lose everything as well as succeed and become wealthy. You must know your risk limits before committing to any business venture. Understand that most businesses do not have an unlimited life span; have an exit strategy before moving ahead. Changes in customer tastes, poor economic conditions, loss of key personnel, or unfavorable environmental conditions (droughts, floods, heat, etc.), all out of your control, can render your company (and investment) vulnerable to failure. Have a good accounting program (like QuickBooks®) which is capable of tracking receivables, payables, and sales. Keep a close eye on the receivables and cash on hand to make sure cash flow will be adequate; review and follow up promptly on accounts receivable if they start to age. Watch profit and loss statements for unusual swings or trends. Reviewing these reports regularly will give you warning of potential problems.

Resources you would recommend?

IRS.gov has great publications for start-ups. SBA (Small Business Administration) has considerable resources including SCORE–a volunteer group of retired business professionals who can help you at no charge. Meetings with your business advisors (banker, accountant, insurance agent, etc.) will prove valuable to get you through the difficult times and prepare for expansion.

Figure 16: Expert Advice from a Certified Public Accountant

In addition to your bookkeeper, your accountant can play an important role in keeping your company focused, in good times and bad (Figure 16). The accountant can usually detect early warning signs that need to be addressed before very serious decisions need to be made…like bankruptcy. They can not only serve to complete your tax returns, but can also offer advice as a business partner to help you through difficult economic times as well as on how to handle exceptional profits. Because finances are not my favorite segment of my business I lean heavily on my accountant (and other financial advisors) to assist me in charting my financial course.

I also depend on our financial advisor to help with our retirement program. Five years ago we switched from a 401k program to a simple IRA profit sharing program. There were several benefits to this decision: a greater dollar amount that could be invested, greater employee control over choosing their investments, and our ability to offer between 1-3% matching at the end of our season. Everyone won with this switch.

WRE Experience

The area of running a business that is my least favorite (finances, budget, cash flow) has resulted in the most consternation for me and the business. That is why I have forced myself to become very comfortable with P&L's, balance sheets, budgets, cash flow statements, and other financial statements. My firm's future success and survival depends on me (and others) to ensure the best financial results–not an easy task. A lesson that I have learned is that when our company is focused– moving ahead with a realistic, detailed budget, established, clean, measurable goals, and all members of the team working together–there is little we cannot accomplish.

Your company's success or failure is dependent on your dedication to creating, following, and adjusting when necessary, your critical financial statements.

Essential Points:

1. Establishing a comprehensive, detailed budget will allow you to achieve specific company goals.

2. To ensure cash flow in slow times during the year, have cash flow projections and contingency plans in place before the season begins.

3. Cultivate a close relationship with your financial advisors. They will help you weather difficult financial times and support you during business expansion.

Chapter 8: COMPANY STRUCTURE, ORGANIZATION, AND LEGAL ENTITIES

There are a myriad of items to consider when beginning a business (and ongoing concerns with an established business) regarding company structure and organization. Will you choose to be a sole proprietor, form a partnership, incorporate, or set up a Limited Liability Company (LLC)? What will your company responsibility flow chart look like? Will there be clear, concise job descriptions for your employees? Are legal entities such as landscape service contracts, confidentiality and non-compete agreements, and written partnership or incorporation papers in place? Do you have the necessary licenses, permits, and certifications to operate your horticultural firm? These items (and numerous others) will need to be addressed before delving into you day-to-day operations. Even established companies can benefit from reviewing these organizational items, making changes, and fully reviewing and refining their company structure and legal entities. Hire a lawyer specializing in business law to ensure you have crossed all of your t's and dotted all of your i's. Let's begin with a look at various types of company organizations, comparing their advantages and disadvantages.

Company Structure

1. Sole Proprietorship

The least complex and easiest company type to form is a sole proprietorship. Many of us in the horticultural industry started our businesses this way. The company is easy to form, you control the profits and make all the decisions, you have less bureaucracy and taxation to deal with, and you can file your own personal tax return. Disadvantages include unlimited liability for all your business debts and obligations (including all of your personal assets), greater difficulty in raising capital and long term financing, and a less professional appearance than a partnership or corporation.

2. Partnership

Partnerships are defined as "an association of two or more persons to carry on as co-owners of a business for profit"[1]. Partnerships, like sole-proprietorships, are easy to form although written articles of partnership would be advisable. Typically there are improved growth possibilities, shared decision making, and more freedom from federal regulations and taxation. Disadvantages include unlimited liability of at least one partner, potential disruption if one partner decides to leave, difficulty in obtaining long-term loans, and buying out a partner can be acrimonious.

3. <u>Corporations</u>

As your business grows, incorporating becomes an appealing option. In the case of being sued, the individual members of the company are protected from liability. Your company appears more substantial and professional in the eyes of the community. You can sell stock to raise capital, and the tax rate maybe lower. Disadvantages include significant government regulations and filings, activities being limited by state chapter and federal laws, and the requirement to pay corporate income tax on earnings and personal income tax on the same earnings.

You can incorporate your business through the Secretary of State's office after filing articles of organization; however, it is advisable to first seek legal advice regarding the process and articles, and whether it is the right step for your business. The Secretary of State in the filing state will issue a charter for the corporation identifying its powers and limitations. Contact your Secretary of State for specific regulations. I have listed websites in Appendix A, Section VI Part D for more information.

There are several types of corporations:

- <u>C Corporation</u> – A C corporation is a corporation in the U.S. that for Federal income tax purposes is taxed under 26 United States Code 11 and subchapter C of Chapter 1 of the Internal Revenue Code. Most major companies (and many smaller firms) are treated as C corporations for Federal income tax purposes[2].

  The income of a C corporation is taxed, whereas the income of an S corporation (with a few exceptions) is not taxed under the Federal income tax laws. The income, or loss, is applied pro rata to each shareholder and appears on their tax return as schedule E income (or loss). Unlike S corporations, a corporation may qualify as a C corporation without any limit on the number of shareholders, foreign or domestic[3].

  Corporations are state entities, and the C corporation status refers to the tax treatment of these corporations by the federal government. The double taxation (taxation of the corporation's income and the separate taxation on its dividends) constitutes the major impact of being a C corporation.

- <u>S Corporation</u> – S corporations, for U.S. federal income tax purposes, are corporations that make an election to be taxed under Subchapter S of Chapter 1 of the Internal Revenue Code. In general, S corporations do not pay any income taxes. However, the corporation's income (or losses) are divided among and passed through to its shareholders who then report the income (or loss) on their own individual income tax returns[4].

S corporations are treated as corporations under state law. As separate legal entities they generally provide shareholders the same liability protection as C corporations. Federal taxation of S corporations resembles that of partnerships where the income, deductions, and tax credits of the S corporation flow through to the shareholders annually.

The income is taxed at the shareholder level and not at the corporate level. Unlike a C corporation, an S corporation is not eligible for a dividends received deduction and is not subject to the 10% of taxable income limitation applicable to charitable contributions.

- Limited Liability Company (LLC) – A relatively new business structure is the Limited Liability Company (LLC), which is a cross between a corporation and partnership. The LLC offers the limited liability protection of a corporation with the flexibility and tax advantages of a partnership. In general the LLC is less restrictive and less expensive regarding taxes compared to an S corporation.

Before making any decisions regarding your company structure, consulting with your accountant and business lawyer would be extremely helpful. Besides the tax issues and limited liability protection questions there are numerous other legal implications on which the legal professionals can appropriately advise you.

Company Organization

Whether you have three or thirty employees, it is wise to create a responsibility flow chart for your company (Figure 17). Particularly when firms are growing, there can be confusion regarding the chain of command and individual responsibilities. Uncertainties can breed turf wars: productivity can be affected, and company morale can suffer. An indication that problems are at hand is the lack of accountability when issues arise, along with that revealing comment "it's not MY responsibility!" There are several ways to improve this situation so that the whole staff is on board.

Prior to meeting with the entire staff to discuss the responsibility flow chart and specific job descriptions, solicit their written input regarding their role, specific responsibilities, and thoughts about the company organization. With the help of your key team members, construct the responsibility flow chart not only using the input of the staff but reflecting the values of your company and its culture. A traditional top-down chain-of-command chart may not fit your more flexible, shared-responsibility philosophy. Both forms can work if they are clearly defined, shared with the staff, and embraced as part of your company's mission, strategies, and goals.

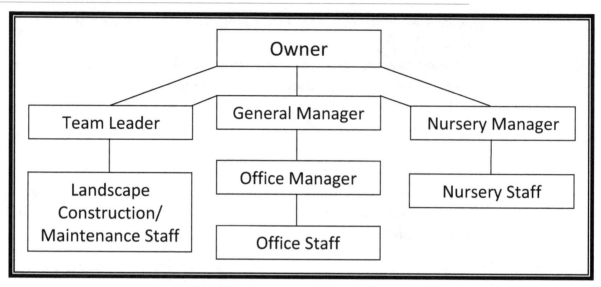

Figure 17: Safe Green, LLC Organizational Chart

Once the responsibilities are clearly formulated, specific job descriptions can be established. My experience has shown that motivation, enthusiasm, and productivity go up dramatically when each team member has a detailed job description. After creating and refining job descriptions for every position at WRE in 2004, our focus, accomplishments, and overall productivity went up considerably. Each team member knew their role, expectations, and position within the company's hierarchy. With greater expectations came greater achievement. Certainly not a new concept, but when applied to your employees the results will be significant.

In addition to the general job descriptions, each position at WRE has a job title, an explanation of to whom they are accountable, requirements, employee classification, and a job level/pay scale explanation (Figure 18). These job descriptions are available to new hires and existing employees who wish to apply for open positions like team leaders and managers.

At the time of completing the job descriptions, each category of employee received a new title. Entry-level positions became Landscape Apprentice, second-level was Landscape Craftsman, third-level was Team Leader, fourth-level was Manager, and fifth-level was General Manager. The benefit of changing the name of the entry level position from "laborer" to "Landscape Apprentice" was evident after our first help wanted ads were placed in the local newspaper seeking Landscape Apprentices. The number and quality of the applicants was significantly higher, and most asked to whom they would be assigned as an apprentice to learn landscaping. The work hadn't changed but the attitude about the position had. By showing a greater respect for the entry level position and presenting potential employees an organized job-level chart with promotion requirements, many saw the opportunities to advance and make landscaping a long-term career opportunity (Table 3).

Table 3: Safe Green, LLC Sample Job Levels

Job Description	Level	Wage Scale	Unit Days/Hours*
General Manager	5	$20 - $25 / hr	14 days / 112 hrs
Nursery Manager Office Manager Division Manager	4	$16 - $20 / hr	10 days / 80 hrs
Team Leader	3	$14 - $16 / hr	7 days / 56 hrs
Landscape Craftsman	2	$12 - $14 / hr	5 days / 40 hrs
Landscape Apprentice	1	$10 - $12 / hr	3 days / 24 hrs

Seasonal Full-Time Employees (mid-March through mid-December, average 40 hours x 40 weeks = 1,600 hours/year).

* Unit time is paid time off: sick days, vacation days, personal time, bereavement time, etc. One day (8 hrs) additional unit time added for each successfully completed year of service.

Every employee is paid for recognized national holidays.

JOB TITLE

Landscape Apprentice –
Reports to Team Leader
Accountable to Division Manager, Director of Operations, and Owner

JOB DESCRIPTION:
The Landscape Apprentice has the skills, experience, and/or desire to support their mentors/team leaders with assigned duties and implied tasks with a focus on efficiency, reliability, consistency and the WRE brand for high quality and outstanding customer service.

The Landscape Apprentice works outside most of the time and will be exposed to cold, heat and severe weather. The Landscape Apprentice may be required to haul and hoist materials, prep the work site to eliminate possible hazards, dig holes for plantings, ditches and trenches, collect and clean tools and equipment, load and unload trucks, etc.

Overtime hours, including Saturdays, are expected when the work schedule or deadlines demand them.

Landscape Construction Division Apprentice –
Reports to Landscape Construction Team Leaders
Accountable to Division Manager, Director of Operations, and Owner

Responsibilities include but are not limited to the proper installation and removal of landscape plantings, installation of hardscapes and garden structures, including patios, walkways, driveways and water features, under the direction of either the Team Leader or the Team Manager.

Heavy physical labor is involved on a daily basis.

Landscape Maintenance Division Apprentice –
Reports to Landscape Maintenance or Lawn Care Team Leaders
Accountable to the Division Manager and Owner

Responsibilities include but are not limited to mowing, weeding, mulching, and pruning of plantings on residential and/or commercial properties and landscapes.

Physical labor involved on a daily basis.

REQUIREMENTS:
- Clean driving record is mandatory.
- Commercial driver's license is desirable.
- Must be able to work productively when unsupervised or as part of a team.
- Good attendance, punctuality, and positive team spirit are expected.

EMPLOYEE CLASSIFICATION
Seasonal full-time position – Late March/early April through mid-December
Typically works 40 hrs/wk for 40 weeks per year

JOB LEVEL / PAY SCALE
Level 1
Hourly wage = $10 to $12 per hour
3 unit days after 90-day introductory period
Plus 1 day for each additional year of employment from start date
4 Paid Holidays

Figure 18: Sample Job Description

Legal Entities

Once you enter a horticultural business there are numerous licenses, permits, and certifications that will be required for you to legally perform your service or sell your product. Whether you are selling a product or service, a written contract between you and the customer will be necessary.

Intellectual property can be protected by copyright law, trademarks, and patents. Your business lawyer can be a great resource for legal entities, especially creating a legal contract for your business and reviewing copyright law and trademarks as they affect your firm.

- Contracts – Many small businesses operate without signed written contracts. Although the handshake deal may be noble, it is a very risky way to conduct your business. Particularly with products or services that are valued in the tens of thousands of dollars, you are at risk of losing money if disputes arise. A sample written contract (Figure 19) spells out the services to be provided, procedures for changes in services or products (namely written change orders), payment terms, start and finish times, provisions for unexpected occurrences, warranties, and client and business owner's signatures. Some states have a 3-day recession clause and other stipulations which may need to be included in your contract; these need to be confirmed with your business lawyer (Figure 20).

  Specific estimates, plant and material lists, plans, etc. that are discussed in Chapter 12 as part of the sample foundation planting project will need to become addenda of the contract and initialed. Remember, the contract is to protect you and the customer by making the written agreement clear and ensuring that it is understood by all parties. Most clients will view the contract as necessary and an indicator of your professionalism.

WOOD RIVER EVERGREENS INC.

101 Woodville Road
Hope Valley, Rhode Island
02832
Telephone: 401 364 3387
Fax: 401 364 3737

LANDSCAPE SERVICES CONTRACT

1. CUSTOMER NAME: _____ CUSTOMER NO. _____

   MAILING ADDRESS: _____
   NO.   STREET

   _____
   CITY   STATE   ZIP

   PHONE: _____
   AREA CODE   NUMBER

   LOCATION OF
   SERVICES: _____
   (IF DIFFERENT THAN ABOVE)

2. DESCRIPTION OF SERVICES TO BE PROVIDED: _____

   _____

   _____

   _____

   (See attachments for design and itemization of nursery stock and materials included in the cost quotation below).
   NOTE: When initialized by both parties, attachments become part of this contract.

3. QUOTATION OF COST FOR SERVICES, AND/OR NURSERY STOCK AND MATERIALS AS DESCRIBED IN ITEM #2 (ABOVE) AND ON ANY ATTACHMENTS:

   $ _____

4. ANY CHANGE IN SERVICES, PLANTS, MATERIALS, AND/OR PRICES MUST BE AGREED UPON IN WRITING SIGNED BY BOTH PARTIES.

5. GUARANTEE: SEE ATTACHMENT ADDENDUM FOR TERMS AND CONDITIONS OF WOOD RIVER EVERGREENS INC. GUARANTEE.

6. PAYMENT TERMS:
   (A) DEPOSIT: A DEPOSIT EQUALING _____ OF THE QUOTED COST (SEE ITEM #3 ABOVE).
   (B) MID-PROJECT PAYMENTS ARE TO BE MADE AS AGREED ON.
   (C) BALANCE: THE BALANCE OF PAYMENT IS DUE AND IS PAYABLE IN FULL ON THE DATE OF PROJECT COMPLETION.
   (D) APPROVED EXTRA COSTS TO BE PAID FOR AS MUTUALLY AGREEN ON.

7. DATE: _____   PROJECT COST: $ _____

                                   MID-PROJECT PAYMENT: $ _____

                                   BALANCE DUE UPON
                                   PROJECT COMPLETION: $ _____

I/We have read this contract and accompanying attachments and agree to fully comply with the terms and conditions herein.

DATE: _____   SIGNATURE: _____

DATE: _____   SIGNATURE: _____
FOR WOOD RIVER EVERGREENS INC.

Figure 19: Sample Landscape Services Contract

Stephen M. Brusini, Esq. has been practicing in the areas of corporate and commercial law for 20 years. His clients are typical Rhode Island and Massachusetts family-owned and privately-owned, small to medium-sized businesses. He also serves as general counsel to a number of larger regional companies as well. Steve, who is a co-founder of Orson and Brusini Ltd. in Providence, Rhode Island, graduated from the College of the Holy Cross (B.A. 1988) and Cornell Law School (J.D. 1991).

The importance of horticultural businesses to have written contracts for their projects.

I am a huge proponent of written contracts for all businesses, specifically including horticultural firms. My corporate lawyer often jokes that if every business owner always did what they were supposed to do, then he would have no business at all- yet he is always very busy! The fact of the matter is that even well-intentioned and honest people can walk away from a meeting, presentation, walk-through, or discussion with radically different ideas of what has been agreed to. This is particularly important for horticulturalists and landscapers for two reasons: (a) like it or not they are peripherally in the construction business, and as such they are faced with the same unforeseen site conditions, customer change requests, coordination with other contractors, and similar issues beyond their reasonable control that will in fact impact job costs and time deadlines; and (b) customers frequently engage a landscape professional immediately on being provided with an estimate, often with an expectation that the estimate itself, or perhaps no more than a handshake, will fully define and describe the contractual relationship between the parties.

How confidentiality and non-compete agreements can protect your business.

Confidentiality agreements are important whenever a business has trade secrets or proprietary information that - if provided to an employee, subcontractor, or vendor without restriction - can be used to the detriment of the business. Non-solicitation, non-competition, and non-circumvention agreements are equally important for all landscape professionals because they provide much-needed protection to prevent (or at least discourage) employees, subcontractors, and vendors from stealing customers, cherry-picking employees, disrupting key business relationships, disclosing sensitive information (such as markups and profit) to customers, and bypassing the landscape professional through direct communication with customers.

Figure 20: Legal Advice: Stephen M. Brusini, Esq.

- Copyrights, Trademarks, and Patents – In the U.S., copyright protection automatically extends to appropriate material like books, advertising copy, and artwork. You should put a copyright notice on all appropriate materials in a highly visible place. This should include either the copyright symbol or the word copyright, the first year the material was issued to the public, and the name of copyright holder.

  The name of your business, your brand name, graphics, or words are essentially trademarks. You automatically have some protection if you were the first to use that trademark, however you should research other business names, brands, logos etc. thoroughly before using a trademark. In many cases trademarks offer geographical area protection, but not nationally or internationally. For national use of trademarks you need to register with the U.S. Patent and Trademark office.

Patents can be granted for a wide range of items including plant patents to protect a particular hybrid tree, shrub, or perennial. A patent must be applied for within the first year of the first commercial use of the product. Most U.S. patents have lifespan of 20 years. Design patents are good for 14 years. The procedure to obtain a patent is complex and may be expensive. For those businesses which have developed a novel and non-obvious design or created a new plant variety the cost to secure the patent will be worth the effort.

- Licenses, Permits, Certifications, and Insurance – There are numerous licenses and permits needed to legally operate a horticultural business. Certifications, even if not legally required, will demonstrate the professional nature of personnel at the horticultural company. The following is a partial list of licenses and permits needed for running a horticultural business in Rhode Island. You will need to contact your state and local governments and trade associations to verify the licenses and permits needed for you particular business. Websites with more information are listed in Appendix A, Section I.

Sales tax permit	Pesticide applicators license	Arborists license
Contractor's license	Hoister's license	CDL drivers license
Nurseryman's license	Composting permit	Landscape architect's license
RI Horticultural Certification	NOFA accreditation	RI Certified Coastal Invasive Manager (CCIM)

Besides licenses, permits, and certifications, you will need various forms of insurance to operate your business: liability, vehicle, workers compensation, fire and theft, etc. A knowledgeable, professional, and dedicated insurance agent is an essential member of your business support team (Figure 21).

John C. Tickner, CPCU is an independent insurance agent and President & CEO of Babcock & Helliwell Insurance and Risk Management in Wakefield, RI.

Whatever your horticultural business type, here are some basic insurance coverages to consider:

- <u>Property Insurance</u> – any building or other property you are required to protect due to leases, etc. Coverage should be tailored to your exposures. Flood and earthquake are areas not normally included in policies so separate discussion is needed to determine exposure.

- <u>Business Interruption</u> – covers your loss of income if a claim to your property causes you to close or interrupt operations.

- <u>Crop Insurance aka Nursery Crop</u>– depending on exposure and amount of coverage needed, this is specialized to the industry.

- <u>Equipment Coverage</u> – Whether you own, rent, or lease equipment, protection for damage to it should be considered.

- <u>Liability Insurance</u> – this is bodily injury, property damage and personal injury that you cause to members of the public emanating from your operations or products/services.

- <u>Pesticide or Similar Pollutant Exposure</u> – Due to the restrictive changes in most policies in the 80's & 90's it is imperative that horticultural entities that use pesticides, etc. purchase this type of insurance.

- <u>Automobile Insurance</u> - Necessary if they own, hire, or "borrow" autos in their operation.

- <u>Workers' Compensation</u> – In all states this is statutory, <u>required</u> coverage. Most states require this if the business has "one employee or more" (that includes businesses with only "one" part-time and seasonal worker, even clerical only, in most states.) Each state has their own law so carefully investigate options. Provides your employees medical, lost wages and rehabilitative costs for employment related injuries and sickness.

- <u>Umbrella Liability</u> – If extra liability limits, higher than $1,000,000, are needed this should be looked into as less expensive than other methods to extend limits.

- <u>Bonding</u> – Some jobs, especially state and governmental projects, may require bid/performance bonds to even quote the job.

Key questions small businesses should ask when choosing an insurance agent include:

- References, references!! What references or people in the industry do you know?

- How informed are you and/or the agency on the horticultural industry? Any involvement with local associations or groups?

- Do you have insurance carriers that specialize in my business?

- Will you be able to handle my account as I grow and offer additional services and products that may be needed in the future? What if we expand into more complex services, etc.?

Your agent should be a great resource, as well as your local, state and national horticultural associations. Some local universities will offer seminars to better understand insurance in general as well as the Small Business Administration (SBA) who will also hold seminars/webinars either on specific insurance coverage or often more of an overview of insurance.

Figure 21: Business Insurance Tips: John C. Tickner

WRE Experience

Like many small business owners, I began my company as a sole proprietorship. Within two years of entering the landscape profession full time, I incorporated my firm as a C corporation. The primary benefit to me was the limited liability protection, especially since we were bringing hundreds of customers onto our property during the Spooky Halloween Hayride season and Christmas tree season in addition to our landscape customers.

Recently I have had discussions about electing for an S corporation, which would eliminate the double taxation of the C Corporation and change our fiscal year from April 1 – March 31 to the calendar year.

Throughout the development of my business, I have depended on my accountants and business lawyers for guidance and legal advice. In 2004 we added confidentiality and non-compete agreements to our Employee Handbooks to protect our firm from breaches of trust and from unhappy employees using our existing clients to begin a competing landscape business.

We have encouraged our team members to obtain as many licenses and certifications as possible, making employees much more valuable to WRE and putting them in a better position for promotions. I cannot emphasize enough how valuable it was to create the detailed job descriptions. With employee input, the delineated job descriptions provided responsibilities, roles, and a source of motivation for employees looking to advance in the company. Changing the names of the specific job levels also created a sense of professionalism, hope for advancement, and pride for all of our employees.

Essential Points:

1. In consultation with your lawyer, determine which company structure (sole proprietorship, partnership, corporation (C or S), or LLC) meets your needs. Realize that as your company grows the legal entity can change.

2. Creating a company organizational chart with staff responsibilities outlined and detailed job descriptions will help reduce confusion amongst employees.

3. Written contracts between you and the customer will be necessary to protect you and the client should disputes arise during and after the project's completion.

4. Research your state's requirements to legally operate your horticultural business including permits, licenses, certifications, and forms of insurance needed.

5. Use your accountant, business lawyer, and human resources professional to help you design legal contracts, employee handbooks, and the type of company structure that fits your business.

Chapter 9: ATTRACTING, HIRING, RETAINING…AND FIRING EMPLOYEES

A major issue facing small businesses, including horticultural firms, is attracting good employees and then finding ways to retain them. Numerous business owners have shared with me that they will not expand their services (or in some cases stay in business) because of the shortage of good, qualified, and motivated employees. Some owners have purposely kept their business small so that they do not have to seek out employees which, if found, would allow them to achieve their long-term vision and goals. Although it is true that the lack of employees will limit the growth, development, and success of your company, hiring the right employees will give you the opportunity to assemble a winning team. With a team of dedicated, talented, and motivated employees there are no limits to what your company can achieve.

Gathering an award-winning team requires a sustained, focused, and year-round commitment to attract, hire, and retain valuable employees. It is not an easy or quick process, but the end results are clearly worth it. Building your team will also require the letting-go of certain employees who do not share the values of your company or who display overt (or covert) negativity, which affects team morale and customer relations. Even though many times the "bad apple" employee is a good worker and dependable, behind the scenes they are destroying the morale of company, which you may not find out until after significant damage is done.

The objective in hiring is to look for talented, motivated, and exceptional people who share your company's values, can align themselves with your management philosophy, mission, and vision, and will thrive personally and professionally within your company culture. Since in many small businesses hiring an employee is like adding a member to your family, the selection process needs to be designed to ensure a match between the employee and your company. There is no magical formula to building a winning team; however, I have used the following ten steps, which have proven successful for us.

Ten Steps to Building a Winning Team

1. Establish a positive, friendly, supportive company culture. Successful companies demonstrate a team spirit and family-like environment. Their company culture is a reflection of established values backed by a positive, friendly, and supportive lifestyle. Firms like Apple Computer, Whole Foods, and locally, Sylvan Nursery Inc., exhibit a defined company culture tied to their mission and values. By hiring employees who embrace their mission and values, the "team" flourishes, contributing to their success.

The owner sets the tone for the company by fostering the friendly, supportive environment. Acting as a coach (rather than a dictator), the owner can motivate, encourage, and set up employees for success. Providing the staff with the resources, tools, and training to succeed at their job will help motivate employees to exceed expectations. Recognizing the diversity of talents, job functions, and employee backgrounds will help in assigning employees to a position for which they are best suited. Employees who serve in roles that they feel fit their skill level and passion will strive for a higher level of performance. In a small horticultural business, employees will be expected to fill many roles out of necessity; however, keeping them connected to their favorite role will be beneficial.

Primary to an employee's continued success is having a role in the decision-making process. Having a participatory management system can contribute to the supportive culture, involve key employees in important company decisions, and create a source of new ideas. Since our company adopted a participatory management program in 1996 (the WRE Planning Committee), all of our major decisions, new services, company changes, and future plans have been proposed, discussed, and acted on within the WRE Planning Committee. The committee meets three times during the winter months and consists of the team leaders (construction and maintenance), managers, marketing director, bookkeeper, nursery manager, and the owner. The success of WRE (and the committee) is based on opportunities for input and consensus decision-making. Smaller, sub-committee meetings precede the major committee meetings, allowing many difficult topics (size of staff, budgets, and compensation issues) to be resolved before the larger committee meetings. With a vested interest in the company and future plans, employees have moved ahead with personal expectations of success and responsibility for the changes.

2. <u>Project a professional image of your company</u>. The image of your company is important for potential employees as well as current employees, clients, vendors, and the community. Your company persona can be a key factor in attracting talented and motivated new employees. Building a strong brand that represents quality, integrity, and service will entice qualified people to seek employment with your company. All team members need to be dedicated to your brand. Your logo (although important) is only one ingredient of your brand. Clean trucks, neat uniforms, the way you keep a job site clean, the professionalism of your staff with clients, and even the way you answer the phone all contribute to the strength of your brand.

WRE has had success in attracting talented, motivated employees, many of whom have previously owned their own horticultural businesses. Having grown tired of performing all the roles to keep their business intact, they were excited to join a professional, award-winning company with a well-recognized brand, a positive company culture, and opportunity to perform the landscape service they enjoy: mowing, masonry, installing hardscapes, or marketing. The experienced and professional nature of our employees is a huge asset as our company plots a course of growth and change.

3. <u>Be specific about job requirements</u>. In Chapter 8 I discussed the value of the specific job descriptions for each position within the company. Using those descriptions can be very useful in attracting and hiring new employees. After analyzing your company's employee needs, carefully design ads to attract the desired employees. With the new job titles we've adopted–landscape apprentice, landscape craftsman, team leader, and team manager–we have been able to solicit a more talented, interested, and motivated job applicant. The first year we advertised for a "Landscape Apprentice" we were pleasantly surprised with the quantity and quality of the applicants. More gratifying was the response of the two employees hired who asked who their assigned mentor would be. They wanted to make landscaping a career, not just a seasonal job.

With all our applicants we request a résumé or an outline of work history. Especially for the apprentice position this requirement raises the level of applicants for the position. Advertising for a landscape laborer will attract applicant who may not be the employee you are looking for.

All applicants complete a comprehensive job application (Figure 22). We encourage people who inquire about a job to fill out an application even if we are not hiring. Building up a résumé reserve, especially in time of high unemployment, can be helpful when someone leaves your company. We are always on the lookout for skilled applicants to complement current staff talents.

Managers and team leaders are involved in the interview process. Depending on the type of employee needed, a set of specific interview questions are written in advance so that all of the interviewed candidates can be compared objectively. The managers and team leaders conduct the initial interview. After the first round I sit in on the final interviews (usually with three applicants) and as a group we choose the candidate who will be invited to join our team. The offer of a job does not happen until references are checked. Experience has taught us that although a candidate may interview well, the follow-up with references is necessary to confirm our initial impressions. Unless the references are positive, we will not hire an applicant and will move on to the remaining choices. If no one meets our requirements we start the search over again. It may mean expanding our search to different geographic areas and new networking sources, and following up on previous leads. With the importance we place on hiring the right person for our team, a delay in our search is preferable to hiring the wrong employee.

Application for Employment

Company Name

(Please Print)

Date of Application: _____

Position Applied for: _____

Other Positions Interested In: _____

_____

Name:_____
           Last   First   Middle

Address:_____
           No   Street

_____
           City   State   Zip

Telephone: _____

Have you filed an application here before?   ____Yes   ____No
      If yes, give date:_____

Have you ever been employed here before?   ____Yes   ____No
      If yes, give dates:_____

Is your spouse/relative employed at this company?   ____Yes   ____No
      If yes, give department:_____

Are you employed now?   _____Yes   _____No

Figure 22: Sample Application for Employment

Work Experience

List current/prior employers: Start with your present or last job. Include all positions which you have held during the past ten (10) years. You may include any verified work performed on a volunteer basis. You may exclude organization names which indicate race, color, religion, sex, or national origin.

Employer:_____   Telephone:_____
Dates Employed:_____   Position:_____
Address:_____

Job Title of Supervisor:_____   Hourly Rate/Salary:_____
Reason for Leaving:_____
_____

Employer:_____   Telephone:_____
Dates Employed:_____   Position:_____
Address:_____

Job Title of Supervisor:_____   Hourly Rate/Salary:_____
Reason for Leaving:_____
_____

Employer:_____   Telephone:_____
Dates Employed:_____   Position:_____
Address:_____

Job Title of Supervisor:_____   Hourly Rate/Salary:_____
Reason for Leaving:_____
_____

May we contact your present employer?   ____Yes   ____No

Are you a citizen of the United States?   ____Yes   ____No
If not, are you legally entitled to work in the United States? ____Yes ____ No

What language(s) do you speak and/or write fluently:_____

On what date would you be available for work?_____

Are you available to work: __Full Time __Part Time __Temporary

What are your hourly/salary requirements? _____

Figure 22, page 2.

Professional Organizations

List professional, trade, business, or civic activities and offices held which are relevant to the position(s) for which you are applying. (You may exclude those which indicate race, color, religion, sex, or national origin):_____

_____

References

Give name, address and telephone number of three (3) professional references who are not related to you: (name, address, telephone number, relationship).

1._____

2._____

3._____

Education

List Highest Education Achieved:_____
        (school, degree)

Honors/Awards:_____

_____

Summarize special skills and qualifications acquired from employment or other experience which are relevant to the position(s) for which you are applying.

_____

_____

_____

_____

_____

Figure 22, page 3.

Military Service

Veteran of the U.S. Military?   _____Yes   _____No

If yes, Branch of U.S.Military Service:_____

Please describe any specialized military training pertaining to the position for which you are applying:

_____

_____

Criminal Record

1. Have you ever been convicted of a felony? _____Yes _____No
If the answer to the above is "yes", please indicate in the space provided the date of all convictions, the particular offenses for which you were convicted, and the final disposition of each matter_____

_____

2. Have you been convicted within the past five (5) years of any misdemeanor other than a first conviction for drunkenness, simple assault, speeding, minor traffic violations, affray, or disturbance of the peace?   _____Yes _____No

If the answer to the above is "yes", please indicate in the space provided the date of all convictions, the particular offenses for which you were convicted, and the final disposition of each matter_____

_____

_____

_____

Figure 22, page 4.

"An applicant for employment with a sealed record on file with the commissioner of probation may answer 'no record' with respect to an inquiry herein relative to prior arrests, criminal court appearances or convictions. An applicant for employment with a sealed record on file with the commissioner of probation may answer 'no record' to an inquiry herein relative to prior arrests or criminal court appearances. In addition, any applicant for employment may answer 'no record' with respect to any inquiry relative to prior arrests, court appearances and adjudication in all cases of delinquency or as a child in need of services which did not result in a complaint transferred to the superior court for criminal prosecution."

_____

Applicant's Statement

I certify that answers given herein are true and complete to the best of my knowledge. I authorize investigation by way of a background check of all statements contained in this application for employment as may be necessary in arriving at an employment decision. I understand that this application is not and is not intended to be a contract of employment. I understand that if I am employed I will have a right to terminate my employment at any time and for any reason, and I understand that this company will retain a similar right to terminate my employment at any time and for any reason. In the event of employment, I understand that false or misleading information given in my application or interview(s) may result in discharge. I understand, also, that I am required to abide by all rules and regulations of this company.

_____   _____
Applicant's Signature   Date

Figure 22, page 5.

4. <u>Network to find new personnel</u>. Many of our new hires are referrals from our current employees. They know the qualifications, the type of individual, and expectations that are needed to fit our team. There is no guarantee that employee referrals will work out, but our employees are encouraged to recommend suitable candidates for interviews. Our managers and team leaders will get a fairly clear indication in the interview whether or not the person would be a good fit for our team. With our 90-day probation period, decisions can be made during the first three months to let the new employee go if they don't work out for some reason.

   I do not recruit competitors' employees based on ethical principles, and I make this clear to my team as well. Occasionally we get applications from a competitor's staff which we treat the same as other job applicants.

   Networking with your local universities, colleges, and trade schools can provide you with a great source of employees. The University of Rhode Island (URI) has been a great source of employees including landscape designers, horticulturalists, turf specialists, team leaders, and apprentices. I maintain close ties with the Landscape Architecture and Horticulture Departments. I serve as a guest lecturer for several horticultural classes at URI, and often members of the graduating class have become WRE applicants.

   Speaking at various public events, appearing on local NBC TV's "Plant Pro" segment, assisting the URI Master Gardener's program, and attending the Rhode Island Nursery and Landscape Association's (RINLA's) educational seminars has provided great networking opportunities to discuss WRE's employee needs especially management positions.

5. <u>Open your doors to the community</u>. One of the most important steps in filling staffing positions is to elevate the importance of attracting and hiring new employees. Building a winning team requires a year-round commitment, not just placing an ad in the local newspaper in March hoping for the answers to your employee needs. If you are going to place an ad, make it targeted for a particular position, larger than a one-line listing, and featuring your company's tagline and logo. Distinguishing your firm from other competing companies will pay dividends in both the quantity and quality of applicants.

   Looking for more productive recruiting alternatives, we have hosted a job fair (in conjunction with a mid-winter open house) in the past–well before help-wanted ads saturate the newspaper.

   Our managers, team leaders, and designers are on site at the WRE Job Fair to meet interested applicants. Staff members hand out sample landscape plans, show applicants photos and videos of our projects, and talk to them about job roles and growth opportunities. Results of this approach have been encouraging; although we haven't attracted huge numbers, we have hired key personnel before they were exposed to other newspaper ads in March. The job fair can elevate the importance of hiring new employees and help build up a résumé file. For small landscape companies, having an open house event or joining up with other major job fairs can help attract new applicants.

The WRE Job Fair is promoted through local newspapers, flyers, local university horticultural classes, a statewide employment website (www.dlt.state.ri.us), and networking efforts with our employees who bring in potential applicants. Participating in other community events like memorial golf tournaments, chamber of commerce events, and speaking at local garden clubs will further expose your company to potential clients…and employees.

6. <u>Define the rules – establish a company handbook</u>. Whether you have three or thirty employees, you need a company handbook. This manual explains your mission, goals, business philosophy, the nature of employment, employee job descriptions, benefit programs, payroll, working conditions, policies and procedures, rules of conduct, and legal guidelines for handling conflicts and leaves of absence. In addition to state and federal rules and regulations, the handbook contains specific confidentiality and non-compete agreements all employees must read and agree to.

WRE has had a company handbook since 1994. It is a written guide which we update each year and hand out to every employee at the spring orientation session. We require that each employee read the handbook and sign the employee acknowledgement form within it. The signed form is kept on file in the office. The handbook has proven extremely valuable during insurance company audits and when negotiating discipline measures and termination issues. The manual also serves as a recruiting and educational tool for new job applicants.

Our handbook is very comprehensive, yet we have it reviewed regularly by a local human resources consultant, David Nichols, for accuracy and being up-to-date (Figure 23). David was extremely helpful in assembling our current handbook and ensuring that it satisfies state and federal laws. Our business lawyer created the confidentiality and non-compete agreements to protect WRE from breaches of confidentiality and from employees leaving our company to start a competing business within a 5-mile radius (and trying to contact our existing clients). These agreements are part of the handbook which each employee signs each year.

David R. Nichols, Sr. is a Human Resource Consultant and Principal of Quality Transitions, Inc. 15 West Beach Road Charlestown RI. He is both retired U.S. Army Officer as well as spending 25 years in corporate America in Human Resources Management. As part of Quality Transitions, Inc. he has serviced small businesses in southern New England for the past 8.5 years and has designed and implemented over 100 employee handbooks.

Why is having a company handbook important?

An employee handbook can be a valuable communication resource for the employer and the employee. It provides guidance and information related to the company's history, mission, values, policies, procedures and benefits in a written format. It is also viewed as a means of protecting the company against discrimination or unfair treatment claims. It is an easily accessible guide to the company's policies and procedures as well as an overview of the expectations of management. In contrast, a policy is a written statement that reflects the employer's standards and objectives relating to various employee activities and employment related matters.

Employers should require every employee to provide a written acknowledgement of having received the handbook. Such acknowledgement should be saved in the employee's personnel file as a way for the company to establish that the employee was made aware of the policies. By no means should the handbook be construed as an employment agreement, which may affect the employer's at-will status. It is imperative to have it reviewed by legal counsel.

How does a small business go about assembling a handbook?

Step 1: Review and make required revisions to the current company policies.

Step 2: Create an outline of what to include in the employee handbook.

Step 3: Create summarized versions of each policy and procedure.

Step 4: Add each summary/statement in the appropriate sections according to the outline.

Step 5: Review the entire handbook.

Step 6: Provide finalized version to legal counsel for review.

Step 7: Select a means of publication.

Step 8: Distribute handbooks during orientation meeting with employees.

Step 9: Update as necessary

Resources that can assist you in development and implementation of an employee handbook:

1. Rhode Island Department of Labor and Training…go to their website www.dolri.gov
2. Bureau of Labor and Training…go to their website www.blr.com
3. Society for Human Resources…go to their website www.shrm.org
4. Quality Transitions, Inc…go to their website www.qualitytransitions.net
5. Google employee handbooks on the Internet and you will find a lot of resources.

Figure 23: Employee Handbooks: David Nichols, Human Resources Consultant

Included in the handbook is a code of behavior which all employees must follow (Table 4). Having this written set of employee expectations has proven useful for our managers and team leaders when they experience problems with their team's workers. Reminding employees of the written code to which they agreed usually is sufficient to bring needed compliance.

Table 4: Code of Behavior

It is imperative to the continued success of our business that all employees understand our mission, and support the Wood River Evergreens brand every day in every way. We expect following the company's code of behavior as follows:

- 100% customer satisfaction 100% of the time
- Reflect our brand image
- Remember our mission
- Work with integrity and self-motivation
- Be accountable and responsible for what you do and say
- Correct professional language at all times
- Dress properly in appropriate uniform attire
- Be on time all the time
- Tolerate the differences of your teammates
- Foster the team spirit

7. Create opportunities for employee advancement. One way to help retain employees is to offer opportunities for employee advancement. Competitive compensation and recognition are very important to retaining key employees, but offering a career path for advancement can be even more valuable. There are many young, talented workers who would like to make a career in the horticultural field. Several obstacles to this desire are the seasonal nature of the business, the need for on-going training, and a clear plan for advancement.

At WRE we have tried to address these issues. For the time our seasonal workers are laid off we continue to pay a portion of their health and dental care, which provides them with year round insurance security. During the winter months we encourage attendance at various green industry conferences, trade shows, and seminars. Employees can also gain useful licenses and certifications by attending pertinent courses when they are offered. WRE offers one-time bonuses for achieving horticultural-related certifications and licenses. Yearly, I meet with each employee to review their evaluation

(Chapter 10) and discuss their long-term plans for advancement at WRE. The resulting Individual Success Plan (I.S.P.) outlines the steps an employee needs to take to qualify for the next job level at our company. With the specific requirements listed on the appropriate job description, they can plan to attend classes, workshops, and seminars to fulfill the requirements. Not only does the plan serve to assist the individual employee, but WRE (and our clients) benefit from the additional training, licenses, and certifications, making our employees more qualified, professional, and effective in the performance of their jobs.

8.   <u>Offer competitive compensation</u>. Instrumental to attracting and retaining employees is a competitive pay scale. We have assigned pay rates to specific job descriptions and levels (Table 3 in Chapter 8) that are in the upper 10% of comparable landscape firms our size in New England. This newer pay scale and our competitive hiring practice has led to higher starting wages for new employees, and has resulted in wage adjustments for current employees who were hired many years earlier at a lower wage.

We have found, however, that certain other adjustments can be made to satisfy employees such as additional benefits (health and dental insurance), more unit days (paid time off), and new positions for those seeking advancements. Additional benefits to attract/retain good employees include:

- <u>Offer Health Benefits</u>
I believe that everyone who works at WRE should have health insurance coverage. After a 90-day probation period, any employee not already covered by a health insurance plan can choose to enter our program. Due to substantial cost increases over the past three years, we have settled on a 50/50 split of the yearly cost. The employees pay their half through regular payroll deductions.

Approximately 85 percent of our team is laid off from late December until mid-March. During the time off, WRE continues to pay 50 percent of the yearly fee, but the employee's 50 percent was collected during the previous work season through extra payroll deductions. This is an important benefit to seasonal workers, as they do not have to struggle paying for this important benefit when out of work. If an employee does not return the next work season, he or she is liable for the portion of winter health plan costs contributed by WRE. Over the years, we have experienced only one or two problems with this policy, and compensation was worked out mutually. I feel our health benefit plan is a significant reason for our low employee turnover rate. Close to 90 percent of our employees return each year.

Continuing to pay for health plan coverage during the winter is a costly item for WRE, but it is far cheaper than hiring and training new employees each year. Clients appreciate that the same employees will be tending their landscapes year after year. Client satisfaction depends on skilled, experienced, motivated employees. We ensure this with our low turnover rate.

- Offer Profit Sharing

    As our workforce aged (our employees range in age from 20 to 60), we realize that a retirement fund was in order. In 1996 we began a 401K account, but later switched to Simple IRA account which has higher owner limits and much less detailed reporting, allows for higher contribution limits, lets employees determine where to invest, and allows WRE to match up to 3% of the employee's contribution. This profit-sharing plan has proved valuable to the employees (especially those of us aged 40 to 55). It is also much easier for me to implement and is a great benefit to include in our compensation package.

- Offer Unit Days for Paid Time Off

    As the business grew and new employees were added (most full-time seasonal, some full time, some year-round), it became more difficult to equitably set standards for sick days, personal time, bereavement time, vacation, etc., so I implemented the concept of unit days (eight hours of paid unit time), which could be used for any purpose and was assigned in amounts that correlated with each position: full-time, part-time or seasonal.

    With few exceptions, this has simplified the whole time-off process. Also, when laid off in December, seasonal employees are paid for their unused unit time, giving them a financial bridge between their last week's paychecks and their first unemployment checks.

- Offer Opportunities for Continuing Education

    We also pay our staff to attend industry meetings, trade shows, and educational seminars. Besides the instructive value of such events, employees get to learn about new products from exhibitors and get to network with fellow horticulturalists.

- Offer Flextime Scheduling

    Several job functions allow completing certain projects at home or working on a variable time schedule. Such job functions are often attractive to employees who are raising families. Flextime schedules can be used to allow parents to care for children, or compensate them with more time off to make up for late-meeting attendance, or, in our case, on-site night-lighting customer visits.

9. Set company and personal goals and perform employee evaluations. Setting company goals before the spring season starts (for example, increase profit by 5%, add ten new maintenance accounts, improve customer satisfaction card rating by 10%, etc.) gives the

staff targets to achieve. Additional goals (for example, winning another landscape award) keep the team motivated and excited to have their work recognized by their peers. Individual goal-setting (being more productive, gaining a CDL driving license, or being a better team leader) helps to motivate each employee to improve their performance.

I feel strongly that a fair, comprehensive evaluation system can help to increase employee performance and identify areas that can be improved. I will describe the WRE evaluation program in Chapter 10.

10. <u>Keep your team motivated!</u> At a recent course at which I was speaking, an attendee stated their belief that you can't successfully motivate employees. I disagree–I think that employees can be encouraged, motivated, and trained to be more productive, efficient, and valuable to your company. I will acknowledge that some employees are easier to motivate than others, but hiring talented, motivated workers at the beginning is a very effective way to run your business.

The best two words you can use to motivate employees to complete a project, make a special effort, receive client compliments, solve a problem, or make suggestions to improve the company are "Thank You". I want all employees, their families, and our vendors to know that their efforts are appreciated. I typically will thank an employee individually and in front of the team for client generated testimonials. You will be amazed at the results generated from positive reinforcement…as opposed to their reaction to undue criticism, manager negativity, and lack of recognition.

Although I make substantial investments in new equipment, tools, and vehicles, I always invest in my team with wages, benefits, training, mentoring, bonuses, and profit sharing. Happy, secure, appreciated employees are a company's most valuable asset.

Firing Employees and Eliminating Negativity from your Team

Although it may sound like an unreachable goal to eliminate negativity from your company, I can attest that it is achievable. Over the last five years WRE has continued to hire talented, positive new employees, not re-hired negative workers who were laid off, and fired several employees who were sources of discontent, negativity, and outright malfeasance. Supporting these moves were the core team players who desired the same positive, motivated, team-oriented employees that I did. The result has been the most talented, cohesive, selfless, and enthusiastic team of employees with whom I have ever worked.

After firing a malcontent employee several years ago, the managers and team leaders came into my office to acknowledge that the long over-due move had raised the morale of the company tremendously. Letting workers go is one of my least favorite responsibilities as owner of WRE; however, I have experienced the ground swell of support, increased motivation, and higher productivity after removing "bad apple" employees that more than justifies the actions.

The end result of having a cohesive, highly productive team is that it allows our company to achieve greater success than was possible with negative influences of certain employees. Team spirit replaces discord, enthusiasm replaces weariness, and high productivity replaces non-achievement. It is a pleasure to come to work each day to "coach" the team which has won 24 Landscape Excellence Awards since 1996…a tribute to their talent, dedication, and penchant for client satisfaction.

Many of the "bad apples" can be encouraged to leave or are not re-hired after our seasonal layoff, but occasionally firing employees is the necessary course of action. Before firing an employee, it is advisable to have documented evaluation reviews, discipline actions taken, or warnings in their employee folder. However, in Rhode Island (and most other states), businesses operate as "at will" employers, meaning the employee or employer can terminate the working relationship at will, with or without cause, at any time, as long as there is no violation of applicable federal or state law or individual state exemptions.

I have found it valuable to have a lawyer who specializes in employee law available for advice when undertaking the firing of an employee to ensure that I am in compliance with all pertinent laws and regulations. Having a comprehensive handbook is also a valuable ally when terminating an employee.

WRE Experience

I have used all the steps described to attract, hire, and retain employees. Happily, the results have been extremely successful as demonstrated by the great team WRE has assembled. Creating a positive, supportive company culture has helped attract numerous skilled employees who had operated their own business, but desired the security of working for an established business where they could perform their specialties and not have the burdens of running their own firm.

Whereas the lack of good employees can limit your growth and success, the building of a cohesive team will allow you to tackle numerous projects and achieve success beyond your expectations. It takes time, a year-round commitment, a willingness to let some workers go for the benefit of the team, and the creating of a company culture that is helpful, supportive, enjoyable, and representative of the company's values. The owner sets the tone through his/her actions, philosophy, and vision. Once a true team is developed the main component of success is in place.

Essential Points:

1. Building an award-winning team requires a sustained, focused, and year-round commitment to attract, hire, and retain valuable employees.

2. Establish a positive, friendly, and supportive company culture to attract top-notch employees.

3. A detailed, comprehensive handbook will be a valuable asset as your company grows.

4. Establishing a strict "Code of Behavior" for your company's employees and holding everyone accountable for adhering to it will help ensure the firm's success.

5. Eliminating negativity from your team and firing "bad apple" employees will help you create a cohesive, highly productive team.

Chapter 10: EVALUATIONS FOR EMPLOYEES AND YOUR COMPANY

One of the most difficult (and most important) elements of our employee retention program is the yearly performance evaluation. Many employers are uncomfortable with this process. This uneasiness can be minimized by having a clear, fair, and comprehensive evaluation program in place. The aim of our evaluation system is to accurately measure job performance in ten categories, reward accomplishments (with wage increases, promotions, or bonuses), identify areas for betterment, and set mutually agreed upon goals for improvement. The ultimate goal of our system is professional growth, increased performance, and personal improvement.

Since 1980, when I was teaching high school biology, coaching, and working on my advanced degrees, I have been intrigued with the evaluation process of athletes, students, teachers, and administrators. I actively researched how to accurately assess current performance and improve future performance, and found that two evaluations of an employee are important to the outcome: the employer's evaluation and the employee's self-appraisal of their performance. In a small horticultural business how does one incorporate team leaders, managers, the owner, and the employee into the process? Additionally, can a system be implemented that includes the evaluation of the owner by the company's managers and team leaders?

The evaluation system we have developed over the years we believe to be fair, comprehensive, and inclusive. The two-part process of our system involves a performance evaluation of all employees completed by his or her managers, team leaders, and myself in December before layoffs, and a self-evaluation and summative evaluation meeting that I hold with each employee before the new season begins in March. The employer evaluation summarizes the performance evaluation score, the employee's self-evaluation, and the employer's overall evaluation and goals for improvement for the upcoming season.

Components of the WRE Evaluation Program

Our evaluation program has three components: the Job Performance Evaluation Score Sheet, the Employee Self-Evaluation Form, and the Employer Evaluation Form.

1. The Job Performance Evaluation Score Sheet (Figure 24) is a scoring form which covers ten employee performance categories: attitude, attendance, communication, dealing with teammates, knowledge of overall duties, dedication, skills, safety, operation of equipment, and productivity. Each of these categories is rated for every employee on a scale from 1 to 10, with 1= poor, 5= average, 10= excellent. The scores are totaled and

divided by the number of evaluations completed to arrive at an average performance score.

There are three different score sheets, each with specific criteria for measuring performance: one form for landscape apprentices, one for team leaders, and one for managers. Each employee is evaluated using the appropriate score sheet by their respective team leaders, manager, and the owner. For an effective assessment, we have found it necessary to have at least three evaluations since each person evaluating the employee emphasizes different job categories. Some evaluators feel that no one should get a 10; others feel 9 and 10 are acceptable. With at least three managers evaluating each employee, the results are more meaningful. To help understand the scores, I have developed a scale that categorizes the results: 86+ is excellent, 76-85 is very good, 66-75 is good, 56-65 is average, 46-55 is below average, and 45 or less means seek employment elsewhere. The key to the scoring system, however, is getting managers and team leaders comfortable with the system and experienced in evaluating team members fairly. You may find there are other categories on which you wish to rate employees; these can be added to this list or replace areas that are not important to you. The important point is that you are objectively rating employees on criteria to measure their performance, generating an average score that will serve as one component of their overall evaluation.

The Job Performance Evaluation Score Sheets are completed in early December before seasonal layoffs. After the results are tabulated, I review them with each employee's divisional manager. During the meeting we discuss potential new job titles, promotions, and compensation changes. I then meet with each employee prior to layoff to discuss the performance score and promotions or potential wage changes for the next year. Wage/benefit changes will not become final until after the new budget is completed in early March (our fiscal year runs April 1st- March 31st each year). Economic conditions, the amount of work finalized, and the budget will dictate what wage increases, if any, will be forthcoming in the spring of the new season. Individual evaluation scores, as well as the overall evaluation, will play a critical role in that determination for every employee.

Apprentice and Craftsman Performance Evaluation

Employee: _____

Date: _____

(Points: 1= poor, 5 = average, 10 = excellent)

CATEGORIES	**SCORE**
1. Attitude towards work	
2. Attendance, tardiness	
3. Follows/takes directions well	
4. Works well with others (team player)	
5. Productivity (works steadily, efficiently, self-motivated)	
6. Operates equipment and vehicles safely and effectively	
7. Safety – performs duties in a manner safe to self and others	
8. Knowledge of overall duties performed regularly	
9. Skills (how good is this person at the jobs done regularly)	
10. Dedication to quality (consistently does job to best of ability)	
Total points	

Personal Comments: _____

_____

_____

Evaluation Scale

86+	Excellent
76-85	Very Good
66-75	Good
56-65	Aim Higher
46-55	Aim Way Higher
0-35	See ya!

Figure 24: Job Performance Evaluation Score Sheet

2. <u>The Employee Self-Evaluation Form</u> (Figure 25) is filled out by the employee in early March before returning to work in the spring. This form gives the employee an opportunity to list positive contributions they have made to WRE in the past year, several areas in which they need to improve, suggestions that would make WRE a better place to work, and their overall evaluation of their job performance at WRE.

       The fact that employees have a way to express their input is valuable for several reasons. First, they can point out what makes them a valuable employee on a written form, for the record and in their own words. Secondly, by identifying areas in which they need to improve, their goals for the next year will be clear. Thirdly, they can make suggestions for improving our company, which will be discussed in our planning meetings. To include employees' input in the evaluation process is not only prudent, but is also effective in gaining suggestions for company-wide improvement. The employee self-evaluation becomes part of the last piece to the WRE evaluation system, the Employer Evaluation.

Employee Self - Evaluation

Employee: _____   Date: _____

1. List several positive contributions that you made to the company this past year:

    a) _____
    _____

    b) _____
    _____

    c) _____
    _____

2. Name several areas you need to improve on next year:

    a) _____
    _____

    b) _____
    _____

3. Make several suggestions that would make the company a better place to work next year:

    a) _____
    b) _____
    c) _____

4. Employee overall self evaluation of their past year's job performance:

    _____
    _____
    _____
    _____
    _____
    _____

Figure 25: Employee Self-Evaluation Form

3. <u>The Employer Evaluation Form</u> (Figure 26) is the final component of the WRE evaluation system. The employer evaluation is a summative collection of the job performance evaluation score, the employee self-evaluation, and the employer's over-all evaluation of the employee. The employer's form contains the job performance average score, the employer's overall evaluation, goals for improvement for the next season, and a comment section. I use the comment section to compliment the employee for one or more special efforts or accomplishments they made during the season. Although there may be several significant improvement goals for the next year, I try to end the written evaluation with several positive, complimentary, and motivational statements. Wages and compensation packages are very important to employees, but recognition and appreciation are equally if not more important to an employee's job satisfaction. This is critical to remember when trying to find ways to retain key employees.

I meet with all employees in mid-March, before they return to work for the season, to discuss the employer's overall evaluation and have them sign the employer evaluation form. At that time, goals for the upcoming season are discussed as are specific training, workshops, or certifications that are needed to achieve their goals. This is part of the ISP (Individual Success Plan) we mutually establish so that each employee has a roadmap to career success at WRE. Many young employees want to make a career in horticulture, they like outdoor work, and they appreciate opportunities to work on high-end clienteles' properties. Helping employees set goals and giving them the tools for success will help make their career choice become a reality.

Employer Evaluation

Employee: _____   Date: _____

1. Job performance evaluation score: _____

2. Employer's overall evaluation of employee:

   _____

   _____

   _____

   _____

   _____

   _____

3. Goals for improvement in upcoming year:

   a) _____

   b) _____

   c) _____

4. Comments:

   _____

   _____

   _____

   _____

   _____

   _____

Employee Signature:_____

By signing, the employee indicates having read the evaluation and acknowledges having been given the opportunity to make his or her own written comments regarding the evaluation.

Employer Signature: _____

Date of Evaluation Conference: _____

Figure 26: Employer Evaluation Form

Employee Evaluation Summary

The owner and managers can use evaluations for many purposes:

- Evaluate each employee's prior season performance by supervisors, managers, team leaders, and the owner.

- Gain subjective feedback from employees about their performance and contributions as well as suggestions for company improvement.

- Through the use of the Job Performance Scoring Sheet, Employee Self-Evaluation Form, and Employer Evaluation Form, develop a "summative" appraisal of all employees' overall performance.

- Use the results to consider promotions, wage/benefit changes, additional training, probationary status, or dismissal from the company.

- Results serve as guide to setting personal and company goals for the next season.

- Areas of employee improvement can be identified and written into the ISP for the upcoming year.

- In an organized, multifaceted, and comprehensive evaluation system, each employee can be fairly evaluated and given an opportunity to be part of the process.

In the business world, evaluation time is synonymous with wage increases. Unfortunately, in our seasonal horticultural business, raises are not automatic. Increases depend upon the economy, the financial health of the company, how many projects are lined up, projected sales, and the increased productivity of employees.

One program we have instituted in lieu of wage increases is a bonus program tied to an increase in profit margins from our landscape projects. Our team leaders and managers are intimately involved in the estimating of our landscape jobs, and the resulting profit margin (%), which is calculated in our estimating program (Chapters 11 through 13). Each team leader is given the parameters of the project: work hours to complete, materials, equipment/vehicles, and profit margin. If, through their efforts, the job is completed under the expected estimate resulting in a higher profit margin, the additional profit is divided equally between the company (50%) and the employees (50%). This employee profit sharing is divided equally amongst all employees and either included in their paycheck or deposited into an employee account. This account would be used for special employee events as decided by the employees.

Effective evaluation takes time and acceptance; probably a major reason why comprehensive evaluation systems are not more prevalent in the horticultural industry. I feel that advancement and compensation increases need to be tied to an employee's level of accountability, responsibility and demonstrated job performance, not just longevity with the company. In conjunction with an evaluation meeting, the setting of goals for the next season and beyond is essential to effective employee management.

I am convinced that effective evaluations improve employee performance while not having regular evaluations will lead to employee stagnation, disinterest, and ultimately lower productivity. If an employee has no meaningful feedback regarding their performance you can be assured that striving for higher productivity will not be a top priority.

Any evaluation program will experience problems, but making adjustments and styling the program to meet your particular needs will improve the system and its results. Making the evaluation more effective, fair, and respected by the employees, managers, and team leaders will be essential. Critical to the evaluation effectiveness is the empowerment and support of all the employees, managers, supervisors, and the owner.

Employee and Customer Evaluation of your Company

Not only do we evaluate our employees, but our employees evaluate our company as well. At our first planning meeting in January we ask all planning team members to evaluate WRE for the previous year: its strengths, weaknesses, accomplishments, shortcomings, what worked, what didn't work, and create a list of improvements and goals for the next season. Smaller sub-committees meet to formalize plans for change, develop specific steps for improvements with the corresponding budget costs, and determine additional training or personnel that will be needed to implement the new improvements. By incorporating team leaders and managers into this process, they develop a vested interest in the changes and work towards the company's success.

Customer evaluation of our services and products is solicited through our Job Satisfaction Survey Card, which is mailed to clients after completing a landscape project (Figure 27). Finding out the level of satisfaction (or in rare cases dissatisfaction) with our services, products, and personnel is critical to generating customer referrals, which are the lifeblood of our business. Approximately 90% of our new business is from referrals, and about 10% are from various forms of yearly advertising like classical radio ads, our website, and direct mailings.

The customer satisfaction card has three categories: design/designer, crew, and services. The design/designer section asks clients to rate the quality of the design, their satisfaction with the design, the knowledge and professionalism of the designer, and the designer's customer service skills. Clients rate the crew on their communication skills, attitude, and customer service, the quality of their work, their dependability and promptness, and their attention to details. The third section rates our services: level of quality/final results, value, and overall experience with WRE. The rating scale runs from 1 to 4, with 1= Did not meet expectations, 2= Met expectations 3= Exceeded expectations, 4= Far exceeded expectations. When completed cards are returned, we add up the points to get a customer average (for example, 3.4). At the end of the

JOB SATISFACTION SURVEY
PLEASE HELP US IMPROVE OUR SERVICES

Using the chart below, circle the ranking that most closely matches your level of satisfaction then drop this card in the mail to us.

1 = Did Not Meet Expectations, 2 = Met Expectations, 3 = Exceeded Expectations, 4 = Far Exceeded Expectations

DESIGN/DESIGNER

Quality of design	1	2	3	4
Satisfaction with design	1	2	3	4
Knowledge & Professionalism	1	2	3	4
Customer service skills	1	2	3	4

Would you recommend our company to a friend or family member?   O Yes   O No

CREW

Communication skills	1	2	3	4
Attitude and customer service	1	2	3	4
Quality of work	1	2	3	4
Dependability and promptness	1	2	3	4
Attention to details	1	2	3	4

What could we do to make doing business with our company easier? _____

Other comments: _____

SERVICES

Ease of ordering & timely delivery	1	2	3	4
Level of quality - final results	1	2	3	4
Value	1	2	3	4
Your overall experience with our company	1	2	3	4

Your name (optional)

Date: _____

We thank you for your time....and your business!

Figure 27: Job Satisfaction Survey Card

season we average all of our clients' scores to get a yearly average, and set a goal for improving that average the next year. Lastly, we ask clients for suggestions on how we can make doing business with us easier, and we inquire if they would refer us in the future. The card can be returned anonymously or their name can be listed.

Although not all of the survey cards that we mail out are sent back to us, we do take the survey results very seriously. This is our report card. Regardless of how we think we are doing, receiving written confirmation and feedback from clients is the dose of reality all companies need. Prior to mailing the cards out, we spend considerable time with clients as their project is winding down making sure there are no loose ends or problems. Each client receives a special WRE thank you card when we are done.

WRE Experience

I have been experimenting with employee evaluation since I entered the horticultural profession full time. The evaluation system I use has evolved, but the major purpose–improving employee performance–has not changed. Involving managers and team leaders in the process has improved the results while teaching supervisory personnel the value of evaluating all employees.

The Job Performance Evaluation Score Sheet has simplified, organized, and clarified the process for evaluations. While each manager doing the evaluations has a different view about the scoring system, calculating the average of their scores provides a good representation of the employee's performance.

As a business owner, it is very important to thank your employees for a job well done and periodically have a quick conversation about how they are doing at work and at home. However, I have found the one-on-one evaluation meeting before the season begins to be extremely important to the employee. They have your undivided attention and enjoy the opportunity to express their excitement, apprehension, or frustration with their job and/or upcoming season. I make sure to highlight their accomplishments, discuss goals for improvement, and express appreciation for their efforts, while leaving time for their comments. This private time between you and your staff can be more valuable than you think. Making sure everyone is on board with the upcoming year's goals and strategies is critical to the success of your company.

You must be willing to commit the time to make the evaluation process work. Since your good employees are your most valuable assets, scheduling the time will be worth the investment.

Essential Points:

1. An effective evaluation program should include a performance evaluation by team leaders, managers, and the owner, a self-evaluation, and a summative evaluation incorporating the performance evaluation and employee self-evaluation.

2. The ultimate goal of this evaluation program is professional growth, increased performance, and personal improvement.

3. Advancement and compensation increases need to be tied to an employee's level of accountability, responsibility, and demonstrated job performance…not just their longevity with the company.

4. Job Satisfaction Survey cards provide valuable customer evaluation of your company's services and potential referrals.

5. Since employees are your most valuable assets, time invested in the evaluation process will pay dividends.

Chapter 11: ESTIMATING FUNDAMENTALS

Few things can influence a company's profitability more than efficient, comprehensive, and accurate project estimating. Next to hiring and retaining a productive team of employees, having a dependable estimating system in place is critical to calculate the price of your landscape service and/or products. Few things are more frustrating (and destructive to your bottom line) than experiencing problems with faulty estimates which result in project losses. Although accurately predicting the labor component is the biggest variable in an estimate, understanding equipment and vehicle costs and providing for their recovery in your estimate can be equally important. Many small businesses do not fully take into account the costs of equipment and vehicles, resulting in lower profitability. Knowing all of your material costs with an established markup will also contribute to the success of your estimates. Another component is to calculate your overhead and make provisions for its recovery. Your company cannot be profitable without recouping all of your overhead expenses. A comprehensive estimating system can ensure your firm's profitability; an incomplete system will prevent you from achieving the financial results you expect.

In this and the next two chapters we will examine the fundamentals of estimating, the implementation of an inclusive estimating program, and job costing to measure a project's profitability. The goal of any estimating program is to identify costs, recover all costs plus overhead expenses, and guarantee a profit. For an estimating system to be effective, an understanding of estimating fundamentals–labor cost, material cost, equipment cost, vehicle cost, and overhead–is the first area to begin.

Estimating Preliminaries

The first step in developing an estimate is to calculate the following: total labor costs, material costs, vehicle costs, equipment costs, and overhead.

Labor Costs

Some employees think (falsely) that their gross wages are the total cost that an employer must pay for their services. Employers, on the other hand, understand all too well that total employee expenses are much higher, contributing significantly to the overall costs that must be included in an estimate. To accurately understand labor costs and budget their overall impact, we produced (in conjunction with a business consultant) an Employee Labor Budget Form[1] (Figure 28).

Employee Labor Budget

Name	Rate	Annual Hours Regular	Annual Hours Overtime	Annual $ Regular	Annual $ Over-time	Gross Pay	FICA	SUI	FUI	Health
Direct Labor										
Employee A	18.00	1,520	200	27,360	5,400	32,760	2,506	1,800	56	-
Employee B	16.00	1,520	100	24,320	2,400	26,720	2,044	1,800	56	1,917
Employee C	18.00	1,250	200	22,500	5,400	27,900	2,134	1,800	56	1,917
Employee D	15.00	1,520	200	22,800	4,500	27,300	2,088	1,800	56	1,917
Employee E	12.00	1,520	200	18,240	3,600	21,840	1,671	1,800	56	-
Total Direct Labor		**7,330**	**900**	**115,220**	**21,300**	**136,520**	**10,444**	**9,000**	**280**	**5,751**
Indirect Labor										
Officer/Sales	25.00	2,080		52,000	-	52,000	3,978	1,800	56	3,837
Administr.	17.00	1,600		27,200	-	27,200	2,081	1,800	56	1,917
Total In-direct Lab.		**3,680**		**79,200**	**-**	**79,200**	**6,059**	**3,600**	**112**	**5,754**
Grand Total		**11,010**	**900**	**194,420**	**21,300**	**215,720**	**16,503**	**12,600**	**392**	**11,505**

Figure 28: Sample Employee Labor Budget Form

This program has proved indispensable in viewing the total cost for each employee by department, the total billable hours for each employee, and the gross revenue generated by each employee. When the expenses are totaled we can see the total employee expense, total G&A (General & Administrative) employee expenses, the total revenue that can be generated by all employees, and the net profit from the difference between revenue generated and total employee expenses. A great benefit of this program is that you can enter "potential" new employee hires and see their projected effect on employee expenses and expected revenue generated. You can then measure the increase in net profit to see if it will make economic sense to hire additional employees. This will allow you to make an informed decision based on actual figures, not just a feeling that you may want more employees because you are busy right now.

Let's examine the Employee Labor Budget Form in detail by looking at employee A. Once their wage rate is established, you plug in that number along with the projected number of annual regular and overtime hours. Their annual pay will be automatically calculated.

In the next series of columns, FICA (Federal Insurance Contributions Act), SUI (State Unemployment Insurance), FUI (Federal Unemployment Insurance), Health Insurance, Dental Insurance, Simple IRA (Individual Retirement Account), Workers Compensation, and Uniforms expenses are entered for each employee.

Employee Labor Budget (continued)

IRA 1%	Wor-kers Comp	Uni-forms	Total EE Costs	Holi-days	Unit Hrs	Total Hours Worked	Bill-able Hrs%	Net Billable Hours	Billable Hourly Rates 45.00	55.00	Total
	1,570	90	38,782	32	63	1,625	80%	1,300	50%	50%	65,000
267	995	90	33,889	32	63	1,525	80%	1,220	100%		54,900
363	1,002	90	35,263	32	63	1,355	80%	1,084	50%	50%	54,200
	991	90	34,242	32	63	1,625	80%	1,300	100%		58,500
	793	90	26,249	32	63	1,625	80%	1,300	100%		58,500
630	**5,351**	**450**	**168,426**	**160**	**315**	**7,755**		**6,204**			**291,100**
520	175	90	62,456								
	70		33,123	77	128						
520	**244**	**90**	**95,579**	**77**	**128**						
1,150	**5,596**	**540**	**264,005**	**237**	**443**						**291,100**

Figure 28, continued.

The next column is a total of all employee expenses–the true picture of what each employee costs the company. For employee A, who had a gross pay of $32,760, his total employee expense is $38,782, a difference of $6,022 (16%). Obviously, when adding new employees, being cognizant of the additional employee expenses is important for the calculation of total labor costs.

Moving across the sheet, the next two columns represent the total of holiday hours and unit time hours for which the employee is paid but is not working. Unit time in our company is time off with pay. Usually one additional day is added for successful completion of each year, as indicated on the employee's evaluation.

The total hours worked is the result of subtracting the holiday and unit hours from the total regular and overtime annual hours. We know that unfortunately, not all of the hours an employee works (particularly team leaders and managers), is billable. By comparing payroll time sheets, daily job reports, and customer billing, we can calculate an approximate billable hours percentage which results in the net billable hours column–the critical number for predicting the total revenue-generating capacity of each employee. Once the billable hourly rates are established (WRE's four rates: maintenance, construction, masonry, and design), each employee can be assigned the expected rate. Some employees work in several departments; their billable rates are allocated according to the amount of time projected in each department. Employee A spends 50% of his time in construction and 50% in maintenance. His total revenue generating capacity is the last column, $65,000, resulting in a net return of $26,218 (40%).

Armed with the projected total labor costs and total projected labor hours you can calculate the average hourly cost by dividing the total employee expense ($168,426) by the number of annual hours (regular and overtime) paid (8230 hrs), equaling $20.47 (rounded to $20) average hourly cost. The average hourly labor cost can be marked up by a factor of 2, 2.5, 3, or more depending on your overhead, overall financial situation, and local market conditions. Within the departments, levels of personnel having several rate structures will afford you the opportunity to generate revenue based on each employee's labor cost and level of expertise (maintenance $40/hr., construction $50/hr., masons $60/hr., etc.).

Material Costs

Regularly checking with vendors who supply materials (mulch, fertilizers, pavers, loam, etc.) for your business is important so that estimates reflect the most current pricing. Volatility in costs for materials can cost you money if pricing updates aren't made frequently. After examining our profit margin on materials several years ago, I realized we were barely exceeding our material costs. By adjusting the markup margin from 15% to 30%, the bottom line began to improve without hiring any new employees. This is one example of ways you can improve profitability without incurring additional costs. The time updating your material costs and adjusting margins will pay dividends on your bottom line.

Several examples of material cost markups are shown in Figure 29. The percentage markup you use will depend on your financial conditions, overhead, and local market situation. The mulch percentage is higher because a truck and driver are sent to the local sawmill to pick up the mulch and deliver it to the site. Products like loam (which we have delivered) are more of a commodity requiring a modest markup. Although there are less expensive loam products on the market, the screened loam we use for clients has been tested for pH, nutrients, and organic matter, making it a preferred product on our projects even at a higher cost. For each of your products you multiply the cost by the % markup and add this to the cost to get the selling price (fifth row in Figure 29). The selling price minus the cost, divided by the selling price = % profit.

Having all of your materials listed on a retail-pricing sheet will make the estimating process much easier. In the early spring before the season commences, we call our vendors to get the new updated prices and make the changes in our estimating program material input sheets. I will discuss the estimating program further in Chapter 12.

Materials Markup

Pavers	$3/sq. ft. (cost) +	35% of cost (35% of $3: 0.35 x $3 = $1.05)	= $4.05/sq. ft.
Loam	$20 (cost) +	40% of cost (40% of $20: 0.4 x $20 = $8)	= $28/yd
Compost	$45 (cost) +	45% of cost (45% of $45: 0.45 x $45 = $20.25)	= $65/yd (rounded)
Total:			
Material	Cost +	Cost x % markup	= selling price
(_____)	_____ +	_____	= _____
Profit:	$\dfrac{\text{Selling price} - \text{cost}}{\text{Selling price}}$ x 100 = % profit		

Figure 29: Examples of Materials Cost Markup

Vehicle and Equipment Costs

Paying attention to your vehicle and equipment costs and having daily or hourly rates to charge for their use will make a significant impact on your profitability. This is an area many small businesses have not fully incorporated into their businesses. Years ago, when I first calculated my vehicle and equipment costs with corresponding daily charge rates, my bottom line was immediately improved. Failure to address vehicle and equipment costs means these costs are coming directly out of your profit.

The sample Vehicle/Equipment Costs (Table 5) demonstrates three examples of vehicle and equipment costs. The first example, a 1-ton dump truck that costs $38,000, is costed out based on a lifetime usage of 1,000 days (200 days/year x 5 years). The daily cost would be $38.00/day (based on $38,000 cost/1,000days). Over the next five years, many other expenses will be incurred: maintenance, insurance, licenses, repairs, taxes, and registrations. These expenses total approximately $26,000; divided by 1,000 days = $26.00/day. The last expense is fuel and oil, which we know has been a very volatile item. For this example we are using $28/day for fuel/oil, which brings the total cost of the dump truck to $92.00/day. At this rate we can recoup the costs of the truck, but we would like to make a profit on the truck charge. We add a replacement cost value to the cost per day rate for all of our equipment and vehicles. In the dump truck example, the new potential purchase (five years from now) was figured at $40,000/1,000 days = $40/day and added to the daily cost, bringing the total charge to $132/day. The replacement value could be whatever value you determine so long as you are making money on the daily truck rate.

Are we able to charge out the daily rate for this and all other vehicles every day? No, but most days the vehicles are recouping their costs, especially with construction projects in which

Table 5: Sample Vehicle/Equipment Costs

Vehicle / Equipment	1 Ton Dump Truck		Riding Lawn Mower		200 Gallon Power Sprayer	
	Initial Cost: $38,000	Cost Per Day	Initial Cost: $9,500	Cost Per Day	Initial Cost: $3,800	Cost Per Day
Lifetime Usage Cost/Day	40 weeks x 5 days = 200 days/year x 5 years = 1,000 days	$38.00	30 weeks x 5 days = 150 days/year x 3 years = 450 days	$21.11	8 weeks x 5 days = 40 days/year x 3 years = 120 days	$31.67
Maintenance, Insurance, License, Repairs, Taxes, Registrations	$26,000 ÷ 1,000 days	$26.00	$2,500 ÷ 450 days	$5.56	$1,700 ÷ 120 days	$14.17
Fuel and Oil	$3.50/gallon x 8 gallons/day	$28.00	$3.50/gallon x 6 gallons/day	$21.00	$3.50/gallon x 5 gallons/day	$17.50
Total Cost Per Day		$92.00		$47.67		$63.33
Replacement	New: $40,000 ÷ 1,000 days	$40.00	New: $10,800 ÷ 450 days	$24.00	New: $4,000 ÷ 120 days	$33.33
Total Charge Per Day (Rounded)		$132.00		$71.67 ($72.00)		$96.67 ($97.00)

estimates include all of the trucking and equipment costs for the entire project. Maintenance services present a more challenging situation. Most maintenance services–mulching, leaf removal, weeding and brush work–will result in vehicle charges. To help offset those times when trucking charges can't be billed, we allocate a portion of disposal fees toward vehicle expenses.

Any vehicle and equipment expenses not recovered reduce our bottom line, encouraging us to be as thorough as we can to recover as many vehicle expenses as possible.

Other examples on the vehicle and equipment cost sheet show daily rates for landscape equipment. The riding lawn mower rate ($72/day) may not be extremely high; however, it is important for mowing companies to figure this rate along with costs for trucks, walk-behind mowers, blowers, weed whackers, etc. into the lawn mowing price charged to the customer. Some lawn mowing companies price to what they think the going rate is rather than based on their true costs, their company's overhead, and a reasonable profit. Your pricing must reflect your own costs, markups, and the profit percentage you wish to achieve…not your competition!

The last example in the vehicle/equipment cost chart is 200-gallon power sprayer. The sprayer example (it could be a sod cutter, slice seeder, or some other equipment) is figured for 40 days per year with a daily charge of $97.00. If the sprayer is only used 20 days the rate jumps to $194/day, making it less likely to recoup its costs and make it profitable. Therefore, it may make more sense to rent the sprayer (or sod cutter, slice seeder) rather than own it. If an item is very specialized and/or it is only going to be used infrequently, renting the item rather than owning it will be more cost effective. If you rent a slice seeder for $90/day, you can mark up the rental charge (40% more) and charge the customer for the trucking and labor to pick up the slice seeder, unload it, and return it at the end of the day.

The sample Vehicle/Equipment Budget Form (Table 6) provides a comprehensive look at all vehicle/equipment costs. From this sheet you can see the cost of every vehicle and piece of equipment as a per-mile rate for vehicles and an hourly rate for backhoes, tractors and other non-road equipment. With the total costs, we can easily arrive at a daily rate for vehicles by dividing the total costs by 200 days. Divide the daily rate by eight hours and we can calculate the vehicle cost per hour.

The form shows the total yearly vehicle/equipment cost and breaks it down amongst the various divisions: construction, maintenance, masonry, nursery, and G&A. Every January we take mileage (or hours) readings to determine the exact miles driven for each vehicle. Using the miles-per-gallon rates, the projected number of gallons of fuel, and the estimated price per gallon, the total fuel expense can be calculated. With the wide fluctuations in fuel prices over time, figuring the budget for fuel has been challenging.

Besides providing the cost factors for each vehicle, the form is helpful to see which vehicles should be kept because of their relatively modest cost. You can also plug in a new vehicle with its corresponding expenses to see its true cost to your firm and the rate you will have to charge to recoup expenses.

Knowing the total vehicle/equipment costs gives you a target amount to meet and exceed. Over the last three years we have paid close attention to vehicle/equipment expenses. One year the total expenses were $165,000 and the amount recouped was only $91,000, meaning we lost $74,000 on our vehicle/equipment expenses. The next year, by paying close attention to vehicle/equipment charges in our estimates, we exceeded expenses by $19,000-adding that revenue to our bottom line. The key was in knowing our total expenses and recouping the costs through careful vehicle/equipment charges in our estimates. The goal is to have each phase of your estimate–labor, material, and vehicle/equipment–cover expenses *and* generate a profit.

Table 6: Sample Vehicle/Equipment Budget Form

Fleet Costs						
	Vehicle 1	**Vehicle 2**	**Vehicle 3**	**Vehicle 4**	**Equipment 1**	**Totals**
Department Charged*	**M**	**G&A**	**C**	**C**	**C**	
Make	Pickup	Pickup	1 Ton Dump	3 Ton Dump	Backhoe	
Year	2002	2004	2005	2000	2006	
Total Miles Driven or Hours Used Annually	*12,000*	*10,000*	*11,000*	*10,000*	*490*	*43,490*
Miles/Gallon (MPG) or Gallons/Hour (GPH)	15 (MPG)	15 (MPG)	12 (MPG)	8 (MPG)	0.29 (GPH)	
Gallons Used/Year	800	667	917	1,250	142	
Cost per Gallon	$3.50	$3.50	$3.75	$3.75	$3.75	
Total Gas/Diesel Costs	*$2,800*	*$2,333*	*$3,438*	*$4,688*	*$533*	*$13,791*
General Maintenance & Repairs	$700	$700	$1,500	$1,700	$750	$5,350
Property Tax	$100	$100	$300	$275	$200	
Road Tax				$300		
Total Taxes	$100	$100	$300	$575	$200	$1,275
Total Insurance	$925	$925	$1,028	$1,168	$350	$4,396
Total Interest	$0	$0	$600	$0	$900	$1,500
Annual Registration	$58	$58	$80	$142	$0	$336
Depreciation	$0	$0	$7,200	$0	$10,400	$17,600
Total Vehicle Costs	*$4,583*	*$4,116*	*$14,145*	*$8,272*	*$13,133*	*$44,249*
Cost per Mile or Hour	$0.38 per mile	$0.41 per mile	$1.29 per mile	$0.83 per mile	$26.80 per hour	

*Department: M = Maintenance, G&A = General & Administrative, C = Construction.

Overhead

All business expenses not directly charged to a project are considered overhead. Examples include advertising, contributions, office payroll, depreciation, health and dental benefits, office supplies, insurance, printing, professional fees, rent, office repairs, taxes, telephone, travel, utilities, and Internet expenses. All overhead expenses need to be recovered during the business fiscal year.

As Charles Vander Kooi, a noted green industry consultant, succinctly states, "You do not make any profit until you recover your overhead."[2]

Determining the overhead costs and the percentage to use in your estimating formula can be challenging; however, the first step is to add up the total operating expenses (or G&A) on your projected P&L (Profit and Loss Statement). To the operating expenses, add interest (from the other expense line on P&L) to arrive at the total overhead from the previous year. Remember that since the previous year's P&L is an historical document, you will need to base your next year's overhead, overhead percentage, expenses, and revenue on projections using the previous figures with line-by-line adjustments for the next year's budget.

Sample overhead calculation

Spending time to understand your overhead recovery percentage will help to make the estimating formula (Chapter 12) easier to understand and allow you to experiment with methods to calculate total overhead, overhead recovery percentage, and allocation of your overhead recovery. The sample Safe Green, LLC 2008 Profit and Loss Statement (Figure 7, Chapter 6) is the source of the figures used to calculate the sample overhead recovery percentage explained below. The following calculations are one way to determine your overhead recovery percentage, which is necessary to ensure the use of the estimating program efficiently and profitably. Although it appears complex, examine the calculations one section at a time and the results will become clear and useful.

---

1. Direct Costs

   a) Purchases: Costs

       (50000*) Plants $31,575

       (51000) Materials $57,345

                 Total $88,920

   b) Direct Labor:

       (55000) Total labor costs $168,426

       (57000) Vehicle, Equipment costs $ 44,345

       (58000) Subcontractor costs $ 18,600

                 Total $231,371

   c) Total Direct Costs (1a + 1b) = $320,291

   *The account numbers in parentheses will give you the line number of the figures used in the calculations from the Safe Green, LLC, P & L (Figure 7, Chapter 6).

2. Overhead (Operating Expenses)

   (60100-69000) Overhead $131,612

   (82000) Interest expense $ 4,870

   (56000) Supplies/small tools $ 3,453

         Total Overhead $139,935

3. Total Direct Costs + Overhead Expenses (Totals of 1 & 2) = $460,226

4. Overhead Recovery Percentage

Total Overhead Expenses	$139,935	
Total Direct Costs	$320,291	= 44%

(Round up to 45%...higher if you anticipate higher overhead expenses during the upcoming year)

5. Desired Profit Percentage

What profit would you like to achieve in the upcoming year? Choose a net profit percentage you would like to achieve: 10%, 15%, 17%, 20%, etc.. For this example, we will use 17%.

6. Necessary Gross Sales

What gross sales will be needed to achieve the desired profit? To determine the gross sales you will need based on a 17% profit, perform the following:

* Divide the Total Direct Costs + Overhead Expenses (line 3), $460,226, by the inverse profit percent (in this example 17% = 0.83)

Total Direct Costs	$460,226	
Inverse profit percentage	0.83	= $554,489 Gross Sales

- The inverse profit percentage for other % profit options: 10% = 0.90, 15% = 0.85, 17% = 0.83, 20% = 0.80.

- The $554,489 projected gross sales figure is the amount needed to generate the 17% net profit figure with the given expenses and overhead recovery percentage. Should any of the expenses, overhead, or sales change then the profit percentage will be different.

7. Profit Percentage

To find the profit number and percentage with the projected gross sales do the following calculations:

a) Subtract the Total Direct Costs and Overhead ($460,226) (line 3) from the projected gross sales ($554,489) (line 6): $554,489 - $460,226 = $94,263 profit

b) To calculate the percent profit divide the profit ($94,263) by the gross sales ($554,489):

$ 94,263	
$554,489	= 17% profit

Chapter 11: Estimating Fundamentals

Overhead Recovery Allocation

Overhead recovery can be entirely allocated to labor; however, I prefer to use a form of multiple allocation of overhead recovery system discussed by Charles Vander Kooi[3]. I believe that each aspect of your business (plants, materials, vehicles/equipment, labor, and subcontractors) should contribute toward overhead recovery.

Table 7 shows a sample overhead allocation for the model company, Safe Green LLC, using their 2008 P & L information (Figure 7, Chapter 6).

Table 7: Safe Green, LLC Overhead Allocation Table

Category	Direct Costs	Percent Overhead	Total
Plants	$31,575	50%	$15,788
Materials	$57,345	30%	$17,204
Vehicles/Equipment	$44,345	30%	$13,304
Subcontractors	$18,600	10%	$1,860
Labor	$168,426	55%	$92,634
Total Direct Costs:	$320,291	Total Overhead Recovery:	$140,790

In this example we have recovered $140,790, slightly exceeding the total overhead ($139,935).

Using the 44% overhead recovery percentage figure, we can multiply it by the Total Direct Costs figures ($320,291) to double check that we will be able to recover our overhead figure ($139,935):

$320,291 x 44% (overhead recovery percentage) = $140,928

Using the 44% recovery, we will slightly exceed our overhead total. Your situation will be different and needs to be designed for your expenses, overhead, percentage recovery, gross sales, and desired profit. These calculations are presented as a way to examine your financials to help predict profit, gross sales, and overhead recovery. Using Figure 30, you can insert your figures to calculate your overhead, recovery percentage, projected profit, and gross sales needed to achieve your financial goals.

Overhead Recovery Calculation

1. **Direct Costs**
    a) Purchases: Costs
        - Plants   _____
        - Materials   _____
                                                        Total =   _____

    b) Direct Labor   Costs
        - Total Labor Costs   _____
        - Vehicle, Equipment Costs   _____
        - Subcontractor Costs   _____
                                                        Total =   _____

    c) Total Direct Costs (a + b) =   _____

2. **Overhead (Operating Expenses)**   Costs
    - Overhead   _____
    - Interest Expense   _____
    - Supplies, etc.   _____
                                                        Total =   _____

3. **Total Direct Costs + Overhead Expenses (1. + 2.) =**   _____

4. **Overhead Recovery %**
        Total Overhead Expenses ÷ Total Direct Costs =   _____ %

5. What profit % would you like to generate in the upcoming year?   _____ % Profit

6. What gross sales will be needed to achieve the desired profit %?
    - Divide the Total Direct Costs by the inverse of the profit %

                                                                     Projected
        Total Direct Costs ÷ Inverse Profit % =   _____ Gross Sales

7. Profit number and %
    - Profit = Subtract Total Direct Costs + Overhead from the Projected Gross Sales
        Gross Sales   -   Total Costs   =   Profit
        _____ - _____ = _____

    - Profit % = Profit ÷ Gross Sales = _____ % profit

Figure 30: Sample Formulas Calculating Overhead Recovery Percentage, Profit, and Gross
Sales to Achieve Desired Profit

WRE Experience

Now I know the importance of understanding your costs, applying your overhead percentage, and using a comprehensive estimating program, but that was not always the case.

My first project after going into the landscape business full time in 1985 was a "real" railroad tie retaining wall project. I met with the client, guessed on the number of ties needed, and thought it would take myself and a helper about four days to complete. I said we could do the job for $2,000. The client asked if I wanted a deposit, and I said no–just full payment when I finished. Two and a half weeks later, with the job still not done, I was frustrated with my lack of planning, inaccuracy in estimating my time, and failure to anticipate the horrendous chain of events working with real, creosote-soaked and trap-rock-filled R.R. ties! I went through two chain saws, eight saw blades, and untold work clothes. The client was extremely understanding– obviously he knew from the beginning it was a much more involved job than I had realized. When the job was finally completed after three weeks, he paid me $3,800–recognizing the low estimate I had verbally given him.

Needless to say, I learned many lessons from that unfortunate experience. From that point forward I calculated my costs before submitting a written estimate and was much more realistic about the time needed to complete projects. I asked for a 50% deposit up front, with the balance due when I completed a job. And, I vowed never to do another real railroad tie job again! I have never broken that vow.

The idea that you must price to what you think a customer might pay or to what you think other companies might estimate is a fallacy. You price based on your labor costs, equipment and vehicle costs, material costs, your overhead, and a reasonable profit. Once you know your costs and profit margin, if a discount is needed to finalize the job you can at least know how, for example, a 10% discount will affect your margin rather than blindly guessing that a discount will be okay. I have found that time spent preparing an estimate will be well worth the effort, especially with large projects on which a small percentage error can have serious financial consequences.

A special note about overhead–it is not a static figure. As the season unfolds, prices change, your overhead expenses may change, and sales numbers will influence the overhead percentage. Better to anticipate changes and start with a higher percentage than to try to recover shortfalls after they occur. Estimating is a dynamic process, not a static per-square-foot formula. You must continually revisit your costs and make the adjustments necessary to produce a fair, complete, and profitable estimate.

Essential Points:

1. Price projects and services based on your labor, equipment, vehicle, and material costs, your overhead, and a reasonable profit.

2. A comprehensive estimating system can ensure your company's profitability; an incomplete system can prevent you from achieving your financial goals.

3. Time spent to calculate your overhead recovery percentage will be critical to the accuracy of the estimating program.

4. Using the Employee Labor Budget Form and Vehicle/Equipment Budget Form will help produce the information needed to use the estimating program effectively.

5. Remember estimating is a dynamic process, not a static per-square-foot formula. Adjustments are necessary to produce a fair, complete, and profitable estimate.

Chapter 12:   IMPLEMENTING THE ESTIMATING FORMULA

With costs for materials, equipment and vehicles, labor, and overhead in hand, you are now ready to enter the data into an estimating formula and calculate a price for a customer's project. In this chapter, I will discuss several estimating methods for construction projects and the effect discounting has on net profit margins, landscape maintenance services, and plant pricing techniques. In addition to demonstrating the estimate formulas with an actual landscape construction project, I will discuss several landscape maintenance service estimates (lawn mowing, mulching, compost tea application) and a plant pricing example. Your estimate numbers may be different from mine, but the inputs and process are what are important. These formulas can be used with any service you perform or product you sell.

There are many ways to estimate projects, services, and products. The two methods we use, The Overhead and Profit Method (O.P.M) and The Retail Method (R.M.), have worked well for us over many years. Any estimating system or method you use, in order to be effective, must be examined regularly for updating. Even a good estimating program can produce poor results if the data are incorrect or not current. The estimating program, in itself, will not be a panacea for improper in use of information or dated data.

The Overhead and Profit Method

The first method (Overhead and Profit, O.P.M.) involves adding an overhead percentage (determined by you for your business) and a desired profit markup to the direct costs of a project. Although we are describing horticultural estimating examples, any small business service or product could effectively use this method. In Figure 31 we can see how the overhead percentage and profit markup percentage are calculated in a sample planting project estimate.

This method is very effective to ensure that overhead recovery is incorporated into the estimate and that a defined profit percentage is figured into the total selling price. Remember, this selling price total is before any adjustments to the estimate; that is, client reduction of plants or materials, changes in material or plant choices, or discounts. As we will see later in this chapter, discounts can be used if needed provided you know the estimated profit margin and the effect discounting will have on your final profit figure.

As mentioned previously, the overhead percentage for your company will be key to recouping your total overhead (operating expenses) for the year. Base your percentage on your figures; do not "assume" that a certain percentage will work for you. Ideally, you should monitor your overhead expenses during the year, and if they rise higher than budgeted projections, you will need to raise your overhead percentage in your estimating formulas. The same can be said

Overhead & Profit Method Sample Foundation Planting Project		Direct Costs
• Plants		$424
• Materials (16 yds loam, 5 yds compost, 5 yds mulch)		$609
• Equipment & Trucking (Kubota backhoe, sod cutter, and trucking)		$360
• Labor (56 total work hours):	56 hrs x $20/hr =	$1,120
	Total Direct Cost	$2,513
	Overhead (Total Direct Cost x 65%) +	$1,634
	True Cost (Direct Cost + Overhead) =	$4,147
	Profit (True Cost x 35%) +	$1,452
	Total Estimate Price (Selling Price) =	$5,599
Selling Price =	$5,599 + tax	
Profit =	$5,599 - $4,147	= $1,452 (Selling Price - True Cost)
Profit Margin % =	($1,452 ÷ $5,599) x 100	= 26% ((Profit ÷ Selling Price) x 100)

Figure 31: Overhead and Profit Method

for the profit percentage. If through a review of monthly or quarterly P&L Statements you find that you are not generating enough profit, consider adjustments in the profit percentage number. Finding the right balance of overhead percentage, profit margin, and a competitive selling price is the ongoing challenge of project, service, and product estimating!

Notice that although we used a profit markup of 35% in the formula, the actual profit margin based on the selling price is 26% (see Appendix B part VIII). This becomes the critical number to keep in mind when considering changes to the project scope and discounts, which will seriously affect the profit margin percentage–the most important number in the estimate!

The Overhead and Profit Method is effective in generating a selling price for a project, but is not appropriate to present to a client. Your overhead percentage and profit margins are your business and no one else's. Therefore, we convert the data generated using this method into a retail format for the customer using the Retail Method (R.M.). This technique uses the same overhead percentage and profit percentage, but converts each of the plant, material, equipment/trucking, and labor costs into a retail price that can be presented to the customer. Using the R.M. also serves as a double check on the accuracy of the estimating technique. In almost all cases the two procedures end up with similar results, confirming the efficacy of the estimate.

Through experience and listening to speakers like Charles Vander Kooi[1], we have developed a system of allocating our overhead in varying percentages to the different cost components: plants, materials, equipment/trucking, labor, and sub-contractors. Most of our overhead recovery is in the labor segment, with lower percentages assigned to plants, materials, and equipment. Certain materials like screened loam, compost, and mulch are commodity products, which could not carry a high overhead recovery and still keep the retail prices you charge competitive. However, each segment of your estimate must help in overhead recovery, even if it is a low percentage. Even subcontractors carry a percentage overhead recovery to help recoup all of your overhead expenses for the year. Remember, there can be no profit until all overhead expenses are paid!

The Retail Method

Let's examine Figure 32, The Retail Method, to see how a retail pricing estimate can be generated from the O.P.M results. Keep in mind that these are sample percentages and that your figures and allocations may be different.

The Retail Method converts the direct costs of a project into a retail (selling) price for each project phase: plants, materials, equipment, trucks, and labor. Each phase has an allocated overhead percentage, from 50% for materials to 85% for labor (the largest overhead recovery at $954). Seeing the percent overhead allocated and the dollar amounts recovered for each project phase in this chart is very useful.

Using the 35% profit markup, the specific profit figure for each phase and the total profit are clearly shown. Adding the True Cost ($4,296) to the total profit ($1,504) gives you the project selling price ($5,800).

Retail Method Sample Foundation Planting Project							
	Direct Cost	Allocated Overhead	Overhead Amount	True Cost*	Profit %	Profit Amount	Selling Price**
Plants (see plant list)	$424	x 65% =	$276	$700	x 35% =	$245	$945
Materials (16 yds loam, 5 yds compost, 5 yds mulch)	$609	x 50.3% =	$306	$915	x 35% =	$320	$1,235
Equipment/Trucking (Kubota backhoe, sod cutter, trucking)	$360	x 68.5% =	$247	$607	x 35% =	$213	$820
Labor (56 hrs @ $20/hr)	$1,120	x 85.2% =	$954	$2,074	x 35% =	$726	$2,800
Totals	$2,513		$1,783	$4,296		$1,504	$5,800
Selling Price =	$5,800 + tax						
Profit =	$5,800 - $4,296		= $1,504	(Selling Price - True Cost)			
Profit Margin % =	($1,504 ÷ $5,800) x 100		= 26%	((Profit ÷ Selling Price) x 100)			

All calculations are rounded to the nearest whole number.
* True Cost = Direct Cost + Overhead Amount, ** Selling Price = True Cost + Profit Amount

Figure 32: The Retail Method

Both methods resulted in a similar total selling price ($201 difference) and an identical profit margin percent (Table 8). With these results I would feel confident moving ahead with this estimate proposal.

Table 8: Comparison of Overhead and Profit Method and Retail Method

Comparison of Overhead & Profit Method (O.P.M.) and Retail Method (R.M.)		
	O.P.M.	R.M.
1. Overhead	$1,634	$1,783
2. Profit	$1,452	$1,504
3. Selling Price	$5,599	$5,800
4. Profit Margin %	26%	26%

But how should it be presented? In what format? I have found the sample customer estimate proposal shown in Figure 33 to work best for our company. It clearly shows the specific retail price totals for the plants, materials, equipment/trucking, and labor, while identifying the specific plants (sizes, quantities, Latin names, and prices) on the plant list, the specific materials proposed (including quantities), the equipment/trucking to be used on the project, and a labor total to complete the job. Overall, this type of presentation has been well received by most clients. Please look at Figure 33 to see the sample landscape proposal using the data and pricing from the Retail Method foundation planting estimate.

Recently, we have added an area at the bottom of the estimate sheet for clients to sign, formalizing the proposal into a contract. For larger projects (over $20,000), we have a separate landscape contract that clients sign, with the detailed estimate proposal becoming an addendum to the contract. Although many small business owners still operate on verbal agreements and a handshake, it makes sense (and cents!) to put your proposals in writing, with services and terms clearly identified, an explanation of how project changes will be handled (change orders in most cases), clear payment schedules, an explanation of how conflicts will be resolved, and signatures of clients and the owner of the landscape firm completing the project. Your lawyer should review any contract you will present to clients regarding legal implications of your document–be sure to incorporate any changes they would advise.

Dick & Jane Customer
Bill Street
Bill Town, ST 10000

Site Address:
Location Street
Location Town, ST 10001

Date   9/15/2010

Landscape Proposal

Phase:	**FOUNDATION PLANTING**	
Scope:	Install shrubs in planting bed. Includes bed preparation, loam, compost, and mulching.	
Plants:	See attached list	$945.00
Materials:	16 yds loam, 5 yds compost, and 5 yds mulch	$1,235.00
Equipment & Trucking:	Kubota backhoe, sod cutter, and trucking	$820.00
Labor:	To prepare planting bed, install plants, mulch bed, and warranty plants for 1 year*	$2,800.00
		$5,800.00
	Tax	TBD
	Total	$5,800.00

Terms:	50% Deposit	$2,900.00
	Balance Upon Completion	$2,900.00
	Quote valid for 30 days	

* See written warranty attached to this estimate

Thank you,

Owner Signature

PROJ #9xx

CONTRACT AGREEMENT

FINAL CONTRACT AMOUNT: _____

I/We have read this contract and accompanying attachments and agree to fully comply with the terms and conditions. Any change in the above services, plants, materials, and/or prices must be agreed upon in writing and signed by both parties.

CUSTOMER

DATE: _____   SIGNATURE: _____

SAFE GREEN, LLC

DATE: _____   SIGNATURE: _____

Figure 33: Sample Landscape Proposal

Additional Example of Estimating

Based on the model company Safe Green, LLC, let's take a look at the Overhead & Profit Method and Retail Method using the overhead recovery percentage that was calculated in the Sample Overhead Calculation (Chapter 11) and the overhead allocation percentage used in the Safe Green, LLC allocation table (Table 7).

In this example (Figure 34), the selling prices were nearly identical, with both methods having a 20% profit margin. When both methods result in comparable selling prices, you can proceed with confidence that the estimate is accurate (based on the information provided). If the two methods produced very different selling prices, you should re-examine the costs, percentage overhead and profit, and the calculations to make sure they were accurate. Taking the average of the two selling prices is an option to arrive at an acceptable selling price for the project.

Overhead & Profit Method		
• Direct Costs (Plants, Materials, Equipment/Trucking, Labor)		$1,130
• Overhead Recovery (Direct Costs x 44%)		$497
	True Cost:	$1,627
• Profit (Overhead Recovery x 25%)		$407
	Selling Price:	$2,034
Selling Price =	$2,034 + tax	
Profit =	$2,034 - $1,627 = $407	(Selling Price - True Cost)
Profit Margin % =	($407 ÷ $2,034) x 100 = 20%	((Profit ÷ Selling Price) x 100)

Retail Method							
	Cost	Overhead Recovery %	Overhead Amount	True Cost[*]	Profit %	Profit	Selling Price[**]
Plants	$300	x 50% =	$150	$450	x 25% =	$113	$563
Materials	$280	x 30% =	$84	$364	x 25% =	$91	$455
Equipment/Trucking	$150	x 30% =	$45	$195	x 25% =	$49	$244
Labor (20 hrs @ $20/hr)	$400	x 55% =	$220	$620	x 25% =	$155	$775
Totals	$1,130		$499	$1,629		$408	$2,037
Selling Price =	$2,037 + tax						
Profit =	$2,037 - $1,629	= $408	(Selling Price - True Cost)				
Profit Margin % =	($408 ÷ $2,037) x 100	= 20%	((Profit ÷ Selling Price) x 100)				

[*]True Cost = Cost + Overhead Amount, [**]Selling Price = True Cost + Profit

Figure 34: Sample Safe Green, LLC Estimates Using the Overhead & Profit Method (top) and the Retail Method (bottom)

The Effect of Discounting on Profit Margins

There are different points of view regarding whether or not to give discounts on project estimates, services, or products. Some small business owners never give discounts based on their business model and philosophy. Some owners judiciously use discounts (particularly in slow, off season months) to improve cash flow. Others indiscriminately offer discounts without a clear understanding of how the reduction in price will affect their bottom line (profit margin).

The key point, regardless of when or if you discount your estimates, is to know what your net profit figure is on each project and be able to understand the effect of discounting the total selling price. Let's take the Sample Planting Project and look at the effect discounting the selling price has on the profit margin percentage (Figure 35). The Sample Landscape Proposal (Figure 33) had a selling price of $5,800 with a profit margin of 26%. With a 10% discount the selling price is reduced to $5,220. To determine the change in profit you need to subtract the true cost ($4,296), which stays the same, from the new selling price. The new profit figure is then divided by the new selling price to arrive at the reduced profit margin percentage.

The Effect of Discounting		
	10% Discount	20% Discount
New Selling Price	$5,800 – 10% = $5,220	$5,800 – 20% = $4,640
New Profit	$5,220 - $4,296 (True Cost) = $924	$4,640 - $4,296 (True Cost) = $344
New Profit Margin (%)	($924 ÷ $5,220) x 100 = 18%	($344 ÷ $4,640) x 100 = %7
End Result	A 10% discount in the selling price resulted in an 8% reduction in the profit margin (from 26% to 18%).	A 20% discount in the selling price resulted in a 19% reduction in the profit margin (from 26% to 7%)!

Figure 35: The Effect of Discounting on Profit Margin

Armed with this knowledge, when confronted with client pressure to discount you can make a decision based on real numbers, not assumptions. If you feel an 18% profit margin is acceptable, then discounting 10% will work for you. However, a 20% discount will reduce your profit to 7%, making it questionable to take on the job. If the reduction in your profit is not acceptable, use sales techniques to justify your price. For example, the quality of materials, level of service, expertise, numerous referrals, and an extensive warranty can be used to explain the value added to your offer compared to your competitors'. I have found selective use of discounts during our off season (January – March) has been effective in generating winter cash flow, ensuring projects for the spring, and giving clients a savings, while preserving the overall economic health of our company.

Estimating Applications

The following figures and tables show you examples of how the estimating formulas can be applied to specific horticultural services: lawn mowing, mulching, and compost tea application (Figure 36, Figure 37, Figure 38, Table 9, and Table 10).

Lawn Mowing Estimate Equipment, Trucking, Fuel, and Labor Costs	Direct Costs
• Equipment/trucking	
(1) Riding mower ($46/day)	$46/day
(2) Walk-behind mowers ($25/day)	$50/day
Fuel	$22/day
Weed whacker	$6/day
Leaf blower	$6/day
• Trucking (pickup/trailer)	$50/day
• Labor: (3) @ 8 hrs = 24 hrs x $20/hr	$480/day
Daily Direct Cost	$660
Overhead (Daily Direct Cost x 50%) +	$330
True Cost (Direct Cost + Overhead) =	$990
Profit (True Cost x 35%) +	$347
Total Retail Selling Price =	$1,337

Selling Price =	$1,337 + tax		
Profit =	$1,337 - $990	= $347	(Selling Price - True Cost)
Profit Margin % =	($347 ÷ $1,337) x 100	= 26%	((Profit ÷ Selling Price) x 100)

Figure 36: Lawn Mowing Estimate

Table 9: Sample Lawns Mowed on a Typical Day

Number	Square Feet	Retail Price lawn	Total
(5)	10,000 sq. ft.	@55/ea.	$275
(5)	12,000 sq. ft.	@66/ea.	$330
(5)	20,000 sq. ft.	@90/ea.	$450
(2)	40,000 sq. ft.	@160/ea.	$320
Total Daily Lawn Income			$1,375*

* Using this gross income ($1,375), the profit margin % would be based on the True Cost ($990): $1,375 - $990 = $385 profit.
Profit margin % = $385 ÷ $1,375 = 28%.

Estimating the Amount of Mulch and Costs for Landscape Beds

1. How to determine the amount of mulch needed:
   - Measure the square footage of landscaped beds (length x width) minus the area taken up by plants and groundcovers. For example, a perennial bed (15' wide x 75' long) = 1125 sq. ft., minus 425 sq. ft. of plants = 700 total square feet to be mulched.
   - New mulching = Approx. 1 yard of mulch will cover 100 sq. ft. (3" thick).
   - Re-mulching = Approx. 1 yard of mulch will cover 150 sq. ft. (2" thick).
   - Example: 700 sq. ft. new mulching = 700 sq. ft. ÷ 100 sq. ft. = 7 yards of mulch.

2. Mulch cost, markup, and selling price.

Mulch Cost	$23.00	/yd
Overhead (x 50%) +	$11.50	
True Cost =	$34.50	
Profit (x 35%) +	$12.00	
Selling Price	$46.50	/yd

   Mulch cost = 7 yds @ $46.50/yd = $325.50

3. Labor to prepare beds and mulch.
   - Labor hours to weed and edge beds:
     2 workers @ 2 hrs = 4 hrs @ $50/hr = $200
   - Labor to spread mulch:
     2 workers @ 2.5 hrs = 5 hrs @ $50/hr = $250
   - Total labor: $450

4. Mulching Estimate:
   - 7 yds mulch = $325.50
   - Labor   = $450.00

   Total Mulching Estimate: $775.50 + tax

Figure 37: Estimating Mulch and Costs for Landscape Beds

Compost Tea Application Estimate			
			Direct Costs
Cost of tea (200 gal. @ $1.25/gal)			$250/day
200 gallon Compost Tea Power Sprayer			$52/day
Trucking			$50/day
Labor: 8 hrs @ $20/hr			$144/day
		Total Direct Cost	$496
		Overhead (Total Direct Cost x 50%) +	$248
		True Cost (Direct Cost + Overhead) =	$744
		*Profit (True Cost x 60%) +	$446
		Total Selling Price =	$1,190
Selling Price =	$1,190 + tax		
Profit =	$1,190 - $744	= $446	(Selling Price - True Cost)
Profit Margin % =	($446 ÷ $1,190) x 100	= 38%	((Profit ÷ Selling Price) x 100)
Retail price/gallon	$1,190 (selling price) ÷ 200 gal	= $5.95	Per gallon

Figure 38: Compost Tea Application Estimate

* For compost tea application, the profit is figured at 60% because of:
- License requirements, training, and certifications
- Expensive testing of the tea for nutrients, microbes, and bacteria/fungi
- Insurance/liability
- Complexity of producing and applying the tea
- Expensive equipment needed for tea extraction and application

Table 10: Compost Tea Applications Typical Billing Day

Square Footage Covered	Gallons*	Price per Gallon	Retail Price
25,000 sq. ft.	50 gal.	5.95/gal.	$297.50
20,000 sq. ft.	40 gal.	5.95/gal.	$238
15,000 sq. ft.	30 gal.	5.95/gal.	$178.50
15,000 sq. ft.	30 gal.	5.95/gal.	$178.50
10,000 sq. ft.	20 gal.	5.95/gal.	$119
15,000 sq. ft.	30 gal.	5.95/gal.	$178.50
Total: 100,000 sq. ft.	Total: 200 gallons		Total: $1,190.00

* Figured at 2 gallons of tea per 1,000 sq. ft.

Using these three estimating applications for specific horticultural services is helpful because:

1. By entering all of the direct cost data and the overhead percentages, you will be able to calculate the true cost of each service–lawn mowing, mulching, compost tea applications, and other services–and not have to guess what they really cost.

2. Determining the profit margin will give you a specific amount of profit to strive for.

3. Armed with the total retail selling price for a day's service (lawn mowing, for example), you can measure your mow team's productivity and profitability based on the number of lawns they mow each day.

4. If a team consistently falls short of the profit goals then changes can be made: adjust pricing, perform more training, change supervisors, or consider not offering the service.

5. Applications of compost tea are relatively new and complex, which helps to explain the premium pricing attached to the service.

Plant Pricing

Plant pricing, like other estimating procedures, involves determining direct costs, adding overhead, and establishing a profit margin (Figure 39). It is important to include costs like shipping and unloading in the direct cost of the plant. Also, notice that dramatic effect discounting the price of the *Stewartia* by 20% has on the profit–reducing the profit margin from 26% to 7%.

Small Tree Pricing Example			
10 gallon *Stewartia pseudocamellia* (Japanese Stewartia)			$120
Shipping and unloading (x 15%)			$18
		Direct Cost	$138
		Overhead (Total Direct Cost x 45%) +	$62
		True Cost (Direct Cost + Overhead) =	$200
		*Profit (True Cost x 35%) +	$70
		Selling Price =	$270
Selling Price =	$270 + tax		
Profit =	$270 - $200	= $70	(Selling Price - True Cost)
Profit Margin % =	($70 ÷ $270) x 100	= 26%	((Profit ÷ Selling Price) x 100)
*Discounting 20% =	$270 – 20%	= $216	(New Selling Price)
New Profit Margin % =	$216 - $200 = $16; ($16 ÷ $216) x 100	= 7%	

Figure 39: Small Tree Pricing Example

Landscape Maintenance Services Estimate Form

In order to make the maintenance services offered more organized and easy to estimate, I developed the Landscape Maintenance Services Estimate Form. Not only is the form convenient for completing maintenance estimates, it also serves as a catalogue of services we offer–many of which clients may not be familiar with. Since we started using the maintenance form, our maintenance sales have increased significantly. Prior to the spring season (in February), a maintenance check-off sheet listing all of our maintenance services is mailed to our existing maintenance accounts. The form asks clients if they would like to continue with previous services, add or delete services, and if there are any special events (weddings, parties, etc.) on their schedule during the upcoming year. Once the check-off forms are returned, we can prepare an estimate for the client's requested services on the detailed Landscape Maintenance Services Estimate (Figure 40) and send them a copy. The completed form serves as a guide for the maintenance manager, who will assign the crews to implement the agreed-to services.

The forms can be adapted to your specific company and services offered. We have created a Microsoft Excel™ template on our computer into which we can input the work hours, equipment, and materials to calculate estimates in a matter of minutes. You can examine the following three pages, which show you a sample Landscape Maintenance Services Estimate for a client.

Sample Landscape Maintenance Services Estimate

Name:		Phone:	
Email:		Fax:	
Site address:			
Mailing address:			

Service

1. **Spring Clean-up** (raking winter debris, leaves, cleaning off patios, drives, etc.)*

	_____ hrs @	$35.00	$0.00
	_____ loads@	$75.00	$0.00
Trucking	_____		$0.00

Fall Clean-up (leaf removal, cutting back perennials)*

	_____ hrs @	$35.00	$0.00
•Disposal fees for leaves, brush, debris, etc.	_____ loads@	$75.00	$0.00
Trucking			$0.00

*Estimate -exact cost to be determined by actual # of hours used to complete services.

Annual Cleanup Total	**$0.00**

2. **Lawn Care Program**   Lawn Area: _____

a) Organic Program (*100% NOFA approved organic lawn care, no pesticides used, safe for pets, children, and applicators.)

•Comprehensive soil/bioassay test		
•Lime application	# of applications	$0.00
•Organic lawn fertilizer program	# of applications	$0.00
•Compost tea application	# of applications	$0.00
•Compost topdressing and aeration	# of applications	$0.00
•Organic weed control	# of applications	$0.00

*(Each organic program to be customized based on testing and previous applications, typically there is a 3-year transition to totally organically maintained lawns from traditional pesticide/inorganic fertilizer programs)

Subtotal	$0.00

b) Traditional Program

•Soil test		
•Lime application	# of applications	$0.00
•Early Spring fertilizer (Crabgrass/weed control)	# of applications	$0.00
•Late Spring fertilizer (with weed/feed control)	# of applications	$0.00
•Early Summer fertilizer (with Merit/grub control)		$0.00
•Early Fall fertilizer (24-5-11 with 5% Fe)	# of applications	$0.00
•Late Fall fertilizer (18-2-18 Fall/Winter)	# of applications	$0.00
	Subtotal	$0.00

c) Additional lawn care services:

•Aeration	# of times	$0.00
•*Slice/over seeding		$0.00
	Subtotal	$0.00

Annual Lawn Service Total	**$0.00**

3. **Lawn mowing/weekly trimming**   Times @

Annual Mowing and Trimming Total	**$0.00**

Figure 40: Sample Landscape Maintenance Services Estimate Form.

4. **Re-mulching**

Labor to prep beds	_____	hrs @	$35.00	$0.00
Pine Bark mulch	_____	yds @	$45.00	$0.00
Bag Pine Bark mulch	_____	bags @	$8.50	$0.00
Hemlock mulch	_____	yds @	$55.00	$0.00
Labor to spread mulch	_____	hrs @	$35.00	$0.00
		Annual Remulching Total		**$0.00**

5. **Feeding: Perennials, shrubs and trees**
    a) Organic Feeding
    •Compost - topdressing for shrubs and perennial beds _____
    •Organic fertilizers - granular and compost tea -

    Subtotal $0.00

    b) Traditional Feeding
    •Granular for perennials
    •Slow release pellets for shrubs
    •Root zone feeding for trees

    Subtotal $0.00

    Annual Feeding Total   **$0.00**

6. **Weed Control**
    a) Organic Weed Control
    •Horticultural vinegar (Burnout)
    •Propane torching of weeds
    •Hand weed beds   _____   hrs @ $35.00 $0.00

    Subtotal $0.00

    b) Traditional Weed Control
    •Pre-emergent control landscape beds
    •Post-emergent (driveways)
    •Hand weed beds   _____   hrs @ $35.00 $0.00

    Subtotal

    Annual Weed Control   **$0.00**

7. **Pruning**

•Selective trimming shrubs and small trees	_____	hrs @	$45.00	$0.00
•Cutting back perennials	_____	hrs @	$45.00	$0.00
•Tree maintenance pruning	_____	hrs @	$45.00	$0.00
		Annual Pruning Total		**$0.00**

8. **Plant Health Care**
    •Monitoring and scouting of landscape trees, shrubs and perennials _____
    •NOFA approved Pesticide applications - (Determined as needed)

    Annual Plant Health Care   **$0.00**

9. **Deer Management Measures:**

•Spray Deer Repellent	May	_____ tanks@	$150.00	$0.00
	October	_____ tanks@	$150.00	$0.00
•Netting installation				_____
•Fencing				_____
•Alternative methods				
		Total Annual Deer Management		**$0.00**

Figure 40, page 2.

10.	**Winter Protection**				
	•Anti-desiccant applications	_____ tanks@	$125.00	$0.00	
	•Windscreens				

Total Annual Winter Protection	**$0.00**

11. **Sprinkler System Maintenance**

•Turn on/check in spring

•Repairs/adjustments (billed as performed)   _____

•Winterize system in Fall   _____

Annual Sprinkler Maintenance Total	**$0.00**

12. **Landscape Lighting Maintenance**

•Bulb replacement   _____   _____ $0.00

(based on bulb type & lifetime hours)

•Service call   _____ @ $50.00 $0.00

   Plus hourly rate for trouble shooting, bulb

      replacement, & maintenance   hrs @ $65.00 $0.00

Total Lighting Maintenance	**$0.00**

13. **Seasonal Changeover Plantings and Maintenance**

    a)   •Spring (bulbs, pansies) - April   _____

           •Summer (annuals) - May - Early June   _____

           •Fall (mums, kale, asters) - September   _____

           •Winter (evergreens for planters, pots, greens for winter interest) - December   _____

    b)   •Decorating services: Fall, Winter (Inquire for details)

Total Annual Seasonal Changeover	**$0.00**

14. **Warranty Work**

Plants covered under our guarantee that do not survive will be replaced at no charge--see attached warranty for details.

15. **Other Services Requested, special events, deadlines:**

_____

_____

_____

Total for Other Services	
TOTAL ANNUAL MAINTENANCE	**$0.00**

DOES NOT INCLUDE APPLICABLE SALES TAXES

Payment Terms: •Billed monthly

                   •Interest of 1.5% per month will be charged on past due invoices over 30 days

Additional services not in this agreement requested and performed will be billed after completion of services. This is an estimate. The exact amount will be determined by the amount of materials, labor and trucking used to complete the maintenance services.

_____   _____

Client   Date

_____   _____

Company Representative   Date

Figure 40, page 3.

WRE Experience

Developing, modifying, and implementing the construction estimating formulas, plant pricing techniques, and maintenance service estimating forms has made our estimating system much more comprehensive and the estimates we present to clients much more professional. The days of guessing at what a project might cost and how much it might generate in profit are long gone. Identifying all direct costs, using a frequently updated overhead percentage, and establishing appropriate profit margin percentages are critical to our company's financial success. Even small mistakes in estimating can have detrimental effects on individual projects and long-term consequences for our company.

Overall there are several distinct benefits that the estimating formulas have provided WRE:

1. An accurate estimating system, which can be adjusted when needed to reflect changes in materials, equipment, or labor costs.

2. Accurate profit margin percentages, which serve as financial goals for the entire project team.

3. The results of the estimating process can be professionally presented to clients in a form they can understand and feel comfortable about.

4. The Landscape Maintenance Service Form has helped us to generate additional business from clients who did not know the extent of our services. Our organic services have particularly benefited from being listed and explained in the maintenance service sheet.

5. Lastly, the detailed estimating system allows us to examine our projects when they are completed. By applying our job costing analysis, we can see if the projects were profitable. Without this last piece of the costing process, it is only a guess or feeling whether a project was profitable. The Job Costing Program takes the guesswork out of the process and will calculate quickly the exact profit margin percentage on each project.

Chapter 13 will detail the Job Costing Program and the information needed to implement job costing successfully. In addition, I will explain our estimating program, which dovetails with the job costing program resulting in an effective, coordinated, and complete estimating system.

Essential Points:

1. Two estimating methods, The Overhead and Profit Method and The Retail Method, can be effective in calculating a price for a project that reflects your overhead and a desired profit.

2. Landscape proposals presented to customers should be clear and comprehensive, and should include retail costs for plants, materials, vehicles/equipment, labor charges, and appropriate taxes.

3. It is important to know how discounts offered to customers affect your profit margin.

4. Use estimating for services performed (mulching, lawn mowing, compost tea applications, etc.) to measure the productivity and profitability of the crews completing these services.

5. The Landscape Maintenance Service Form can be valuable in generating more business from existing clients through offering additional services to those clients. The form also provides an efficient way to estimate the yearly costs of services clients choose to have you complete.

Chapter 13: THE WRE ESTIMATING PROGRAM AND JOB COSTING TO MEASURE PROFITABILITY

In order to fully explain Job Costing, I will describe the computer program that WRE had developed for estimating and job costing. As our company grew in the mid to late 1990's, I realized the importance of having a comprehensive, accurate, and efficient estimating program. We needed a program that would calculate an estimate quickly with a predictable profit margin and overhead recovery. Although I had researched other estimating programs on the market, none of them fully accomplished what I wanted for my business. Custom designing our program was not an easy, inexpensive, or quick process, but the resulting estimating/job costing program meets our needs. It is also relatively easy to update and provides us with accurate estimates that clients can easily understand. If there are changes to the proposal, discounts, or certain phases to be completed, the information in the program can be saved or adjusted in minutes. Where estimates used to take us many hours, they can now be completed in a fraction of that time. Integrated into the program is the job costing segment which, with the input of the actual costs when a project is completed, can quickly produce the actual profit margin percentage and compare all actual costs to the estimated costs. This comparison of actual costs to estimated costs is extremely valuable in finding out what went as expected and which areas did not meet projections. With these "lessons learned," changes can be made on future estimates to achieve the most accurate, profitable results.

The WRE Estimating Program

The components of the WRE estimating program are: the Customer Contact Information Sheet, the Job Estimate Input Sheet, the Material, Equipment/Trucking, Subcontractor, and Labor Rate Sheets, the Financial Summary Sheet, the Retail Estimate Proposal Sheet, Plant Picking Ticket Form, and the Job Costing segment (which will be explained in detail in the next section).

All the estimating components are shown in Figure 41 through Figure 43. Let's examine each one to see how they work and contribute to the resulting final estimate.

1. <u>Customer Contact Information Sheet</u> – This form is filled out when a customer first makes contact with our company (Figure 41). Phone numbers, email, and mailing addresses are important in allowing us to quickly and efficiently communicate with the client. Every new customer is asked how he or she heard about us so that we can track the most effective forms of marketing. Areas of interest and directions to their site are included along with any special notes obtained at the first meeting. This information is then stored in our customer database.

CUSTOMER CONTACT INFO

CUSTOMER MAILING/BILLING ADDRESS

NAME _____

ADDRESS _____ CITY _____ STATE _____ ZIP _____

EMAIL _____

TELEPHONE _____ FAX _____ CELL _____

CUSTOMER SITE ADDRESS

NAME _____

SITE ADDRESS _____ CITY _____ STATE _____ ZIP _____

AREAS OF INTEREST

		NOTES
LANDSCAPE DESIGN		
LANDSCAPE LIGHTING		
LANDSCAPE MAINTENANCE		
LANDSCAPE SERVICES		
MASONRY		
CARPENTRY		
NURSERY STOCK		
EDUCATIONAL PROGRAMS		
CONSULTATIONS		
SEASONAL CHANGEOVERS		
OTHER		

REFERRALS

HOW DID CUSTOMER HEAR ABOUT US?

DATES

SITE VISIT   FOLLOW UP

DIRECTIONS TO SITE

MEETING NOTES

PREPARED BY: DATE:

Figure 41: Customer Contact Information Sheet

2. <u>Job Estimate Input Sheets</u> – The input sheets, which are part of a Microsoft Excel®
    spreadsheet program, have revolutionized our estimating process. All of our team leaders and
    managers are involved in the estimating process for each project. It makes sense that they
    should play a critical role since they are the team members who will be implementing the
    project. For each project, they will study the plan, visit the site, make calculations as to the
    square footage of beds, patios, walks, lawn, driveways, etc., and check off the quantities of
    materials, equipment, and trucking needed, any sub-contractors to be used, and the labor
    needed to complete the project. The input sheets (Figure 42 pages 1-4) contain almost all of
    the materials and equipment/trucking options they would need; if something is not listed
    there is a section to enter a new material or equipment, which will then be added to the
    program.

    There is an investment in time having team leaders visit the potential job site and
    complete the data input for the estimate, but the effort pays huge dividends through more
    accurate estimates. There is a tremendous time savings on the estimate process compared to
    prior methods, when one estimator did all the calculations by hand and with little, if any,
    input from the team that would actually do the job. Now there is ownership of the proposal
    and the profit margin, which becomes a goal to exceed with efficiency, high productivity,
    and self-pride.

JOB ESTIMATE INPUT SHEET

CUSTOMER INFORMATION

NAME	
SITE ADDRESS	
EMAIL	

TELEPHONE	**FAX**	**CELL**

DESCRIPTION OF JOB (SCOPE)   PHASE # ____

PHASE TITLE:

DATES

SITE VISIT DATE	**ESTIMATED START DATE**	**ESTIMATED COMPLETE DATE**

PLANT REQUIREMENTS

Plant pick ticket will be generated separately if plants are included in job.

Enter the following information from the pick ticket: **TOTAL COST** ____

TOTAL RETAIL

MATERIAL REQUIREMENTS

	UNITS		NOTES
BLUESTONE (up to 24"x36")		SF	
BLUESTONE CAP & TREAD STOCK		LF	
BLUESTONE, CRUSHED 3/4"		TON	
BLUESTONE, CRUSHED 3/8"		TON	
BURLAP		FT	
CEMENT, PORTLAND TYPE 2		BAG	
COBBLES (JUMBO)		EA	
COBBLES (REGULAR)		EA	
COMPOST		YD	
CONDUIT, 2", 10'		EA	
DIRT, YELLOW (SCREENED)		YD	
DUCK BILLS 1/8 X 30		EA	
FERTILIZER, STARTER		BAG	
FERTILIZER, TABLETS 20-10-5		EA	
FILL		YD	
FLAG (FIELD) STONE IRREGULAR		PALLET	
GRAVEL, BANK RUN 6"		TON	
GRAVEL, PROCESSED 3/4"-1 1/4"		TON	
LANDSCAPE FABRIC		LF	
LIME, PELLETIZED		BAG	
LOAM, SCREENED		YD	
MORTAR MIX, QUIKRETE		BAG	

Figure 42: Job Estimate Input Sheet (page 1)

JOB ESTIMATE INPUT SHEET

CUSTOMER INFORMATION

NAME			
MULCH, BAG	_____	BAG	_____
MULCH, DARK PINE BARK	_____	YD	_____
MULCH, HEMLOCK BARK	_____	YD	_____
MULCH, PINE BARK	_____	YD	_____
PAVER EDGING, 16' ALUM W/SPIKES	_____	EA	_____
PAVER EDGING, 8' PLASTIC	_____	EA	_____
PAVERS, BOSTON COLONIAL	_____	SF	_____
PAVERS, BRUSSELS	_____	SF	_____
PAVERS, CAMELOT	_____	SF	_____
PAVERS, GRASSY	_____	SF	_____
PAVERS, HOLLAND STONE	_____	SF	_____
PAVERS, IL CAMPO MIX	_____	SF	_____
PAVERS, ROMAN WALL, 1 1/2 UNIT (FACE FT)	_____	FT	_____
PAVERS, ROMAN WALL, 1/2 COPING UNIT (EACH)	_____	EA	_____
PAVERS, ROMAN WALL, CAP UNIT (FACE FT)	_____	FT	_____
PAVERS, ROMAN WALL, CORNER UNIT (FACE FT)	_____	FT	_____
PAVERS, YANKEE COBBLE	_____	SF	_____
RIP-RAP, 6"	_____	TON	_____
SAND, JOINT	_____	BAG	_____
SAND, MASON	_____	TON	_____
SAND, PIPE (CONCRETE)	_____	TON	_____
SAND, SCREENED	_____	TON	_____
SAND, STONE (STONE DUST)	_____	TON	_____
SEED, ENDOPHYTE	_____	LB	_____
SEED, PERENNIAL RYEGRASS	_____	LB	_____
SEED, GRASS URI #2	_____	LB	_____
SEED, HARD FESCUE	_____	LB	_____
SEED, NE WILDFLOWER MIX	_____	LB	_____
SEED, SHADY	_____	LB	_____
SEED, WRE SEASIDE MIX	_____	LB	_____
SOD	_____	SF	_____
STONE, CRUSHED - ALL SIZES	_____	TON	_____
STONE, RIVER ROCK	_____	YD	_____
WALL STONE, BULK	_____	TON	_____
WALL STONE, PALLET		EA	

IF YOU NEED TO ENTER OTHER MATERIALS NOT ON THIS LIST, ENTER HERE

MATERIALS	QTY	UNITS	

Figure 42, continued (page 2).

JOB ESTIMATE INPUT SHEET

CUSTOMER INFORMATION

NAME	

EQUIPMENT REQUIREMENTS

	# DAYS	NOTES
AERATOR		
AUGER		
CEMENT MIXER		
CHAINSAW/POLE PRUNER		
COMPOST TEA (per gal. applied)		
CUTOFF SAW		
DISPOSAL FEES, BRUSH/LG LOAD		
DISPOSAL FEES, BRUSH/MED LOAD		
DISPOSAL FEES, BRUSH/SM LOAD		
DISPOSAL FEES, COMPOST/LG LOAD		
DISPOSAL FEES, COMPOST/MED LOAD		
DISPOSAL FEES, COMPOST/SM LOAD		
DISPOSAL FEES, DUMPSTER/ 1/2 PICKUP		
DISPOSAL FEES, DUMPSTER/ 1/2 TON		
DISPOSAL FEES, DUMPSTER/1 TON		
DISPOSAL FEES, FILL/LG LOAD		
DISPOSAL FEES, FILL/MED LOAD		
DISPOSAL FEES, FILL/SM LOAD		
DRILL, HAMMER		
DUMP, 1 TON		
FREIGHTLINER		
GAS COMPACTOR (PACKER)		
GAS SPADE		
GENERATOR		
GRAVELY		
GRINDER		
KUBOTA R520 (1-5 DAYS)		
KUBOTA R520 (6+ DAYS)		
KUBOTA TRACTOR + ATTACHMENTS		
LEAF BLOWER		
MOWER (WALK BEHIND)		
PICKUP		
RENTAL-ROTOTILLER		
RENTAL-SOD CUTTER		
SAW, CIRCULAR		
SAW, WET		
SLICE SEEDER		
SPRAYER (300GAL)		
TRENCHER		

IF YOU NEED TO ENTER OTHER EQUIPMENT NOT ON THIS LIST, ENTER HERE

EQUIPMENT	# DAYS	

Figure 42, continued (page 3).

JOB ESTIMATE INPUT SHEET

CUSTOMER INFORMATION

NAME	

SUBCONTRACTOR REQUIREMENTS

	# DAYS	NOTES
BACKHOE	_____	_____
BULLDOZER	_____	_____
ELECTRICIAN	_____	_____
EXCAVATOR	_____	_____
IRRIGATION	_____	_____
MINI/SKID LOADER	_____	_____
TREEWORKS	_____	_____
TRUCK, 10 WHEEL	_____	_____

IF YOU NEED TO ENTER OTHER SUBCONTRACTORS NOT ON THIS LIST, ENTER HERE

SUBCONTRACTOR	# DAYS	

LABOR REQUIREMENTS

	# MEN	# DAYS	NOTES
CARPENTRY			
CONSTRUCTION			
MASONRY			
PLANTING			
PRUNING			

CONSIDERATIONS

Is there sufficient access for machinery?	yes/no	Where is the septic located? _____
Is there a water source (where)?	yes/no	Has dig save been called? yes/no

NOTES

PREPARED BY: **DATE:**

Figure 42, continued (page 4).

Sample Equipment, Trucking, Subcontractor, and Labor Rates		
Equipment Rates	Cost/Day	Retail/Day
AERATOR	$75.00	$150.00
CEMENT MIXER	$50.00	$125.00
CUTOFF SAW	$95.00	$190.00
DISPOSAL FEES, BRUSH/LG LOAD	$75.00	$150.00
DISPOSAL FEES, COMPOST/LG LOAD	$75.00	$150.00
DISPOSAL FEES, DUMPSTER/ 1/2 PICKUP	$25.00	$50.00
DISPOSAL FEES, DUMPSTER/ 1/2 TON	$35.00	$70.00
DISPOSAL FEES, DUMPSTER/ 1 TON	$50.00	$100.00
DISPOSAL FEES, FILL/LG LOAD	$50.00	$100.00
DUMP, 1 TON	$85.00	$170.00
FREIGHTLINER	$110.00	$220.00
GAS COMPACTOR (PACKER)	$35.00	$70.00
HEDGE TRIMMER (1 DAY)	$55.00	$110.00
KUBOTA R520	$200.00	$500.00
KUBOTA TRACTOR	$75.00	$150.00
MOWER (WALK BEHIND)	$50.00	$100.00
PICKUP	$60.00	$120.00
RENTAL ROTOTILLER	$95.00	$190.00
SAW, WET	$90.00	$180.00
SLICE SEEDER	$75.00	$150.00
SOD CUTTER	$75.00	$150.00
SPRAYER (300 GAL)	$70.00	$140.00
Subcontractor Equipment Rates	Cost/Hr	Retail/Hr
BACKHOE	$85.00	$128.00
BULLDOZER	$125.00	$188.00
EXCAVATOR	$150.00	$225.00
TRUCK, 10 WHEEL	$100.00	$150.00
Labor Rates	Sample Cost/Hr	Retail/Hr (Estimates)
CARPENTRY	$26.00	$65.00
CONSTRUCTION	$22.00	$55.00
MAINTENANCE	$18.00	$45.00
MASONRY	$30.00	$75.00
PLANTING	$20.00	$50.00

Figure 43: Sample Equipment, Trucking, Subcontractor, and Labor Rates

3. Rate Sheets – Critical to the estimating program's calculations are the material, equipment/trucking, sub-contractor, and labor rate sheets (Figure 43). Producing these sheets must take place before using the estimating program, and the sheets must be updated frequently to reflect changes in costs of materials, rates for labor, equipment, and sub-contractors. The process of creating the rate tables will have an additional benefit besides estimating–it will help to organize your business. Researching and establishing costs will give you the important data needed to produce accurate estimates without "guesstimating".

4. <u>Financial Summary</u> – After the input sheets are completed, our marketing manager enters the data into the MS Excel® estimating program to calculate the estimate. The result of the input is the financial summary, which displays the direct costs for the plants, materials, equipment, sub-contractors, and labor, plus the true cost with the overhead added in (Figure 44). The program allocates overhead automatically. The exact overhead allocation will depend on your particular overhead, type of business, and market place. The financial summary shows the result of the Retail Method and a retail price including profit.

The summary also calculates the profit margin (profit divided by selling price) in the form of a percent, which becomes the target profit goal for the project…barring any adjustments from discounts. Another helpful feature of the summary sheet is a discount option, which will calculate the discounted retail price and adjusted profit margin percentage, all from the entry of the discount percentage number. This is extremely valuable to see what the effect of discounting will have on your bottom line, giving you real numbers to consider when discounting.

FINANCIAL SUMMARY (For Sample Landscape Proposal)

CUSTOMER:	Dick & Jane Customer		PHASE # 1	FOUNDATION PLANTING
	DIRECT COST		**TRUE COST**	**RETAIL METHOD**
PLANTS	$424		$700	$945
MATERIAL	$609		$915	$1,235
EQUIPMENT	$360		$607	$820
LABOR	$1,120		$2,074	$2,800
SUBCONTRACTOR	$0		$0	$0

TOTAL DIRECT COST:	$2,513	
OVERHEAD (DIRECT COST + 70.95%) =	$1,783	
TRUE COST (DIRECT COST + OVERHEAD) =	$4,296	

	RETAIL METHOD
TOTAL QUOTED RETAIL: TRUE COST + 35% PROFIT	$5,800
PROJECTED PROFIT OVER COST: RETAIL COST – TRUE COST	$1,504
NET PROFIT: PROFIT ÷ RETAIL PRICE	26%

DISCOUNT

Enter Desired Discount: 10% Discounted Price	$5,800 - $580 (10%) = $5,220 (Retail) - (10% Discount) = (Discounted Price)
New Profit =	$5,220 - $4,296 = $924 (Retail) - (True Cost) = (New Profit)
New Net Profit % =	New Profit : $924 = 18% New Retail : $5,220 (New Net Profit)

Figure 44: Financial Summary Sheet

5. <u>Retail Estimate Proposal Sheet</u> – In Figure 33 (Chapter 12) you can see the retail estimate proposal that will be given to a customer. It lists the scope of the job (and succeeding phases, if there are any), the plant total, the materials total (with individual quantities of products), a listing of equipment and trucking to be used on the job, a sub-contractor total, and the labor price to complete the project. At the bottom of the page are the payment terms–usually 50% deposit, 50% when completed for jobs under $20,000 and 40% deposit, 40% mid-payment, and 20% final payment for larger projects (over $20,000).

    Recently, we have added a contract segment for the clients to sign, turning the estimate proposal into a contract. Clients with projects exceeding $20,000 sign a more detailed Landscape Service Contract (shown previously in Figure 19, Chapter 8).

6. <u>Plant Picking Ticket</u> – Specific plant picking tickets (Figure 45) are generated separately from our FileMaker® plant database. The resulting plant picking ticket contains all of the plants chosen for the job, with Latin names, common names, quantity, size, individual price, and total price. This sheet accompanies the Retail Estimate Proposal and becomes part of the signed contract. After the job is completed, the plants actually used are entered and a revised picking ticket is given to the client, a copy is placed in their file, and the exact plants used are removed from our inventory database.

Customer ID: cust-3289			Number: 1580	Date Created: 8/23/2010			Print Date: 8/23/2010

Product ID	Description	Size	Qty On Hand	Qty Out	Qty Back	Qty Used	Price	Extended Amount
N800KA	NYSSA SYLVATICA	1.5/2" Cal	0	1		1	380.00	380.00
H162GE	HYDRANGEA MACROPHYLLA PINK BEAUTY	#5	0	1		1	50.00	50.00
S180GC	SPIREA BUMALDA ANTHONY WATERER	#3	2	3		3	30.00	90.00
V048GC	VACCINIUM CORYMBOSUM DUKE	#3	0	5		5	35.00	175.00
P260GC	PIERIS JAPONICA VALLEY VALENTINE	#3	0	5		5	50.00	250.00
							PL Item Total:	945.00

Figure 45: Plant Picking Ticket

Job Costing Program

The last component of the estimating program is the Job Costing segment. This component is valuable to find out how profitable the estimated project was after completion.

For years we operated our business without this important aspect of the estimating process. We "assumed" certain jobs were profitable…and ignored those that we knew might have lost money! However, as the business grew, our overhead climbed, competition became more prevalent, and our bankers became concerned about profitability, we embraced the job costing segment in our estimating program. I can tell you that it was not easy to implement–a well-qualified and meticulous person needs to oversee the program, and everyone needs to be prepared for some eye-opening results. I was amazed (and at times dismayed!) with some of the results. "I think we did OK on the job" was replaced with "I can't believe we actually lost money on that project." But having the actual figures and profit margins has made us a stronger company by permitting the analysis of each job completed to see where we can make changes in future jobs to be more efficient and profitable.

Job Costing Components – The job costing program requires the following information: accurate Job Reports (with all slips for the project, rentals, etc. purchased for the project), a Project Estimate Sheet, and a Job Costing Summary Sheet (Figure 46 through Figure 50). These are described below.

1. Job Reports – The most important components of completing the job costing analysis are accurate, complete, and legible job reports (Figure 46 and Figure 47). Our team has improved significantly in this area through patience, prodding, and pleading from our managers. These reports are given to our office manager, who enters the data into the MS Excel® spreadsheet form. Instructions on how to complete the forms and how to accurately allocate hours, materials, and equipment/vehicles to various phases of a large project has helped tremendously to ensure that the reports contain all the necessary information to compile the job cost report. Having employees turn in all receipts from purchases for the specific job phases (mulch, grass seed, bluestone, rototiller rental, processed gravel, etc.) is essential to compiling accurate results. This year we have assigned a team leader whose responsibility is to ensure that all slips are turned in at the end of each day, ensuring that the data entered into the program will be accurate and complete.

CONSTRUCTION SERVICES JOB REPORT			Date:		
			PROJECT NO.		**ORIGINATOR**
CUSTOMER					

CREW		HOURS (excl lunch)	CREW		HOURS (excl lunch)
	TOTALS			TOTALS	

PHASE:

MATERIALS USED:				VEHICLES USED:	1/2 DAY	FULL DAY
Bluestone	Size:	SF:		Dump, 1 Ton		
Bluestone, Crushed	Size:	Tons:		Freightliner		
Cobbles	Size:	Each:		Pickup		
Compost	Yds:			Truck		
Conduit, 2"	Size: 10'	Each:				
Dirt, Yellow	Unscr/Screened	Yds:		EQUIPMENT USED:	1/2 DAY	FULL DAY
Fertilizer, Starter	Bags:			Kubota R520		
Fertilizer, Tablets	Each:			Cement Mixer		
Gravel	Type:	Tons:		Compost Tea Sprayer		
Loam	WRE/Screened	Yds:		Cutoff Saw		
Mulch	Type:	Yds:		Compactor		
Mulch	Type:	Bag:		Rototiller		
Paver Edging	Type:	Each:		Saw, Circular/Wet		
Pavers	Type:	SF:		Trencher, Small/Large		
Sand	Type:	Tons:				
Sand, Joint	Bags:					
Seed	Type:	Lbs:				
Sod	SF:					
Spikes, Edging, 10"	Each:					
Stone, Crushed	Tons:					
Stone, River Rock	Yds:			DISPOSAL FEES:		# LOADS
Wall Stone, Bulk	Tons:			Brush	Small Load	
Wall Stone, Pallet	Each:			Brush	Medium Load	
				Brush	Large Load	
				Compost	Small Load	
				Compost	Medium Load	
				Compost	Large Load	
				Dumpster	1/2 Pickup	
SUBCONTRACTOR USED:	1/2 DAY	FULL DAY		Dumpster	1/2 Ton	
Backhoe				Dumpster	1 Ton	
Excavator				Fill	Small Load	
Truck, 10 Wheel				Fill	Medium Load	
				Fill	Large Load	

DESCRIPTION OF WORK DONE AND PROGRESS:

TOTAL MAN HOURS ON THIS PHASE: WORKERS X   HOURS

Figure 46: Construction Services Job Report

PHASE: _____

MATERIALS USED:

Bluestone	Size:	SF:
Bluestone, Crushed	Size:	Tons:
Cobbles	Size:	Each:
Compost	Yds:	
Conduit, 2"	Size: 10'	Each:
Dirt, Yellow	Unscr/Screened	Yds:
Fertilizer, Starter	Bags:	
Fertilizer, Tablets	Each:	
Gravel	Type:	Tons:
Loam	WRE/Screened	Yds:
Mulch	Type:	Yds:
Mulch	Type:	Bag:
Paver Edging	Type:	Each:
Pavers	Type:	SF:
Sand	Type:	Tons:
Sand, Joint	Bags:	
Seed	Type:	Lbs:
Sod	SF:	
Spikes, Edging, 10"	Each:	
Stone, Crushed	Tons:	
Stone, River Rock	Yds:	
Wall Stone, Bulk	Tons:	
Wall Stone, Pallet	Each:	

VEHICLES USED:

VEHICLES USED:	1/2 DAY	FULL DAY
Dump, 1 Ton		
Freightliner		
Pickup		

EQUIPMENT USED:

EQUIPMENT USED:	1/2 DAY	FULL DAY
Kubota R520		
Cement Mixer		
Compost Tea Sprayer		
Cutoff Saw		
Compactor		
Rototiller		
Saw, Circular/Wet		
Trencher, Small/Large		

DISPOSAL FEES:

DISPOSAL FEES:		# LOADS
Brush	Small Load	
Brush	Medium Load	
Brush	Large Load	
Compost	Small Load	
Compost	Medium Load	
Compost	Large Load	
Dumpster	1/2 Pickup	
Dumpster	1/2 Ton	
Dumpster	1 Ton	
Fill	Small Load	
Fill	Medium Load	
Fill	Large Load	

DESCRIPTION OF WORK DONE AND PROGRESS:

TOTAL MAN HOURS ON THIS PHASE: _____ WORKERS X _____ HOURS

Figure 46, continued (back of form).

MAINTENANCE SERVICES JOB REPORT

Date:

ORIGINATOR

CUSTOMER _____

CREW	HOURS (excl lunch)	CREW	HOURS (excl lunch)
TOTALS		TOTALS	

DESCRIPTION OF WORK DONE:

LABOR HOURS:	# MEN	X HOURS
Maintenance		
Pruning		
Spraying		

MATERIALS USED:

Material	Unit		Material	Unit
Anti Desiccant	Gals:			
Burlap	Feet:		Loam, WRE Screened	Yds:
Compost Tea	Gals:		Mulch, Bag	Bags:
Deer Repellant	Gals:		Mulch, Dark Pine Bark	Yds:
Duck Bills 1/8 X 30	Each:		Mulch, Hemlock Bark	Yds:
Fertilizer, 8-4-24	Bags:		Mulch, Pine Bark	Yds:
Fertilizer, HOLLY TONE	Bags:		Mulch, Starter (2500 sf)	Bags:
Fertilizer, Kelp Booster Organic	Bags:		Seed, ENDOPHYTE	Lbs:
Fertilizer, Lawn Booster, Organic 8-1-1	Bags:		Seed, GOALKEEPER Perenn, Ryegrass	Lbs:
Fertilizer, Root Feed (MACRON 20/20/20)	Gals:		Seed, HARD FESCUE	Lbs:
Fertilizer, SUSTANE 5-2-4	Bags:		Seed, NE WILDFLOWER MIX	Lbs:
Fertilizer, Tablets 20-10-5	Tablets:		Seed, SHADY	Lbs:
Herbicide, RAZOR BURN	Gals:		Seed, WRE SEASIDE MIX	Lbs:
Horticultural Oil	Gals:		Seed, WRE WILDFLOWER MIX	Lbs:
Insecticidal Soap	Gals:		SOD	SF:
Lime, Pellitized	Bags:		Stakes, Wood Guide, 2"	Each:
Loam, Screened	Yds:		Tape, Arbor	Feet:

Figure 47: Maintenance Services Job Report

VEHICLES USED:	1/2 DAY	FULL DAY
Dump, 1 Ton		
Flatbed		
Pickup		

EQUIPMENT USED:	1/2 DAY	FULL DAY
Aerator		
Chainsaw/Pole Pruner		
Compost Tea Sprayer		
Leaf Blower		
Mower (Walk Behind)		
Power Washer		
Slice Seeder		
Sprayer (300GAL)		
Weedwacker		

DISPOSAL FEES:		# LOADS
Brush	Small Load	
Brush	Medium Load	
Brush	Large Load	
Compost	Small Load	
Compost	Medium Load	
Compost	Large Load	
Dumpster	1/2 Pickup	
Dumpster	1/2 Ton	
Dumpster	1 Ton	
Fill	Small Load	
Fill	Medium Load	
Fill	Large Load	

ADDITIONAL NOTES/COMMENTS:

Figure 47, continued (back page).

2. <u>Estimate and Actual Spreadsheets</u> – (Figure 48 and Figure 49). The Estimate Spreadsheet (MS Excel®) containing estimated plants, materials, equipment/trucking, and labor costs is derived from the estimate proposal's data produced during the estimate process. In spreadsheet form, the various phases are summarized in specific columns, breaking down the estimate into plant, material, equipment, and labor costs for each phase.

Estimated Job Cost Spreadsheet

Dick & Jane Customer

ESTIMATED COSTS	COST	TOTAL UNITS	FOUNDATION PLANTING				ESTIMATED COST TOTALS	CONTRACT AMOUNT	RETAIL
LABOR	COST	HRS	HRS	TTL	HRS	TTL			
PLANTING	20.00	56	56	1,120.00		-	1,120.00	2,800	$50.00
TOTAL LABOR		56	56	1,120.00		-	1,120.00	2,800	
PLANTS		QTY	$ EA	TTL					RETAIL
TOTAL PLANTS				424.50			424.50	945	
MATERIALS	COST	UNITS	UNITS	TTL	UNITS	TTL	TOTALS		RETAIL
COMPOST	$30.00	5	5	150.00		-	150.00	400	$80.00
LOAM, SCREENED	$22.75	16	16	364.00		-	364.00	560	$35.00
MULCH, PINE BARK	$19.00	5	5	95.00		-	95.00	275	$55.00
TOTAL MATERIALS		26	26	609.00		-	609.00	1,235	
EQUIPMENT & TRUCKING	COST	DAYS	DAYS	TTL	DAYS	TTL	TOTALS		RETAIL
DUMP, 1 TON	$85.00	1	1	85.00		-	85.00	170	$170.00
KUBOTA R520	$200.00	1	1	200.00		-	200.00	500	$500.00
SOD CUTTER	$75.00	1	1	75.00		-	75.00	150	$150.00
TOTAL EQUIPMENT		3	3	360.00			360.00	820	
TOTAL COSTS				2,513.50		-	2,513.50	5,800	

Figure 48: Estimated Job Cost Spreadsheet

The actual data are entered into the Actual Job Cost Spreadsheet from the job reports and slips to create an exact economic picture of the completed project. The Actual Job Cost Spreadsheet will reveal the exact time and materials cost compared to the estimated spreadsheet cost. Individual areas can be examined to see where the project did well and where it came up short. The final analysis is made with the Job Costing Summary Sheet.

Actual Job Cost Spreadsheet

Dick & Jane Customer

ACTUAL COSTS		TOTAL UNITS	10/22/2008		DATE		ACTUAL COST TOTALS	TIME & MATERIALS	RETAIL
LABOR	COST	HRS	HRS	TTL	HRS	TTL			
PLANTING	20.00	60	60	1,200.00		-	1,200.00	3,000	$50.00
TOTAL LABOR		60	60	1,200.00	-	-	1,200.00	3,000	
PLANTS		QTY	$EA	TTL					RETAIL
TOTAL PLANTS				449.00			449.00	988	
MATERIALS	COST	UNITS	UNITS	TTL	UNITS	TTL	TOTALS		RETAIL
COMPOST	$30.00	4	4	120.00		-	120.00	320	$80.00
LOAM, SCREENED	$22.75	18	18	409.50		-	409.50	630	$35.00
MULCH, PINE BARK	$19.00	6	6	114.00		-	114.00	330	$55.00
TOTAL MATERIALS		28	28	643.50		-	643.50	1,280	
EQUIPMENT & TRUCKING	COST	DAYS	DAYS	TTL			TOTALS		RETAIL
DUMP, 1 TON	$85.00	1	1	85.00		-	85.00	170	$170.00
KUBOTA R520	$200.00	1	1	200.00		-	200.00	500	$500.00
SOD CUTTER	$75.00	1	1	75.00		-	75.00	150	$150.00
TOTAL EQUIPMENT		3	3	360.00	-	-	360.00	820	
TOTAL COSTS				2,652.50		-	2,652.50	6,088	

Figure 49: Actual Job Cost Spreadsheet

3. Job Costing Summary Sheet - (Figure 50). The Job Costing Summary Sheet consolidates the estimated cost and contract amount with the actual cost and time and materials billing. It tabulates the actual true cost, overhead, total billable amount, and profit margin. The sheet allows the comparison of estimated costs with actual costs so that you can see where the project may have gone off course. This will provide you with valuable information to make corrections for the next estimate.

The Adjusted Retail Billing column shows what the retail price should have been, based upon the actual costs ($6,088). Since in this example a contract was signed to complete the job for $5,800, the actual profit was reduced from $1,504 ($1,504 ÷ $5,800 x 100 = 26% profit margin) to $1,364 ($1,364 ÷ $5,800 x 100 = 24% profit margin). The actual direct cost plus overhead ($4,436) was $140 more than the estimated direct cost plus overhead ($4,296). The contract price ($5,800) minus the actual direct cost + overhead ($4,296) equals the reduced profit of $1,364. Having a provision in your contract to allow for add-ons based on the actual plants, materials, and labor used to complete the project and communicating with the client may allow you to charge the Adjusted Retail Billing amount ($6,088).

It is important to share the project results with your managers and team leaders so that they can see where changes might be made to increase profitability. This is essential, since our team leaders are a vital part of the estimating process. Not sharing job costing results is like having your team play an entire baseball game with no scoreboard. Unless they are made aware of the final score, they will lose motivation and wonder why they work hard to be productive with no numerical measure of their success–or shortcomings. The job costing results are a visual report card on how the project did financially.

Job Costing Summary

CUSTOMER: Dick & Jane Customer			PHASE # 1	FOUNDATION PLANTING
	ESTIMATED DIRECT COST (A)	CONTRACT AMOUNT (B)	ACTUAL DIRECT COST (C)	ADJUSTED RETAIL BILLING (D)	DIFFERENCE (B - D)
PLANTS	$424	$945	$449	$988	-$43
MATERIAL	$609	$1,235	$644	$1,280	-$45
EQUIPMENT	$360	$820	$360	$820	$0
LABOR	$1,120	$2,800	$1,200	$3,000	-$200
SUBCONTRACTOR	$0	$0	$0	$0	$0
TOTAL	$2,513	$5,800	$2,653	$6,088	-$288

PROJECTED			ACTUAL	
TOTAL DIRECT COST	$2,513	(COST)	$2,653	(DIRECT COST)
OVERHEAD @ 70.95%	$1,783	(DIRECT COST x 0.7095)	$1,783	(SAME AS ESTIMATE)
SUBTOTAL	$4,296	(DIRECT COST + OVERHEAD)	$4,436	(DIRECT COST + OVERHEAD)
PROFIT @ 35%	$1,504	(TRUE COST x 0.35)	$1,364	(= $5,800 - $4,436): 24%
TOTAL BILLABLE AMOUNT	$5,800		$5,800	

Figure 50: Job Costing Summary Sheet

WRE Experience

From the time we developed a comprehensive, custom, estimating program, our estimates have been professional in appearance, more accurate, and well received by our customers. With the involvement of our managers and team leaders in the estimating process (along with my review and final approval), our estimates now reflect a more realistic view of the actual time to complete the project. Prior to employee involvement, unrealistic expectations of completion time were common, leading to manager and employee conflict when projects significantly ran over the projected time frame. Team leaders now have a vested interest in the outcome since they are involved in setting the time to complete construction projects.

Job costing has had a dramatic impact on our estimating process. When jobs do not achieve the desired profit margin, team members diligently work on the next estimate to make the necessary adjustments to increase profitability. I can certainly state that without job costing, there would not be a thorough review of completed projects. This review drives the commitment to make changes and be more accurate with the estimates. At times it has been frustrating to see poor job costing results, but the alternative of not knowing until the end of the fiscal year, when it is too late, makes the bad news more palatable.

With the instability in our economy, the pressures to be productive and profitable, and the uncertainty of guessing at financial results, it has been comforting knowing that our estimating system works for us.

Essential Points:

1. An effective estimating program requires detailed, accurate data sheets and rates for materials, vehicles/equipment, and labor, with frequently updated information.

2. A financial summary sheet shows the results of estimating using the Overhead and Profit Method and the Retail Method, with a calculated profit margin which becomes the financial goal for the project.

3. Job costing is essential to determine if completed jobs were profitable or if they lost money. Accurate job reports are needed to provide actual figures for determining the profit (or loss) on a specific project.

4. The Job Costing Summary Sheet will provide the comparison of estimated costs with actual costs and the resulting profit margin.

5. Sharing job costing results with your managers, team leaders, and crews is important so that they can see where changes might be made to increase profitability.

Chapter 14: **INCREASE SALES TO IMPROVE PROFITABILITY**

Sales are the lifeblood of a business. Even with a well-designed marketing plan, if there are not enough sales the business will deteriorate. Given sufficient sales a business can grow, prosper, and plan for a successful future. Sales are important all year long, but are especially so in times of an economic slowdown. In this chapter I will discuss ten steps to better sales, share sales tips, and provide information about including contracts, written estimates, and change orders in all of your proposals. Previous chapters have identified ways to create a marketing plan, develop your brand, implement promotions to attract business, and use a comprehensive estimating process for projects–now you need to generate and close sales to support your company's efforts!

Ten Steps to Better Sales

1. <u>Timely Response to Customers</u> – One way to separate yourself from your competitors is by promptly responding to all customer calls and emails. A few years ago, a new client hired our firm because their landscaper hadn't returned phone calls made to him over a 3-4 week period. New customers are surprised (and pleased) to be able to call during the week and actually talk to one of our team members. When we are completing a major project, the client will have my cell phone number so that they can reach me with questions, concerns, and any changes. We offer a toll free number for our out of state clients. The easier and more pleasant you can make contacting your company the better satisfaction a customer will have in dealing with your firm. Email has become a preferred choice of communication with many of my clients. I check and answer emails when I arrive at the office at 6:30 a.m., at mid-day, and later in the afternoon, ensuring quick response and customer feedback. Emails have several other advantages including the ability to send emails when convenient, compile a written record of communication, and send proposals and sketches as attachments, speeding up the process of finalizing jobs without the slowness of the U.S. Postal Service.

2. <u>Look Professional, Act Professional</u> – As previously discussed in Chapter 4, developing a strong brand is essential to your long-term business success. Your brand is more than a nice logo; it includes clean trucks, neat uniforms, appropriate crew conduct, and professional communication and sales tools. Important to our sales success is our coordinated communication tools–letters, letterheads, bills, proposal forms, fax sheets, thank-you notes, customer survey cards, warranty forms, website, and other forms of communication. All contain our logo, the same print font, the same style of paper, and business contact information so that the message we send is consistent and uniform.

Our primary business sale tool is our marketing folder and image brochure. The tan folder with Wood River Evergreen's logo on the front upper corner is 50% recycled paper and contains all of the handouts we want to give to the client. These documents include our mission statement, business history, division descriptions, customer referrals, testimonials, an owner biography, and company awards. The ivory paper is also 50% recycled, with various symbols on each sheet for the different topics and divisions.

The folder also contains our image brochure with a thicker cover and native twig attached to the top binding, containing five pictures of our business. The marketing folder and brochure say professional, well-thought-out, green, and yet subtle. If we want to include any color pictures we tuck them inside the folder. When presenting an estimate, the typed proposal is included in one of the folder jackets. It is very important to make a positive impression when soliciting business or presenting a proposal. Using professional presentation materials will go a long way toward impressing your customer and separating you from the competition. Numerous times I have closed a sale even though I was a higher bidder, and the professional sales brochure and folder made a significant difference.

3. Listen to the Customer – By carefully listening to the customer you can usually ascertain their needs. For example, if the customer identifies privacy as an issue because of a new house being built next door, you can begin to consider alternative screening methods, fencing, columnar evergreens, or well-positioned trees. Before suggesting solutions, however, confirm the need with the customer and determine the level of privacy they envision (6', 10', 15', etc.) and an approximate budget. Many clients will not reveal their budget, but I find that asking questions like "Do you envision spending more or less than $12,000" usually produces a response. If a client is embarking on a major landscape project, it is especially important to know the approximate budget in the design phase so that a $300,000 project is not proposed for a $75,000 budget! Carefully listening to a customer (and taking notes) will point you in the direction of offering an appropriate solution. The suggested solution should be formulated, planned, and estimated prior to meeting the client again to present your proposal. Giving "rough" estimates at the initial meeting can be dangerous since you have not researched the solution nor completed a cost analysis to develop an appropriate estimate using your overhead and profit formula! When clients request a "ballpark" estimate and promise not to "hold" you to it, be wary. No matter how the actual estimate comes back for the work proposed they will compare your written estimate with the "off-the-cuff" figure, creating questions in their mind. The better choice is to decline giving an inaccurate or un-professional quote and to promise to return soon with a detailed proposal containing an estimate for plants, materials, equipment/vehicles, and labor, a sketch of the work to be done, and pictures of similar projects you have completed.

4. Position Your Benefits Before the Buyer – Once a need has been identified, begin to position your capabilities before the customer. Create a perception of added value that your company

has that the competition does not. Using the privacy example, if you recommend 12'-14' native red cedar (*Juniperus virginiana*) as the solution, describe your company's expertise: we specialize in privacy screening plantings, have the plants in stock, use equipment designed for large tree installation, are an award-winning company, have a talented, dedicated team of employees, offer the industry's best warranty (three years), and have an extensive referral list. Point out that the owner will not only make the sale, but will be on-site to see that the plants are properly installed and that everything else is running smoothly. The goal is to highlight your strengths and advantages so that the client can see a clear difference between your company and the competition, which is worth a premium price.

5. <u>Sell the Solution…not the Price</u> – After you have designed the solution to their needs (for example, the privacy evergreen screen) and calculated an estimate, contact the client for an on-site meeting to discuss the proposal. Mailing a proposal does not have nearly the same effect as a face-to-face meeting. The closing rate for mailed-out estimates is fairly low, while direct presentations offer you the opportunity to read the customer's facial expressions and body language, ask questions, offer options, negotiate an agreement, sign a contract, and receive a deposit…the goal of all successful sales presentations!

   At this meeting, lead with the need (the customer needs privacy from the new house next door) and present the solution: Plant (10) 12'-14' red cedars along the border. Once established the plants will grow approximately 2 feet per year and they are wind, salt, and disease resistant. We have the cedars in stock and ready for installation within two weeks. The 14' hedge will give you instant privacy from your porch. Our team is very experienced in planting large trees for hedges, and with our specialized equipment the job can be completed in three days. We offer a 3-year warranty on the plants and can provide watering services if you need them.

   You have sold the solution, your expertise, and even offered to schedule the job within two weeks…now you can present the estimate!

6. <u>Anticipate a Client's Objections to the Estimate</u> – Before you present an estimate, have responses and project options and alternatives ready in anticipation of client objections. Part of your sales preparation, besides designing the solution and estimating the cost, is to have well-prepared responses to a customer's concerns. The cost of the project is often a major objection. Have alternative options ready: reducing the size of plants will save a certain amount, as will phasing the project over two seasons, reducing the number of plants, etc. As a last resort you could offer a 5-10% discount, provided you know your profit margin and are comfortable with the resulting lower margin.

   Do not lose hope due to hearing client objections as they may actually indicate customer interest in buying your service. Even after hearing objections and concerns, continue to emphasize your solution to the problem, the quality of your product, the quality of the team implementing it, and your warranty backing up the investment. The better prepared you are to respond to objections with alternatives, the more successful the negotiations will turn out.

7. Close the Sale – After you have proposed the solution for a customer's need, presented a detailed estimate, and successfully answered all their concerns, ask for the business! Unless you specifically ask for them to agree to the project terms, there is no sale. "The sale belongs to those who are closers" (Jeffery H. Gitomer[1]).

   In the evergreen screen example, the original estimate presented was for $15,000 ((10) 12'-14' red cedars) but the client felt they needed to reduce cost. Thus, a size smaller ((10) 10'-12' cedars) were agreed to with a project cost of $12,500. The closing statement could be: "With a 50% deposit we can schedule your job within two weeks. Would you like to sign the contract confirming the project details and write a deposit check today?" Once a question has been asked confirming the sale, be quiet and wait for the customer to agree. When they have agreed, pull out a contract, have the customer(s) sign the agreement, and acknowledge receipt of their deposit! This closes the sale, but important steps still remain.

8. Follow-up – Follow-up with a customer after the contract is signed to confirm the starting date for their project is extremely important. This demonstrates your commitment to scheduling and provides an opportunity to address other questions, issues, or concerns. Making sure that the assigned starting date is when the team actually arrives to install the cedars will go a long way toward establishing trust…and the potential for referrals if the job is completed satisfactorily. After the project is completed, a walk-around is scheduled to review the project, deal with any concerns, explain after care for the plants, and request final payment. Once the project is completed and final payment has been received, a thank you note along with a customer survey card seeking their feedback for the job our team has done (our report card!) are sent to the client. Those customers who are extremely happy also include testimonials, which are a great resource for future marketing.

9. Keep in Touch! – Staying in touch with customers via newsletters and targeted postcard mailings can go a long way toward creating "client advocates" who will use your services again and recommend your company to friends. Having very satisfied clients recommending your company is the goal of many businesses. With a referral, a new customer will have talked with the client referring you to learn about the quality of your work, pricing information, examples of your work, and what your company was like to deal with…all significant hurdles to attracting new business. You need to treat referrals like gold because they are an extremely valuable asset, which if used properly will help fuel company growth and profitability.

10. Exceed Expectations! – Unfortunately, in today's competitive environment, "satisfied customers just aren't good enough[2]". The goal today is to exceed customer expectations, and as Ken Blanchard and Sheldon Bowles stated in their book Raving Fans, you must create

raving fans. I refer to these very satisfied customers as "client advocates"; clients who have a high degree of loyalty to you and your company and will go to significant lengths to recommend your company and find projects to keep your business busy. Advocates are particularly helpful during slow economic times and when there is a lot of competitive pressure in your market. Client advocates are to be treated like part of your company–because they are!

Unfortunately, not all customers will become client advocates, and a few may actually be dissatisfied with your best efforts. The goal, however, is to exceed all of your clients' expectations with excellent service, clear communications, high quality products, on-time execution of the project, meaningful follow-up, and 100% backup of the work completed. To ensure a steady revenue stream establish a network of client advocates who will not only provide years of referrals but will find many additional projects for your company at their home!

Written Estimates, Contracts, and Change Orders

This is not the most exciting or glamorous topic to discuss, but spending time with developing and using written estimates and contracts will save you aggravation, legal problems, and thousands of dollars in the future! There are many reasons to have written proposals and signed contracts. The agreement becomes binding when both parties agree to the terms and sign the contract. Included in the contract will be the contents of the estimate, scope of work, tentative time schedule, cost (with tax), payment terms, agreements as to how the project can increase or decrease in cost, procedures for deciding disagreements, and other stipulations that your lawyer may insist on.

Not only is a written contract advantageous for both parties, it demonstrates clearly that you are a professional business owner–following professional procedures to ensure that the project is backed up with a clear, legal, understood agreement. A contract does not guarantee that there won't be problems, but it will give both parties a frame of reference and legal standing.

Prior to signing the landscape contract it is highly recommended that a written (preferably typed) estimate be presented and discussed with the client. Along with any changes made in the proposal, it will provide the details about the project: specific materials, plants, equipment and trucking, and labor to complete the job. Once initialed, the estimate can be attached to the contract to become part of the approved agreement. If you have a written guarantee, it also should be included with the landscape contract. WRE's guarantee is shown in Figure 51.

WOOD RIVER EVERGREENS INC.
GUARANTEE

All trees and shrubs planted by Wood River Evergreens, Inc. (WRE) are fully guaranteed for a period of THREE YEARS from the original date of planting. Any trees or shrubs which die during the guarantee period as a result of poor health at time of purchase, or improper planting when installed, will be replaced free of charge, in accordance with the following limitations and as long as the necessary growing conditions have been met.

1) The customer must provide, or have WRE provide, proper care for the trees and shrubs in accordance with the planting guidelines, growing conditions and or other WRE provided stipulations, if any. Such care includes but is not limited to regular watering, fertilizing, and proper protection from extreme weather, deer, insects, disease, etc.

2) The WRE guarantee does not cover replacements for damage or death due to deer or other animals, unusual events such as fire, extreme weather (extended drought and/or water bans, persistent rainfall, floods, hurricanes, etc.) or any other natural or man-made disaster that would affect the normal growth and vitality of the trees and shrubs. If a plant is determined to be damaged but healthy, WRE has the option to replace the plant or fertilize and prune it to stimulate growth.

3) This guarantee is not transferable. Should the real estate which is the subject of this contract change ownership during the guarantee period, the guarantee will no longer be in effect.

4) This guarantee covers 100% of the original cost of the trees and shrubs and original installation fee. It does not cover plant costs or installation fees for larger replacements than plants originally purchased. Cost for second and subsequent replacements and installation fees will be billed at full price if the damage was not due to inferior health at time of purchase or improper installation by WRE.

5) If the customer purchases a WRE Landscape Maintenance Agreement, this guarantee will be extended for the duration of WRE's Landscape Maintenance Agreement.

CLIENT NAME

_____

PROPERTY LOCATION

_____

WOOD RIVER
EVERGREENS INC.

PLANTING DATE

_____

**WOOD RIVER EVERGREENS, INC.
FRANK CRANDALL, OWNER**

_____

Figure 51: WRE's Guarantee

Few things can create more angst during a project than client changes, especially when there is no acknowledgement of additional cost by the contractor until the end of the project. As soon as the client brings up a change, complete a change order with a description of the change and its estimated cost and present it to the client for approval and payment. Change orders can be burdensome, but they must be a part of your operating procedures if you are to effectively be compensated for work done outside the contract. Most of the problems I have experienced with client changes have been as a result of failing to use a change order.

With written materials you are clearly identifying the scope, specifics, and cost of the project, eliminating ambiguity. The written contract protects you and the client, giving legal standing to your project agreement. You also are providing a method to deal with project changes with the change order process. Finally, you are demonstrating a professional approach to finalizing a project, separating you from other less qualified individuals.

Sales Tips

I want to share several sales tips I've gathered through my experiences and through researching the topic. One book on sales which I highly recommend is <u>The Sales Bible</u> by Jeffery H. Gitomer. His book is comprehensive, insightful, and full of practical ideas you can quickly adapt to your business.

<u>Frank's Seven Favorite Sales Tips</u>:

1. <u>Keep appointments: be on time, or call the client</u>. Your time *and* the client's time are valuable–treat both with the utmost respect. It only takes a minute to call ahead if you are going to be late. This demonstrates your respect for the client and your professionalism.

2. <u>Do your homework</u>. Be well prepared for your client meetings: have reference books, handouts, company marketing folders, business cards, and albums. If the meeting is about screening trees, research alternatives for the area, have resources showing pictures, and check your own inventory for plants that could fit the plan. Clients appreciate preparedness!

3. <u>Understand the 80/20 rule, which in sales means 80% of your new referrals will come from 20% of your customers</u>. Once you identify the 20% (they are not hard to locate), treat them like gold! Clients that are willing to refer new customers and serve as an advocate for your firm are the building blocks for success and profitability.

4. <u>If your clients are a couple, request meetings and times that both partners can attend</u>. Lack of involvement of either client can spell frustration when decisions need to be made but one member of the couple is not present. Not having the involvement of one partner can be disastrous if the project begins and the other client objects to the work being done. Try to keep both parties engaged, informed, and part of the process to minimize the inevitable bumps in the road.

5. <u>Give the clients space, if needed</u>. In the final negotiations for a job, before the contract is signed, if you sense the couple may need a few private moments to discuss whether to finalize the sale, excuse yourself and head to your vehicle for a few minutes (to pick up a contract!). Many times after you return, the customers have discussed the proposal and made a decision to move ahead. You can present the contract, reiterate the final agreement, ask them to sign, and request the deposit. The short break can save having to come out to the site again to finalize the contract.

6. <u>Your goal has to be 100% satisfaction, every time</u>. I know not every job goes smoothly and not all clients will be happy with your efforts, but your objective is to strive for satisfaction with every customer. Surveys show that customers will talk to ten people if

you do a great job and 50 people if you do a bad job! Exceeding expectations will generate tremendous positive buzz from your happy customers, leading to more opportunities, new jobs, and potentially greater profits.

7. <u>Jeffery H. Gitomer talks about sales people using the "Wow Factor[3]"</u>. Your interactions with clients should be professional, courteous, and prepared–but they should be much more than that. You should strive to be creative, real, and funny. Be knowledgeable, offer a compelling presentation, and use your skills to get a customer to agree to a contract. Leave a lasting, positive impression with the customer; show your personality and enthusiasm. Connect with the client in a way that shows you're genuine. Make your visit and sales call memorable! By using the "wow factor," you can finalize more projects and generate many more referrals…the lifeblood of your business!

WRE Experience

For many years, I have been involved in generating landscape sales for my business. Sales have ranged in size from the modest $1500 job to the exceptional $1.8 million residential project. Although there is a wide range in sales scope, the sales techniques remain remarkably similar. Making a professional, comprehensive presentation is a prerequisite to landing any size job. Being well prepared for client objections and questions shows you are serious about closing the sale. Particularly when given a referral to develop a plan and estimate, you have a high percentage chance of finalizing the job (in my experience, about 70% are finalized). During economic recessions, the closing rate can drop to 50% or less, meaning more potential clients must be contacted to ensure enough work to support your current staff. Obviously, when given a referral you have a great opportunity to close a sale and add to your satisfied client base. If you exceed expectations, you can potentially add another "client advocate" to your marketing team!

Approximately 90% of our business each year is the result of referrals and 10% is the result of classical radio advertising, the Evans Mobil landscape, and targeted mailings. Knowing what works helps us plan our marketing strategy and wisely invest our advertising dollars. We ask all new customers which of our marketing methods are working and which ones are not effective. Without this type of feedback you may continue spending significant amounts of money on a marketing strategy that is not working.

Contrary to popular wisdom, we fully support, and in some cases increase, our marketing budget during economic slowdowns. With fewer businesses having a presence in the media, we have a greater frequency and exposure resulting in more potential sales. Combined with a traditionally lower sales-closing ratio during recessions, the additional exposure and sales calls result in an acceptable level of closings.

Recently I finalized a $42,000 project even though I was the high bidder. The customer had received a $31,000 bid from a competing landscape company but chose WRE for several reasons: first, she liked my landscape design along with the clear and comprehensive estimate for the plants, materials, equipment/trucking, and labor. Secondly, I had caught several potential problems and addressed them in my proposal. Third, she enjoyed my patient and professional approach through the design and estimate process. Fourth, she had seen numerous examples of our work in the surrounding neighborhood, which made her comfortable choosing our firm. Lastly, our 3-year warranty gave her a great measure of confidence that if any plant died it would be replaced. Your sales technique can spell the difference between landing a job or not. With a professional, prepared, and personal sales presentation you can close on a very high percentage of your sales calls.

Essential Points:

1. Sales are the lifeblood of a business, which ensures growth, success, and prosperity.

2. Separate your business from your competitors' through timely responses to all customer's calls and emails.

3. After designing a solution to a client's needs and calculating an estimate, contact the customer for an on-site meeting to discuss the proposal.

4. In today's competitive environment satisfied customers are not good enough…you must exceed a customer's expectations!

5. Exceeding expectations can in many cases create a "client advocate" who will be a great source of referrals and additional projects.

Chapter 15: LEADERSHIP WITH INTEGRITY

I have always been fascinated with great leaders and their leadership styles, strengths, and resiliency in the face of defeat. Any business, without strong, effective leadership, will find it difficult to succeed. Many owners are good managers (maintaining an organization moving ahead in a certain direction), but are not true leaders. Leaders can effect change, influence people, and attain goals that will ensure company success, even in the face of adversity. The ultimate profitability and success of your horticultural business will be determined by the leadership strength of the owner and/or management team.

Therein lies the significance of learning about leadership: its definition, styles of leadership, and characteristics of a "serving leader". Equally important is to examine leadership in the context of integrity: a true measure of a person's character and personal values, doing what is right all the time. John C. Maxwell, noted author on leadership, points out that great leaders win the hearts of their followers by showing commitment and consistency and by acting with integrity.

Let's look at several definitions of leadership, discuss various styles of leadership, and describe the characteristics of the "serving leader".

Definitions of Leadership

There are numerous definitions of leadership to consider. I have listed five for you to compare and contrast:

1. Leadership is the art of motivating a group of people to act towards achieving a common goal. Put more simply, the leader is the inspiration and director of the action. He or she is the person in the group that possesses the combination of personality and skills that make others want to follow his or her direction.

    In business, leadership is welded to performance. Effective leaders are those who increase their company's bottom line. To be effective, a leader certainly has to manage the resources at his/her disposal. But leadership also involves communicating, inspiring, and supervising; just to name three more of the main skills a leader has to have to be successful[1].

2. "Effective leaders do not blame others. Strong leaders do whatever they can to encourage and champion their team to become stronger themselves."[2]

3. "John Adair believes that leadership matters deeply, that good leadership is good leadership irrespective of whether it's within a business, charity, sports team, political

party, or army regiment. He also believes that good leadership can be learned and that everyone can improve their leadership ability."[3]

4. "In its essence, leadership in an organizational role involves: a) Establishing a clean vision; b) Sharing (communicating) that vision with others so that they will follow willingly; c) Providing the information, knowledge, and methods to realize the vision; and d) Coordinating and balancing the conflicting interests of all members or stakeholders. A leader comes to the forefront in case of crisis, and is able to think and act in creative ways in difficult situations. Unlike management, leadership flows from the core of a personality and cannot be taught, although it may be learned and may be enhanced through coaching or mentoring."[4]

5. "The true measure of leadership is influence nothing more, nothing less."[5]

As you can see from these samples, definitions of leadership run from the very simple to the long and complex. I have assembled the following definition of leadership I find to be appropriate: "Leadership is the power of persuasion used to achieve company goals with the tacit support of your team, especially in times of difficulty."

Regardless of your definition of leadership, there are certain qualities leaders possess that we can identify. Although some researchers maintain that leaders are born and individuals cannot be taught to be leaders, I maintain that individuals have leadership qualities that can be strengthened. What are some of these leadership qualities that can be enhanced?

Leadership Qualities

Writers about leadership have identified numerous qualities that leaders possess; some leaders having many of the qualities, a few have all of the qualities, and certain leaders have a select few of these qualities. John C. Maxwell, a noted author on leadership, wrote The 21 Indispensable Qualities of a Leader[6], published in 1999, identifying critical qualities leaders possess. I will list ten qualities that many leaders exhibit; most of these qualities, with work, can be improved upon:

1. Character – We define our character every time we make choices, and reveal our true character when under pressure to make difficult decisions.

2. Attitude – This characteristic will shape how we approach our leadership role–with positive energy or with a lackadaisical outlook. Our attitude will not only affect the outcome of our decisions but will impact our employees' attitudes at the same time.

3. <u>Communication</u> – Every effective leader has the ability to communicate with their audience clearly, simply, and truthfully. Asking for and receiving feedback will confirm that your message was received and understood.

4. <u>Listening</u> – Successful leaders will make a practice of listening frequently and intently to their employees, customers, and competitors. Customer and employee complaints are a great learning opportunity–if they are heard.

5. <u>Focus</u> – With numerous challenging situations presenting themselves every day, a good leader learns to prioritize, ensuring that the critical decisions are made and solutions implemented. Without a clear focus, even mundane decisions that are forgotten can result in serious disruptions to the company.

6. <u>Self Discipline</u> – Leaders will make their priorities, develop a plan to achieve their goals, and work in a disciplined way to accomplish their objectives. Eliminating the use of excuses will strengthen your discipline to achieve the results you seek.

7. <u>Delegation</u> – Delegating responsibilities is an important step for leaders to achieve their goals. True leaders realize they cannot do everything themselves.

8. <u>Adaptability to Change</u> – The one constant all leaders can expect is change! Effective leaders anticipate, embrace, and adapt to change. Those leaders who resist change will not experience the success they seek.

9. <u>Vision</u> – All leaders have visions. Those leaders who express their visions clearly and compellingly to employees, customers, and others will have much more success with implementation of their plans. Unless a vision is written down and shared with the needed individuals it will only be a dream.

10. <u>Serving Leader</u> – The successful leaders realize they are serving not only the customers but also the employees, vendors, and support staff. The leader's role is to support the employees and customers in any way possible to ensure that they will succeed.

Styles of Leadership

To me, no one exemplifies positive leadership characteristics more than Winston Churchill. Criticized and ridiculed by countless British politicians prior to 1940, his "radical views" were eventually embraced. He was elected prime minister of Great Britain, and experienced his finest hours as a wartime leader in the defeat of Nazi Germany…only to be defeated at the polls following the conclusion of World War II.

Many owners of businesses, however, do not display a leadership style which employees embrace. Many times the owner's leadership style causes great frustration and stress amongst the staff. The effect is confusion, lack of focus on company goals, and considerable angst among the staff members. The solution to this problem can be found in situational leadership.

Ken Blanchard, Patricia Zigarini, and Drea Zigarini, authors of <u>Leadership and the One Minute Manager</u>[7], detail the effectiveness of four styles of situational leadership–directing, coaching, supporting, and delegating–when used with the appropriate professional level of employees:

- <u>Style 1: Directing</u> – The leader provides specific direction and closely monitors task accomplishment.

- <u>Style 2: Coaching</u> – The leader continues to direct and closely monitor task accomplishment, but also explains decisions, solicits suggestions, and supports progress.

- <u>Style 3: Supporting</u> – The leader facilitates and supports people's efforts toward task accomplishment and shares responsibility for decision making with them.

- <u>Style 4: Delegating</u> – The leader turns over responsibility for decision-making and problem solving to people within the company.

To ensure success in achieving goals it is essential that the leader's style match the professional level of the employees. When the style is not appropriate for the employee level, frustration, lack of progress, and low achievement are the results.

I have held a variety of leadership positions during my lifetime: student council president, football captain, head track and field coach, association president, chairman of the Master Gardener Foundation, Worshipful Master of Charity Lodge, and President of my own company. Yet, in spite of all this experience, I often felt uncomfortable serving as the "boss" of my growing staff. The mounting responsibilities of managing and directing the business, as well as hiring, training, and disciplining workers, caused me great frustration, anguish, and considerable stress. It often became obvious that the staff wasn't very happy with my leadership style or behavior either.

After reading <u>Leadership and the One Minute Manager</u> and listening to Charles Vander Kooi (a noted motivational speaker) remark that today's workers do not respond well to the "command and control" leadership style, I realized that my leadership style was the problem–for my workers and for me! None of us liked a style of giving orders to be followed without question and handing out punishment when the orders were not followed. Further, my years of coaching experience left me with a natural leadership style that not only fit my personality better, but also the personalities of my talented, experienced, and self motivated employees as well.

I preferred directing, planning, monitoring progress, motivating, praising, and supporting my employees with what they needed for success (also the ingredients of a "serving leader"). The wisdom of this leadership style was demonstrated years earlier, when the high school track team I coached won numerous conference titles and a state title. I changed my leadership style at work, began delegating responsibilities, and invited my staff to share in the day-to-day decision making process. These were simple steps that had a profound effect on everyone in the company…including me.

If you have an experienced, talented staff, delegation of responsibilities can produce unexpected benefits. I used to control the entire scheduling of daily jobs and weekly projects, which usually resulted in last minute changes and incomplete instructions because of my own hectic schedule and responsibilities. Out of frustration I delegated the responsibility to a manager, and as a result the schedule was organized, shared with the crew, and coordinated with clients on a daily basis. The tasks (like scheduling) that the staff now handle are completed in a more professional, efficient, and timely fashion. This emphasizes an important point: for any leadership style to be effective, you need the right people in the right roles…and a leader willing to delegate and trust his staff.

Over the years, hiring and retaining key personnel, properly training team members, and shifting people to roles they enjoy have been priorities of mine. I make sure that everyone understands their value and the effects their roles have on the success of our company. It is important to frequently extend praise, recognition, and rewards for employees' efforts to let them know they are appreciated. Mark Twain once said "I can live for two months on a good compliment"[8]. Praise is an important component of successful leadership–you will be amazed at the effect that thoughtful, appreciative remarks can have.

The Serving Leader

One of the qualities of a leader I described earlier was that of a serving leader; one that understands his/her role to be one who serves not only the customers but also the employees in their quest to satisfy the customer's needs. The serving leader will do whatever is necessary to support the employees–with training, equipment, supplies, and backing to achieve their objectives. One great leader I mentioned earlier, Winston Churchill, exhibited a leadership style that was predicated on responsibility, optimism, decisiveness, and clear direction. He also displayed the secret of all great leaders by being a "serving leader" to all his constituents.

In The Serving Leader, Ken Jennings and John Stahl-Wert write about "upending the pyramid"[9]. The organization chart of a traditional business typically consists of leaders at the top, followed by managers, team leaders, staff, and finally customers, in descending order (Figure 52). However, to be a true "serving leader", the chart needs to be inverted with the customers at the top, followed by staff, team leaders, managers, and the owner at the bottom. Because this is a vastly different model, some members of my staff are still learning how this works. If asked, some team members will say they work for the owner and support their supervisors. What I remind them and show by example is that we ALL work for the customer, and it is my job to train, motivate, support, and assist employees so they can serve clients better.

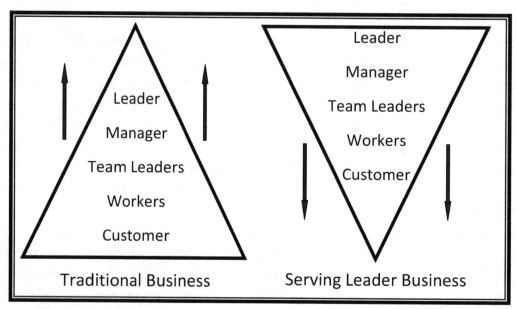

Figure 52: Traditional and "Serving Leader" Organizational Models

Foremost, a leader has to articulate a vision of the future, assemble a capable team to carry out the vision, and work passionately to see it implemented. By embracing the idea of being "in service" to others, the steps required to achieve the vision can be taken. Creating and nurturing the relationships between the customer, team members, and the leader are the key to bringing visions into reality.

Integrity: A Leader's Compass

A true measure of a person's character and personal values is when he or she lives with integrity; that is, doing what is right all the time. In The Six Fundamentals of Success[10], Stuart R. Levine notes that conducting yourself and your business with integrity strengthens your brand.

I know this to be true. The credibility I have gained since first opening Wood River Evergreens has transformed our brand into a well respected, trusted, and recognized name in our market. In today's competitive market, a trusted brand is a powerful asset. But, I also know that the positive reputation associated with our brand name can be ruined overnight. Everyone at WRE strives to maintain our values and high standards every day. We aim to act consistently with our values: integrity, tolerance, generosity, fairness, and respect. This helps us make good choices–the right choices.

You will find it difficult to serve and help others unless you respect yourself. I try hard to build up each team member's self-esteem, self-respect, respect for his or her position at WRE, and respect for the job they perform. I do not tolerate disrespect of themselves, their teammates, managers, or clients. Employees show respect for each other by showing up on time, being courteous, giving their undivided attention when communicating, helping their teammates, being active listeners, and concentrating on the team–not themselves.

Doing what you say you will, honoring your agreements, and being accountable for your actions and performance makes you reliable, trustworthy, and dependable. As a result, your good reputation will grow and prosper.

Many times, WRE picks up new clients because competitors do not return phone calls, miss appointments, do not finish a job, or refuse to be accountable for lack of performance. This lesson drives the high standards we apply within our company as well as our choices of subcontractors: accountability is the key to client satisfaction.

One of our best clients paid us a high compliment recently. He said we were the most accountable company he ever has dealt with: always operating with integrity, always reliable and trustworthy, and always accomplishing what we promised, on time. In short, we always exceed expectations. These types of compliments humble me. I am honored when clients recognize our talented and dedicated team members who strive for excellence with every landscape project they install. WRE has rarely missed an agreed-upon deadline for a landscape project – a feat that motivates us to strive even harder.

Inherent in acting with integrity is to always be honest with the client and strive never to promise more than we can deliver. It is better to do what we promise and exceed expectations than to not accomplish all that was agreed upon and disappoint the client. Effective leadership based on integrity, appropriate styles, and sound character will ensure your company's success. Time spent learning about leadership qualities, various leadership styles, and matching appropriate styles with employee levels can result in dramatic gains in company morale and goal achievement, and ultimately lead to greater profitability.

WRE Experience

Discovering my most effective (and employee-accepted) leadership style was a turning point in the development and success of WRE. Up until that point the company had grown, expanded into many new areas, and assembled a hardworking crew, but we had not reached our potential. It took me becoming "serving leader" and adopting the coaching leadership style for there to be a synergy with our team.

I also learned that a positive attitude equals positive results. It took me a while to realize just how my moods, problem solving techniques, and communication style affected staff morale. When I was angry, short-tempered, relaying bad news about current projects, or expressing my concerns about our financial status, I was lowering the morale and motivation level of the staff. Conversely, as I learned to be calm in the face of difficulties, friendly, supportive, appreciative, and more careful with my selection of words, the morale of the staff got better, the working atmosphere improved, and motivation levels were raised. This may not be a surprising discovery, but it's an important one that I try to apply to my daily actions.

These results illustrate the "Hawthorne Effect": people who believe good, positive things are happening are motivated to do better. However, the more you believe things are getting worse, the lower your motivation will be. It is not easy to look at yourself as the owner (or management team) and objectively evaluate your leadership style and effect on your staff, unless you are willing to look at yourself in a mirror and make adjustments as necessary. Only then will you and your company reach their full potential. Once you identify the appropriate leadership style(s) and match them with your employee level(s), you will be on your way to achieving the success envisioned by you and your team!

Essential Points:

1. The ultimate profitability and success of your horticultural business will be determined by the leadership strength of the owner and management team.

2. "Leadership is the power of persuasion used to achieve company goals with the tacit support of your team, especially in times of difficulty." -Frank Crandall

3. The leader's role is to support the employees and customers in any way possible to ensure that they will succeed.

4. To ensure success in achieving goals it is essential that the leader's style match the professional level of the employees.

5. Doing what you say you will, honoring your agreements, and being accountable for your actions and performance makes you reliable, trustworthy, and dependable.

Chapter 16: **EMBRACING TECHNOLOGY TO IMPROVE EFFICIENCY AND PROFITABILITY**

It is truly amazing how information technology has impacted our horticultural industry, my landscape business being no exception. In 1993 we were using a simple computer to type letters and do basic accounting–until the computer died. When we purchased a new computer, I hoped that we could put our written mailing list on it and print labels instead of handwriting several thousand of them for our mailings–a tiresome process at best.

Fortunately for WRE (and me), a local computer retailer sent Ken Mazur to our office. Ken not only solved our immediate problem, but over the next 17 years helped me grow my business by reorganizing the way I did things–helping our company look more professional and increasing our profitability. We now use computers for many tasks: PCs are used for accounting tasks, and Macs are used for our customer database and product inventory, pricing, catalog and label-making, word processing, email, quarterly newsletters, promotion color post cards, job estimating and job costing, digital scans, data storage, Microsoft PowerPoint™ presentations, and spreadsheets. There is no facet of our business that hasn't benefited from the information technology revolution. Our website has been operational since 1996 and plays an ever-increasing role in attracting new clients and providing valuable information for existing customers. The Internet plays an important role for gathering information, communicating, and finding sources of needed products and supplies.

How has all this technology benefited my business? As Mazur states, "View information technology as an opportunity to simplify, streamline, and improve your business process."[1] The real benefits of computerizing don't come from the technology at all–they come from changing the way you do business. If your business is a mess now, when you automate it will be an automated mess. The biggest productivity gains you can realize from computerization stem from changing the way you work, not from buying machines.

Let's examine the benefits of computerizing: identifying the tasks to computerize, ways to change working in your business, kinds of software and fundamental applications, and determining hardware choices. The goal of this chapter is not to teach you how to become a computer programmer, but to provide you with basic information that will assist you in streamlining your business and developing a plan to effectively computerize.

Benefits of Computerizing

The biggest obstacle to any business owner trying to grow their business is time: there's just not enough of it. No matter how long the day, no matter how long the week, no matter how long the season, there's always more to do to improve your business, whether getting new customers, cementing relationships with current customers, streamlining your operations for cost savings, or performing any number of other tasks to improve your profit picture.

For example, if you were to use a desktop computer to do customer labels for a quarterly newsletter, the time savings would be approximately 25 hours over hand labeling, giving you substantial money savings as well as the extra hours for other important tasks.

In addition to saving time, computerizing has many other benefits:

1. <u>Break Bottlenecks</u> – One technique to get business owners into a more receptive frame of mind in regard to computers is to computerize something the owner hates to do. Find something that's taking up time he/she resents giving up (for example billing, estimates, or scheduling), but is deemed essential to the operation of the business. Once bottlenecks are broken everyone wins–the customers, employees, and the owner!

2. <u>Automate Repetitive Tasks</u> – For small businesses, avoiding tedious labor isn't just a way of avoiding unpleasant tasks–it is crucial to your success. You make money by concentrating on the tasks with the high profit margins – you can be sure that summing and alphabetizing aren't among those tasks.

   Task automation can save you time. The best application programs provide task automation with a minimum of user input, keyboard fussing, and command memorization. Look for programs that minimize the need to perform such tasks as summing numbers, alphabetizing lists, sorting in order, and making identical copies.

3. <u>Make Work More Efficient</u> - If you have ever worked with power tools in your business, you know the advantage that these tools can give you. You can dig a hole for a root ball with a shovel or you can use a backhoe—which is faster and more efficient?

   Personal computers provide power tools for your management and office tasks. You can reorganize a filing system with hundreds of documents just by clicking a button. You can archive thousands of client records and print hundreds of bills just by choosing a command from a menu. You can search a 100-page technical report for errors just by choosing a spell check command.

   Using a computer doesn't guarantee that you will do a better job of running your business with a computer than you did before. A power saw doesn't guarantee a good carpentry job! If you start with a bad plan…you get bad results.

4. <u>Avoid Errors</u> – Many computer programs come with features that can help you avoid embarrassing or costly errors, such as spelling mistakes, calculation errors, and incorrect data entry. Keep in mind that these features aren't foolproof!

5. <u>Produce More Professional Output</u> – If you want your business to look professional, the materials you use to interact with customers and potential customers have to look like professionals produced them. Typed estimates with whiteout mistakes and mimeographed

price lists send a different message than professional looking estimates, price lists, and contracts.

This is not to say that a handwritten message or "thank you" isn't very effective–customers appreciate the personal touch of a handwritten note when appropriate. However, your computer tools can generate a consistent look for all your routine business communications–letters, bills, estimates, newsletters, etc.–contributing to the "branding" of your business. Clients will notice and appreciate the consistent, professional image your company demonstrates, as opposed to those operations whose communications look unprofessional and inconsistent with their brand image.

6. <u>Acquire New Skills</u> – This benefit makes available to ordinary employees some of the skills and competence of professionals and experts. In doing so, the computer saves you the money you otherwise would pay to hire experts in design, newsletters, and financial analyses.

In a spreadsheet program, you can choose from many built-in formulas for performing complex financial analyses–the kind of analyses (such as computing the net present value of an investment) that you would learn if you were to study finance at a business school. In a desktop publishing program, you can use many layout techniques that would otherwise require years of experience with layout boards, razor knives, and sharp blue pencils.

Computer programs can give you some of the tools of trained professionals, but only you can ensure that the output is of the highest professional standards.

7. <u>Extend your Reach into New Areas</u> – Reducing the time it takes to perform certain tasks will give you free time to investigate new areas of opportunity. With additional free time, you can pursue new marketing opportunities and contacts with potential clients, research new products, plants, or services to consider, or devote time for employee coaching and other useful business pursuits.

Identify Tasks to Computerize

This process can be very helpful to understanding how your business is currently functioning and how computerizing some tasks will improve its operation. Gather all of the papers you use to run your business (billing, communicating, ordering, inventory, estimating, etc.) and rank those documents that are fundamental to the central objectives of your business. Take on one task at a time. Try to determine the task areas most likely to produce the biggest gains in productivity, profitability, and time savings through computerizing. Some examples:

1. <u>The task is routine, but it takes a lot of time</u>. You should spend as much of your work time as possible doing things that make the most money for you. If you're spending lots

of time doing paper-shuffling tasks that fall far below your level of professional competence, consider taking advantage of the computer's capacity to automate certain routine tasks (such as spell checking, alphabetizing mailing lists, calculating estimates, and keeping track of who hasn't paid their bill).

2. <u>The task requires skills you don't possess, so you've become dependent on the assistance of professionals</u>. It may be worth it to pay accountants to handle the payroll, but maybe it isn't. Just how many computer-based skills you are willing to acquire depends on your needs, interests, and motivation. Be sure you at least consult with the professionals so that you choose the right software application and use it according to professional standards.

3. <u>Your present methods don't enable you to adapt rapidly enough to changing conditions</u>. Restaurants that depend on printed menus can't respond quickly to variations in the availability of fresh foods, the cook's favorite new dish, and the changing demands of customers. Green industry price lists are also dynamic, and there is often one list for retail customers and another one for wholesale accounts. In a spreadsheet, you can use the same price list template for both lists and just change the pricing. Using a database program will allow many customized lists and changes in prices to be done quickly and accurately.

4. <u>Performing the task is too tedious or (outright impossible) with current methods</u>. If you use a simple paper-based accounting system, can you figure out quickly whose bill is more than 30 days late? More than 60 days late? More than 90? How long does it usually take for clients to pay their bills? At the end of the season, it is useful to see all of our customers' billing totals arranged by invoiced amounts. This would be a daunting task by hand, but with a computer the task can be done in seconds–leaving more time for analyzing, not calculating.

5. <u>You envision a computerized approach that would give you a strategic advantage over your competition</u>. Having a well-designed website will give you an edge over most of your competitors. Featuring before and after landscape project photos, service and product information, and easy contact procedures will make your site valuable in attracting and retaining clients.

6. <u>Your current system fails to provide the level of service you want for your valued customers</u>. Have you ever found yourself saying, "I'd like to help you but I just can't find the information," or "I'm not sure what to tell you. I think it's been ordered but could you call back tomorrow?" or "I'll have to see what's in inventory and call you back with a price"? By making information more readily available and by bringing you some of the skills of experts, personal computers can help you provide the level of service your customers and clients deserve.

7. <u>You want to improve the quality of the product you deliver to your valued customers</u>. The time you gain from increased efficiency can be used in two ways: you can spend the time doing something else or you can reinvest the time in the task you are already doing and aim for higher quality. For example, completing estimates for customers using the estimating program and then emailing them along with attached plant picking tickets will speed up the review process, ultimately leading to finalizing jobs more quickly.

It is important to set realistic goals in identifying tasks to computerize. Do not expect productivity to zoom upward immediately–you must allow time for training and implementation. Remember, your goal is not to become a computer programmer but use the computer as a tool to improve your business.

Change the Way You Work

You can't put computers on everyone's desk and somehow expect productivity to improve immediately. To computerize effectively, you must target the most promising tasks to computerize, choose the right software, train yourself and your employees to use it, and guard against computer-related catastrophes such as accidental data loss.

Personal computers have the potential to benefit your business, but the key word is POTENTIAL! As you ponder your computerization strategy, consider some of the ways that you can change the way you work.

1. <u>Avoid reinventing the wheel</u> – Develop and refine template versions of important letters, memos, reports, worksheets, newsletters, business forms, and data management forms. A template is a generic (empty) version of a document that you can load, modify, and print without having to repeat all of the tedious formatting and design operations that go into creating the original document.

    One of the main purposes of this handbook is to provide you with proven template formats that you can adapt to your businesses and begin using immediately, without having to "reinvent the wheel."

2. <u>Combine and simplify</u> – Creating our plant inventory database at WRE was straight-forward; however, developing the "customer picking ticket," which was central to what we were doing, necessitated changes in the way we did things. This included changing the estimating process, the inventorying of a customer's plants, the organization of the nursery, and the processes we use to maintain control of the pass-through inventory.

3. <u>Reorganize Work Patterns</u> – Nursery personnel had to learn new inventory procedures, new ways to organize plants for projects in the nursery, how to monitor plants used and returned from projects, and how to maintain an up-to-date plant inventory database.

Employees have learned new skills, perform more varied work, and express more satisfaction with their jobs.

4. <u>Never Type the Same Information Twice</u> – Computerization provides an excellent opportunity to avoid needless duplication of effort. Once the customer plant picking ticket list is created, it can be easily changed without having to re-enter data or re-type the plant names and price.

5. <u>Use the Computer to Produce Knowledge, Not Data</u> – Using a typewriter, you can produce a five-page document that lists information without any intelligent analysis. Using a personal computer and word processor, you can produce a 50-page document that lists information without any intelligent analysis. The real benefit of computer technology isn't its unfortunate capacity to increase the amount of unanalyzed, meaningless data; it's the computer's much less frequently utilized capacity to reduce information to the essentials!

Kinds of Software and Fundamental Applications

There are basically two kinds of software: systems software and application software.

A. <u>Systems Software</u>: Programs used to control and maintain a computer. Commonly used operating system software includes Microsoft's Windows (Windows XP, Vista, etc.), Apple's Macintosh System (now up to OS X 10.6); Linux, Unix, and others less commonly used by most people.

    The operating system is absolutely essential and indispensable for the computer's proper functioning. System utilities are programs for day-to-day system maintenance (such as backing up files, system clean-up, or defragmenting disks).

B. <u>Application Software</u>: Programs that enable computer users to apply computer technology to their own needs (write letters, balance a checkbook, complete an estimate, etc.). Although there are countless programs written for computers, there are essentially five fundamental applications useful for most business tasks:

- To write – word processing
- To calculate – spreadsheets
- To store/retrieve data – database
- To illustrate – photo editing, graphic design
- To communicate – Internet browsers, websites, email, social networking, and system security/firewall software

1. <u>Word Processing</u> – The objective is to create well-written, letter-perfect, and pleasing printed documents. All word processors do some basic things: enter, edit, format, and print text.

2. <u>Electronic Spreadsheet</u> – A spreadsheet is a computerized version of an accountant's pad. Its advantage is that you have rows and columns that form cells with distinct addresses. You can put numbers, labels, or formulas into these cells and relate them to one another.

    The fabulous thing about spreadsheets is their ability to make "what-if analyses" quick and easy. The point of creating a spreadsheet isn't to just solve a problem. When the worksheet is completed, you can type in new values and the spreadsheet is recalculated instantly. This is a form of data exploration in which key variables are changed to see their impact on the results of the computation. Spreadsheets make valuable templates for such calculations as estimating and job costing. Spreadsheets are ideal for the following conditions:

    -   The calculations you perform depend on many variables that are unique to your line of work (labor, fertilizer costs, vehicle costs, and plant costs).

    -   You must perform the calculations repeatedly.

    -   Your planning ability is enhanced by exploring the bottom-line impact of changing key variables and assumptions (How much markup can you manage and still be competitive?).

3. <u>Database Management</u> – When you use a database, your primary objective is to store, organize, and retrieve information. A database is a collection of related information about a subject that has been organized in a useful manner, enabling you to retrieve information, draw conclusions, and make decisions (our plant inventory is stored on a FileMaker™ database). The ideal database should allow you to:

    -   Define data fields so that you can store and retrieve information that is unique to your business (mailing list, plant inventory, etc.).

    -   Create an on-screen data entry form that facilitates easy, less error-prone typing and correction of data.

    -   Place filters on each data field to prevent the user from typing the wrong kind of information (such as text in a numeric field).

    -   Prevent duplicate information from being entered.

    -   Sort the data in a variety of ways, using any data field as the key for the sort.

    -   Select only the records that meet the criteria you specify.

    -   Create printed reports that include subtotals, totals, and averages.

- Print mailing labels.
- Create a complete menu driven application customized for your business needs.

4. <u>Illustration and Graphic Design</u> – Graphics and layout programs are for the creation, alteration, display, and printing of images and documents. Adobe Photoshop®, Illustrator®, and PageMaker®, paint programs, file conversion programs, and QuarkXPress® are examples of these types of programs.

5. <u>Communications</u> – The Internet (Web browser, websites, email, and social networking) enables online communications. To go online, most small businesses need two essential items:

- Modem (translates digital signals into analog signals and back).
- Communications programs – A Web browser to access the Internet (for example, Microsoft Internet Explorer, Safari, Google Chrome, Mozilla Firefox, etc.), plus email for communicating with another computer. Security software (firewall) to protect against computer viruses is also highly recommended.

The benefits of computer-based communications:

- Store all the information needed to communicate with another computer user with a keystroke or click of the mouse.
- You can store all of your personal information and have it entered when you log on.
- You can address email to one or many recipients.
- You can retrieve messages and files from others anywhere in the world.
- You can access online data resources.
- You can communicate at your convenience.
- Leaves a "paper trail" documenting back-and-forth communications.

Five-Step Plan for Computerizing

You need to do some homework before you shop for software. Here is a five-step plan of attack for computerizing your business:

1. Develop a problem statement that succinctly and accurately analyzes what is wrong with the way you are doing things right now.

2. Choose the critical areas to which you want to apply computer technology.

3. Develop a list of the features and capabilities that the software must have in order to suit your needs.

4. Decide whether single-purpose, integrated, or special purpose (vertical market software) best meets your needs.

5. After talking with an information technology expert, choose programs that meet your needs.

Choosing Computer Hardware

- Computers – Given the speed of today's computers, just about any one you buy will have more power than you'll ever need. If it is important enough to have one computer in your business, you should have two.

  It is easy to be lulled into a state of complacency with today's powerful desktop computers. Most of the time they run so well that we take them for granted and become lax in maintaining safeguards to protect our important information. But these machines are, after all, only machines, and they will eventually break down, either mechanically or through a software glitch. It is not a question of if a computer will crash, but when.

  Given that fact, the following statement is true: the most important computer files in your business aren't the business plan, customer list, inventory database, or even the tax records–the most important files in your entire business are the up-to-date backups of those files. Maintaining current copies of vital files is a simple process that can ensure that a company conducts day-to-day activities with minimal interruption or disruption, while not having backup copies could easily bring an enterprise to its figurative knees.

- Laser Printers – The image is baked onto the surface of the paper. You can use a variety of papers and letterheads. Even relatively cheap laser printers do excellent printing– usually, graphics are printed flawlessly. They are more expensive than inkjet printers, and toner cartridges are relatively expensive but last a long time.

- Inkjet Printer – Ink is sprayed onto the paper. These produce excellent documents when you use the right paper. The ink is usually water-soluble. Inkjet printers are relatively inexpensive, but the ink cartridges are expensive.

- Scanners – Device that scans images into a computer file. With Optical Character Recognition (OCR) software, you can scan and convert large quantities of text without having to type it in yourself.

- <u>Digital Cameras</u> – Another way to get images into your computer. Newer cameras range from several megapixels to professional 20+ megapixel cameras.

- <u>File Servers</u> – A dedicated, networked computer in the office allowing shared access to files by multiple users.

- <u>Backup Uninterruptable Power Supply</u> – Gives you time to save your work and shut down your system without corrupting or losing open files.

- <u>Surge Protectors</u> – To (hopefully) protect against lighting strike or other power surge damaging your computer equipment.

- <u>Furniture</u> – Choose computer furniture that is ergonomically correct. Fatigued workers make more mistakes than those who are in comfortable positions, and poor working posture can lead to injuries such as back/neck pain and carpal tunnel syndrome.

WRE Experience

Computerizing our business has had numerous positive effects, including an overall streamlining of our operations, enhancing of our brand image, and increased profits. Additionally, some of our other business systems have improved, including our cost estimating, client billing, plant inventory and pricing, and accounting system.

1. <u>Streamlining Operations</u> – Take a look at your business and determine how many tasks are repetitive: customer mailings, label creation, job estimates, product pricing, and inventory. How many of these tasks do you do manually? How do you check the status of a project? How do you find an address or phone number, or retrieve and distribute directions? Technology automates repetitive tasks, keeps running records for accuracy and knowledge sharing, provides your team with valuable, up-to-date information in a matter of seconds, and reduces errors with software products that take the guesswork out of calculations. Technology saves you time and money.

2. <u>Enhancing Brand Image</u> – We use graphic design software products such as QuarkXPress® and Adobe Photoshop® to create many materials that enhance our professional image. Formatted templates are used to generate invoices, estimates, letters, newsletters, and postcards which match our brand identity. Preferred type fonts and attractive layouts with our logo present a unified, consistent appearance. We create and publish multipage, full-color newsletters in-house. Our website promotes our spectrum of

products and services to current and potential customers. Microsoft PowerPoint ™ software allows me to create dynamic lectures that enforce our company's professional image when I speak to various groups and horticultural organizations. A company that looks professional has a competitive edge when it comes to attracting customers.

3. Increased Profits – Computer technology allows WRE to access information and to respond to clients faster, monitor inventory better to keep popular items in stock, estimate jobs more accurately, and create an appealing, consistent, professional image for our communication materials. All these things add up to greater productivity and efficiency higher profit margins, and increased customer satisfaction.

4. Cost Estimating – Using Microsoft Excel® software, we have created an estimating and job costing template for our landscape construction projects and maintenance services. After inputting the amount of materials, plants, equipment, vehicle hours, and labor hours required to complete the job, the program automatically calculates an estimate with profit margin percentages in a matter of seconds.

   After a project is completed, the actual time, materials, and equipment/vehicle costs are entered in the job costing program to calculate the actual profit margin. The results give us an accurate measure as to our success with the project, and if we fall short of our goal, specific areas we can adjust on the next proposal.

5. Client Billing – Computer technology also helped us tackle the biggest frustration for the office staff, the clients, and me: customer billing. As our business grew, accurate and regular monthly billing was essential for generating the cash flow that we needed to meet monthly expenses. Initially, I controlled all of the billing, which over time proved to be a huge bottleneck.

   By fine-tuning the project job reports, all of the information needed for billing is given to the office manager. Using pricing templates, our office manager is able to enter the billing information directly into Intuit's QuickBooks™ accounting software, creating a "pending" customer bill which I review and approve. The approved copies are converted to the final bill, which I sign and then are mailed out to clients. Since I removed myself from the bill creation process, it is now done much more quickly and smoothly, and bills go out on time every month!

6. Plant Inventory and Pricing – Keeping track of our plant inventory, creating labels, establishing prices, and organizing customer orders were tasks rarely done accurately and efficiently by hand.

   Taking over a year, a plant inventory database was created in FileMaker Pro™. A standardized retail pricing formula was established that automatically calculates a percentage markup above wholesale costs. The inventory program also allows us to generate plant labels that list each plant's Latin name, common name, size, price, and the name of the client who purchased the plant, all within a matter of minutes.

A customer "picking ticket" was developed for the plants included on landscape plans. The picking ticket lists all of the designer-specified plants for a project by site location, Latin name, quantity, size, and price. Once a job is complete, the final picking ticket, with the total number of plants actually installed, is generated for the final billing. The plants are automatically removed from inventory, giving us a greater awareness and control over the number of plants we have in stock.

7. Accounting – To keep up with our business's growth we had to acquire an accounting program that could provide the financial data we needed, be compatible with our accounting firm's software, and be networkable.

    We purchased Intuit's QuickBooks® software to manage all of our accounting functions. The program provides us with valuable, "real-time" information which we can use to improve company operations, develop and monitor budgets, and regularly evaluate our financial condition.

We have come a long way since purchasing our first computer in 1993, and will continue to invest in new and improved technology. Besides the improved efficiencies and time savings, the investments in technology have paid huge benefits in streamlining and improving the processes of operating our business. The result has been a more professional, organized, and profitable company.

Essential Points:

1. Information technology provides the opportunity to simplify, streamline, and improve your business's processes. Benefits can include enhanced brand image and increased efficiency–and profits.

2. The biggest obstacle to any business owner trying to grow their business is time—there's just not enough of it. Technology can help.

3. It is important to set realistic goals in identification of tasks to computerize. Remember, your goal is not to become a computer programmer but to use the computer as a tool to enhance your business.

4. The most important computer files in your business aren't the business plan, customer list, inventory database, tax records, or accounting–the most important files in your entire business are the up-to-date backups of those files.

Chapter 17: MANAGEMENT TIPS FOR SUCCESS

After spending so many years in the horticultural industry running my own landscape design, construction, and maintenance firm, I can state definitively that fluctuations in gross sales and profits are to be expected! As with other businesses, horticultural firms are subject to the vagaries of the economy–leading to hiring employees and purchasing new equipment/vehicles in boom times, and downsizing to survive during recessions. The real objective is to take advantage of the boom times to become profitable and efficient so that you can weather the recessions with preparedness and a sufficient financial buffer. Ideally, adopting the major tenets of this handbook will help prepare your business for oscillations in sales, which are a certainty.

In the 25 years I have operated Wood River Evergreens full time, I have experienced the joy of a very profitable year and the despair of finishing the season with a financial loss. Almost every time there has been a loss it was because I strayed from following the tenets described in this handbook. Financial difficulties were exacerbated by not adhering to the following: a business plan or marketing plan, an efficient estimating and job costing program, employees with positive attitudes, the appropriate leadership style, or not delegating responsibilities. However, it was remarkable how well our company performed when these tenets were followed.

I recently have read Spencer Johnson's new book Peaks and Valleys,[1] which I found useful in explaining ways to deal with the ups and downs of running a business (and life's daily challenges). Johnson outlines steps to manage your good and bad times. Whether you are temporarily up on a peak or down in a valley – "avoid believing things are better than they really are when you are on a peak or worse than they really are when you are in a valley; make reality your friend."

I am reminded of the quote "Success is not forever, or is failure fatal"[2]. It is important not to get too down when things are not going well, nor too overconfident when the boom times are upon us. The seeds of future downturns are sown during exuberant good times, and the seeds for recovery are planted during slow times.

To get out of slow times Johnson recommends, "Relax, knowing that valleys end. Do the opposite of what put you in the valley. Get outside of yourself: be of more service at work and loving in life. Avoid comparisons. Uncover the good that is hidden in a bad time and use it soon to our advantage." To stay on a peak longer, "…appreciate and manage your good times. Be humble and grateful. Do more of what got you there. Keep making things better. Do more for others. Save resources for your upcoming valleys."[3]

Most seasonal horticultural businesses experience the ups and downs of the national economic cycles as well as the seasonal nature of their cash flow cycles. Not only do horticultural businesses have to overcome the business challenges identified in Chapter 1, but also we have to produce enough profit to carry the company through several months of limited or no income, even though the bills and expenses continue. I have certainly experienced these challenges over my time in business and will share my "Fifteen Management Tips for Success". When followed together, they have a synergistic effect that can create the type of business you envisioned when you first thought of owning your own company.

Frank's Fifteen Management Tips for Success

1. <u>Lead with a Vision</u> – What is your "grand strategy" for the future? Where do you (and your company) want to be in 3 years? 5 years? 10 years? From the moment you decide to open your own business there is an idea or vision of what you believe your company will develop into. Eventually, all of your decisions, purchases, and services you offer contribute to the attainment of that goal. However, unless your employees, management team, bankers, accountant, and other advisors are aware of your vision, it will be difficult to achieve. Articulating your vision, writing it down, and sharing it with your team are the first steps toward achieving your overall goal.

    If your vision is to become a large, successful maintenance firm offering numerous services like mowing, lawn care, pruning, weeding, mulching, plant health care, and property clean-ups, writing down your vision with specific objectives and a tentative timeline will give your employees (and financial advisors) a roadmap to the future path of the company. When your team knows where they are headed it is easier to get their support, dedication, and enthusiasm. With employee support, your written vision can affect change that is needed to achieve your goals.

    Sometimes, in spite of a clear vision for the future, fear prevents our pursuit of a dream. Perhaps it is a fear of failure or of making a wrong decision. Perhaps it is fear of the unknown or of taking a risk. Speaking from experience, risk-taking in life and in business is unavoidable. In fact, there are just as many risks to standing still as there are from taking action.

    Stepping upon a path is the first step to overcoming your fears, as this simple activity often distracts the mind from becoming paralyzed by "what if" scenarios. Inviting others to join in your undertaking–a partner or a capable team–can help you analyze and negotiate difficult experiences. Know who your lifesavers are, share your vision with them, empower them, and they will be there to help you survive the tough business or personal landscapes you may encounter on your journey.

2. <u>Develop a Business Plan</u> – This particular management tip has proven critical to my business success. Some of my business difficulties over the years have resulted from the plan not being followed. In 1992, my creation of a detailed business plan was the key

element in getting my local banker to restructure our loans and allow us to establish a credit line – necessary steps to save our company from financial ruin.

Besides helping to obtain loans from banks, the business plan also alerts the company when certain aspects of the company aren't working. When setting goals in the plan, be sure to gauge your current situation and use it as a benchmark to track your progress (or lack of it). Several times in the past ten years, we eliminated business divisions when they were no longer meeting our goals, particularly in the financial arena. Our Spooky Halloween Hayride and Christmas business divisions were eliminated because of liability concerns, lagging sales, and financial losses.

The business plan acts as a roadmap for the future: where we are now, where we are headed, how we will get there, and what we will need along the way to achieve our goals. Over time the plan will need to be updated and revised as conditions change. With the plan as a benchmark, we can track our growth and keep our eyes on the bottom line. Remember, the plan is organic, requiring frequent visits, modifications, and adjustments to accurately reflect changing conditions and actual results along the way.

3. <u>Leadership Style is Consequential</u> – I have always considered myself a leader, but my foray into running my own business severely tested my assumptions about my leadership ability. Without recognizing the style I was employing, I soon found out that the directing, military style of running my company not only didn't work, it was the wrong style for my natural instincts and previous training. Once I adopted a more "serving leader" style, becoming more of a coach, supporter, and delegator, the employees were happier and more productive, and I was more comfortable with a style I enjoyed– coaching.

Determining your leadership style is very important. Equally important is knowing your employee's level of training and abilities. Matching the appropriate leadership styles to the professional level of your employees is the key to having successful, happy employees and achieving the highest productivity. Less-trained individuals will need a more directing style, while experienced employees will benefit from coaching. Long- term, talented employees will respond well to the delegating style, giving you more time to spend selling, marketing, and operating the business in a way to achieve your goals.

As the leader, it is not only your responsibility to have a plan but to clearly communicate the plan to everyone on your team. Make sure everyone is working toward clearly defined goals – a higher degree of awareness will increase enthusiasm, passion, and motivation. Using the appropriate leadership style will bring huge dividends for your company, employees, and yourself.

4. <u>Empower your Managers: "Let go and Delegate"</u> – My company began to truly reach its potential and achieve a high level of success when I finally learned to delegate

responsibilities to my managers and team leaders. As the owner of a company, it is extremely difficult to relinquish control, especially if you are not sure the employee to whom you are delegating will do the job well. What I have found out over the years is that the responsibilities I have delegated to others–scheduling, marketing, estimating, and billing–have been done better, more efficiently, and on-time than when I tried to "do it all." When given specific responsibilities, guidance, and accountability most empowered employees will relish the opportunity and work diligently to succeed.

One caution in delegating–you must not only allow the employee to succeed but also to fail. If at the first sign of problems you take back the responsibilities, the employee will never learn the important lessons of overcoming difficulties. Think back to the valuable lessons you learned from your own failures…you must give your employees the same learning opportunities. Your growing company may never achieve the success you envision if you tightly hold on to all of the operation's responsibilities.

Participatory management is another way to share responsibilities and decision-making in your business. We have planning meetings in the winter months to review the previous year's activities and to establish a budget and goals for the upcoming year. Attending the meeting are our team leaders, nursery and office managers, bookkeeper, marketing director, and the owner. Each team member is given an opportunity to give input and serve on sub-committees to decide the critical items for the next year: equipment and vehicle needs, employee needs, policy changes, wage and benefits suggestions, and ideas for new services. By including team members in the formulation of policy and decision-making, they have a vested interest in the success of the company.

5. <u>Make Customer Satisfaction the #1 Priority</u> – You are exposed to countless ads that profess that customers are number one in their business. Unfortunately, in reality many times that is not true. If your business is to succeed, actually making customers the number one priority is necessary. In a competitive market, those firms who truly try to exceed customer's expectation will survive and prosper.

You can begin by reviewing your mission statement with your staff and posting it in the office. Answering phone calls in a timely, friendly, and professional manner will demonstrate your commitment to customer service. Following through on your promises will establish trust. If you promise to start a project on Monday, be sure to begin on Monday. If there is a delay, communicate with the client promptly. Never leave a customer hanging about what's happening with their project. Good communication is essential, even if it is to discuss delays or problems.

If a plant dies in a customer's landscape, be sure to honor your warranty and replace the plant. Few things can destroy a company's reputation (and your own) faster than failing to stand behind your guarantee. So that everyone is well informed about your warranty policy, make sure each customer is given a written copy along with any conditions of which they should be aware.

This may sound obvious, but when the project is completed, review the job to make sure there are no loose ends or problems. Once the project is completed and final payment is made, thank the customer for their business. We follow up each job with a thank you note and customer survey postcard to obtain valuable feedback on our design, installation, and team. Exceeding expectations will (hopefully) gain us a "client advocate" who can be counted on for new landscape referrals and future projects.

6. Build a Strong Brand – Today's buying decisions are made based upon promises that transcend your products or services. An expectation of performance, a mark of trust and integrity, your reputation, and a collection of memories all make up your brand. Those companies with a strong brand continue to attract customers even in slow economic times. That is why creating and maintaining a loyal brand is so significant to your long-term success.

    Our company frequently has new customers who will describe several landscapes they like because of the style of the design, quality of the plants, the professional workmanship of the stonework, and the over-all appropriateness of the completed landscape. Many times the landscapes they identified were WRE-designed, installed, and maintained projects! Our brand is typified by quality, professional application, and pleasing results, which we continue to strive for and improve upon with each project we complete.

    Instilling customer dedication to your brand, from your construction and maintenance team to your office staff, is critical to strengthening your brand. The way you and your staff answer the phone, bill customers, keep your trucks clean, stake trees, and interact with clients are all components of your brand. Everything you do reflects your brand. Why is branding important? In a competitive market new customers will be more likely to do business with those companies that have a recognizable, strong brand. In a slow economy, the well-branded companies will continue to receive a good number of job requests because of their brand recognition and reputation.

7. Foster a Company Culture that Promotes a Supportive Team Spirit – Your company culture can play a key role in attracting and retaining good employees. Beginning with your mission statement and management philosophy, you can set the tone for the type of culture your company exhibits. A supportive, positive, and encouraging philosophy will entice quality employees to seek employment with your company and to make a long-term commitment to your firm. Those companies with non-supportive, unappreciative cultures will find it difficult to retain key employees.

    Company cultures that are based on positive values such as integrity, honesty, tolerance, a great work ethic, a family atmosphere, a supportive philosophy, and fun, will develop a team that will be understanding, motivated, and successful. This type of culture will attract top-quality employees who will thrive in this type of environment. It is no secret why the successful teams (the New England Patriots, for example) continue to attract talented players who contribute year in and year out to the team's success–it is their supportive, winning, team-first culture. This same principle applies to small businesses and always starts at the top, with the owner and management staff.

I have found that when you ensure that every individual on your staff is in alignment with your company's principles and values, your culture will be harmonious, productive, and happy. I'm reminded of John C. Maxwell's quote, "Loyalty fosters unity, and unity breeds team success."[4] The loyalty exhibited to and by our employees has a unifying effect on the whole team. Communicating with your employees on a daily basis, being attentive and aware of their concerns, and letting them know that you care will encourage that winning company culture. Another key principle to developing a winning culture is to set up each employee for success. I firmly believe that when my team members head out to install or maintain a landscape, they will succeed even under difficult conditions because they have the resources and the owner's support to complete the project effectively and efficiently.

8. <u>Hire Employees Who Complement Your Strengths</u> – Our goal as a company is to build a strong, talented, diverse team by hiring motivated and exceptional people. Our employees share our values, align themselves with our management philosophy, mission, and vision for the company, and will thrive personally within our company culture. Additionally, I look to hire individuals who have skills and talents that I do not possess, such as mechanics, equipment operators, carpenters, computer users, and bookkeepers. This way I can offset my own weaknesses with the strengths of others.

The number one complaint I hear from business owners I meet is how difficult it is to find good employees. And, if they are fortunate enough to find one, it is extremely difficult to retain them. We have had success in attracting and retaining employees, especially former business owners, by creating a supportive company culture, having a brand that stands for service, quality, and the promise of satisfaction, being specific about job descriptions, offering a very competitive wage and health insurance benefits, and offering employees opportunities for career advancement. Creating a winning team of employees does not happen just with "help wanted" advertising in March, but requires a year-round commitment to attracting and hiring key personnel.

To maintain a positive, supportive company culture, it will be necessary to eliminate negative employees who do not share your values or team-first philosophy. Although at times this can be painful, the sooner you remove negative influences from your team (even though they may be good, dependable workers), the sooner your employees will gel into an unbeatable team. "Bad apples," even one, can contaminate your carefully constructed team, causing a significant lowering of morale–without you even seeing it until it's too late.

Over the last five years I have removed negative influences from our staff, leaving the most dedicated, talented, positive team possible. It is a pleasure coming to work each day to coach this wonderful group, which continues to succeed at their jobs beyond my expectations. With a great team of employees, there is no landscape challenge we cannot overcome.

9. Remember to Make a Profit – Although profit is not a dirty word, sometimes it can be an elusive word! As with the variability of the economy, profitability has also been changeable. I have adopted several programs and processes which have helped mitigate some of the unsteady nature of company profitability.

Developing a comprehensive cost estimating system and job costing program has formalized the whole estimating process, creating an efficient and accurate way to price our projects. This system also allows us to measure the results and see what the actual profit margin is after job completion. Basing the results on actual figures (and not gut feelings) is very important to determine the financial condition of the company.

Establishing a detailed budget has also put us on a better financial footing. We monitor our financial progress during the season to give us time to make adjustments before the end of the season. With the unpredictability of gross sales from month to month, it is vitally important to have a handle on the economic health of the company at all times. We haven't always followed this process, but now we realize that well constructed budgets are essential to the path to profitability each year, regardless of sales projections.

Lastly, it is extremely helpful to hire key financial advisors (accountants, bookkeepers, and financial planners) to help monitor and maintain the financial health of the company. The advice from these experts on changes that are needed in times of financial crises is invaluable. Keeping yourself intimately involved in your company's financial matters and being regularly informed of the condition of the company is, without question, a vital function for the success of the company.

10. Computerize to Create Efficiencies – When the computerizing of WRE began in the mid 1990's I was a reluctant supporter of this time-consuming process. However, now I am a huge fan of the results and will support using additional technology in the future. Our whole company has benefited from embracing technology: our inventory database programs, accounting software, estimating and job costing programs, catalog and label making, word processing, email, website, quarterly newsletters, photo presentations, and spreadsheets–all made possible by our computerization over the last 17 years.

Interestingly, the major benefits from computerizing our operation have been the changes we have adopted in running our business. Yes, there has been a much greater efficiency and time savings with all our daily company functions, but the streamlining and re-structuring of processes like plant inventory, estimating, billing, and the way we communicate with clients proved extremely valuable in making WRE a better, more professional firm.

With our investments in and commitment to technology, we have enhanced our professional brand image. A company that looks professional has a competitive edge when it comes to attracting potential customers. Having a website is expected in today's market; having a high-quality website featuring pictures of landscape projects and listing our services is also necessary to meet our customer's expectations.

11. <u>Be Active in Your Industry's Trade Organizations</u> – Since the first days of opening my business, I have been involved in many trade organizations: The Rhode Island Christmas Tree Growers Association (RICTGA), The New England Christmas Tree Alliance (NECTA), The Rhode Island Nursery and Landscape Association (RINLA), The Master Gardener Foundation of R.I. Inc., and most recently the Northeast Organic Farming Association (NOFA).

I became involved in these organizations to learn more about issues affecting our industry such as new market trends, new products, and new sales techniques. Also, I began networking with speakers, association members, and vendors in order to stay abreast of the latest developments in my field, allowing me to maintain the highest degree of customer satisfaction through a job done with the best products and latest techniques.

Being a member of an organization is important, but taking on a leadership position within that organization will be even more rewarding. The lessons you can learn and the people you meet will make you a better leader, owner, and person. If you want to advance your business (and grow as an individual) it is vital that you become involved in industry trade organizations, particularly in leadership positions. Extended involvement helps you become a sought-after expert in your field.

Becoming a public speaker in your industry can demonstrate your knowledge on a particular topic, increasing your professional visibility. I enjoy public speaking because it allows me to indulge in my true passion as a teacher–sharing my knowledge and experiences in hopes it will help others.

12. <u>Appreciate People…Daily!</u> – The two most important words an owner or manager can use are "Thank You." People want to be compensated appropriately, have an interesting job, and work in a safe environment, but most of all they want to be recognized and appreciated. I make an effort to appreciate all of the people in my sphere of contact…every day. I praise team members for their achievements, congratulate family, friends, and staff on their successes, thank clients for their business, recognize subcontractors and vendors for their contributions, and sincerely empathize and sympathize with those experiencing hardships.

Adopting "an attitude of gratitude" can be the most effective leadership style you embrace. It begins with a focus on the positive qualities of the individuals you come in contact with each day: cheerful, optimistic, thorough, thoughtful, meticulous, friendly, supportive, focused, caring, cooperative, dependable, trustworthy, passionate, and appreciative. When you "see" or experience these attributes, praise them. When you regularly notice someone's positive attributes, their self-confidence is bolstered and their faith in (and loyalty to) the company is strengthened. When team members feel unique, special, and competent, you begin to develop a workforce that is passionate, motivated, and successful.

There are many ways to show your appreciation: a verbal thank you, a phone call, a card of thanks, a small gift, a gift certificate, or a simple handshake or pat on the back. The important point is that a sincere, timely act of appreciation establishes trust, encourages further cooperation, and strengthens a relationship that benefits both parties.

Showing gratitude has helped us build a wonderful team of employees, a network of dependable, professional subcontractors and vendors, and dedicated group of clients who are happy to refer our services–fitting testimony that the two most important words you can use every day are "Thank You."

13. Hire Professionals for Crucial Business Functions – When you reach critical stages in the growth and development of your company, the hiring of professionals to assist you in getting organized or reaching that next level can be extremely valuable. Experienced professional consultants can significantly reduce your learning curve, while guiding your company to more efficient organization, greater expansion of services, and increased profitability. Consultants can be hired hourly, by the day, or by the project. Over the years we have hired professional consultants for numerous business functions:

- Human Resources – I hired a human resources consultant when we needed to update our handbook. He was able to ensure that all the state and federal regulations were met.

- Employee Law – When an employee "situation" arose, I hired a lawyer specializing in employee law. He also was able to create our Confidentiality and Non-Compete Agreements, which are included in our employee handbook.

- Team Building – Several times in the past seven years I have hired a Team-Building Consultant, who ran a several-hour workshop for our entire staff. Everyone found value in the sessions, which have brought our employees much closer together.

- Budget Program – When I was having difficulties creating a budget, I hired a consultant who implemented a power budget system. This system has transformed (and made bearable) our financial projection and budgeting process.

- Accounting – Having an excellent accountant is extremely valuable, not just for completing our financial statements, yearly corporate tax returns, and personal tax returns, but also for his advice in planning for the future. In difficult economic times, his guidance is valuable in preparing for potential cash flow problems. In profitable times he can be helpful in effectively preparing for tax liabilities.

- Organic Landscaping – We are on a 5-year plan to convert our company to organic methods. In order to speed up the process, we hired a consultant to help with the production of compost tea, which we have found to be quite a learning process. With the consultant we have saved considerable time and are on the path to producing a high grade of compost tea.

Although good business consultants can be expensive, they can make a huge difference in the effective growth, organization, and profitability of your company.

14. Anticipate, Embrace, and Adapt to Change – Whether in prices, markets, new technology, additional competitors, environmental crises, employee problems, or new regulations, tomorrow will bring changes that you will need to address. Long-term, the changes that may occur will have profound effects on your business. Unless you anticipate, embrace, and adapt to the changes you may find your business without customers, leaving you no option but to close. However, anticipating changes, adapting to new conditions, and being a leader in re-inventing your company for new challenges will put you in a great position to succeed and remain profitable.

Spencer Johnson, M.D., in his bestselling book Who Moved My Cheese[5], asserts that those who anticipate change can adapt to it quickly–putting them in a better position to survive and even prosper. In the horticultural industry, change is ever-present, offering new opportunities for those ready and willing to embrace them. Those leaders who are inspiration for change will make the adjustments to move forward and succeed, while those tied to the status quo will flounder. I firmly believe that keeping abreast of changes in the green industry will give our company and other progressive firms an advantage in devising business plans for future directions. This will put them in a competitive advantage for new clients, services, and profits.

15. The Journey Never Ends – Even though this handbook has identified many ideas, techniques, and methods to improve your business, there is one other valuable lesson I wish to share with you. Physics proves that things in this universe eventually expire when out of balance with other forces in their surroundings. Remember that your work is only one part of life's equation. Your professional career should be a means to an end, not the "end-all, be-all" of your life. Create a balance between work and family, scheduling time for both. I learned this lesson the hard way, and the price I paid was my 32-year marriage and risking my close relationships with my children. Since reducing the amount of time I spend at work, I have reconnected with my three children and my grandchildren. I spend as much quality time with them as I can.

It is important to overcome your fears and move forward with confidence and determination. With the support of your family, friends, employees, and clients you can accomplish the goals set out in your vision. By looking back along the path I have traveled, I am able to advise people with great enthusiasm and certainty to never give up, in spite of setbacks and let downs. For every step backward, be determined enough to take the next two steps forward and you will eventually reach your goals.

Don't get complacent in today's success. Move on with each new day. Continue to improve your business methods, operation procedures and communications. This keeps your business healthy and vibrant and alive – ready for any new trends that might require a shift in marketing strategies or business tactics. Everything worthwhile in life takes effort, persistence, and drive to make it happen. Keep your eye on the future, use your sense of integrity and life's lessons as your road map, expect the landscape to have hills as well as valleys, draw energy from your friends and family as your fuel, and you will find the fortitude to push on with your dreams.

Essential Points:

1. The real business objective is to take advantage of the boom times to become profitable and efficient so you can weather recessions with preparedness and a sufficient financial buffer.

2. Articulating your vision, writing it down, and sharing it with your team are the first steps to achieving your goals.

3. Your company may never achieve the success you envision if you tightly hold onto all of the operation's responsibilities and don't learn to delegate.

4. If your company culture promotes a team and family environment, you will soon share in your employees' personal successes, milestones, and setbacks.

5. The two most important words an owner or manager can use are "Thank You."

Chapter 18: THE FUTURE OF SMALL HORTICULTURE BUSINESSES

Several months ago, my sister Lorie gave me the book <u>The Art of the Long View</u>[1] by Peter Schwartz. This book prompted me to really think about the future of horticulture. Schwartz's book describes the art of "taking the long view" of decisions you need to make today, and how those actions will be compatible with prevailing trends, attitudes, forces, and influences. The method he uses to examine potential actions and outcomes is called "the scenario." In developing the scenario, individuals consider several stories that may be possible in the future, based on research and potential future conditions. These "what if" stories for your business may include your worst nightmare, your most desired outcome, or something completely unexpected. From pondering these stories, your resulting strategic decisions will be able to take into account many possible future scenarios.

I am fascinated by this way of thinking about the future of the horticultural industry for several reasons. First, there is a tendency to concentrate our efforts, resources, and planning for the near-term: tomorrow, next week, this season, but not much further into the future. Secondly, with the vast amount of change occurring in our world–oil availability and price, fresh water usability, climate change, the move to sustainability, and the continued technological innovations–strategic planning for three, five, or twenty years into the future will require considerable research, resources…and luck! Thirdly, those businesses willing to think about the future and support that thinking with specific plans, resources, and commitments to embrace and adapt to change will have a better chance to survive and prosper. Those companies who continue to run their firms on a short-term basis, with no thought of the future changes coming to the horticultural industry (and society as a whole), will probably not survive.

Experience has shown us that dramatic changes can happen practically overnight, with profound effects on our industry:

1. The rapid rise of oil to over $145 a barrel impacted all phases of our business. Although the price has fallen from its historic high, it is only a matter of time before it increases dramatically again, presenting significant challenges for our industry.

2. Water shortages affect our industry severely each summer, especially in communities that adopt water bans. I believe that next looming crisis will be the availability of sufficient, non-polluted, fresh water for our nurseries, farms, customers, and other green businesses that depend on water for their survival (turf farms, golf courses, garden centers, etc.).

3. Sustainability of the plants and lawns installed, and crops planted, has become more of a concern. There is a distinct movement towards "organic", "sustainable", and "eco-friendly" landscape methods because of concerns about pesticide use, shortages of water, and the environment, and a sincere desire to become more "green" in the way we live,

work, and play. Some of the changes to become more sustainable are the result of state and community laws or regulations requiring organic methods of lawn care, as well as consumer driven demand for non-pesticide alternatives for landscape installation and after-care.

4. Climate change is not only affecting our geographic area, but has a worldwide impact. We in the horticultural field are in a unique position to reduce our carbon footprint with the activities we do; planting trees and shrubs, using organic and eco-friendly methods, and recycling our garden wastes into compost. Landscape architects and designers can create plans which feature sustainable landscapes using native plants, low water demanding selections, carefully placed trees to help with winter heating and summer cooling of homes, and collecting and recycling runoff water in the landscape.

5. Establishing permaculture systems will increase out of choice and necessity. Permaculture refers to an ecological design incorporating plants, animals, structures, and the land. It involves an integrated process which can happen in urban and rural properties.

Change is fundamental in our landscapes as well as our horticultural industry. The future will be filled with expected, unexpected, and surprising changes that will challenge our abilities to adapt, succeed, and prosper.

Let's take a closer look at these five changes. Then, I will conclude with a scenario of what landscaping in 2025 might be like.

1. The Impact of Oil and Energy

Most scientists and geologists believe that we are at or very near the oil production peak, with roughly half of the world's oil supply already consumed. The end of "cheap oil" is upon us, with expensive and rising oil prices in our foreseeable future. We all must begin the process of moving toward a post-oil world.

As we progress toward renewable energy sources such as wind, solar, tidal power, fuel cells, and others, there may be significant changes to our lifestyles and industries unless the transition begins soon. If the journey to energy independence begins today, there will be time to prepare for an energy use descent until we re-establish our population in balance with the surrounding ecosystem (Earth stewardship scenario). As prices of fossil fuels escalate, we not only have to switch to alternative energy sources but also drastically cut energy demand.

The end of cheap oil means the end of cheap broad-scale cultivation, the end of cheap fossil fuel-based fertilizers, and the end of cheap long-distance transport. In an expensive, reduced energy situation horticulture and productive gardening will need to become more local, shifting back to communities where they have traditionally been more sustainable. The movement to support local farms, grocers, and Community

Supported Agriculture (CSA) gardens will continue to expand. Homeowners will want to combine food production with their seasonal, aesthetic landscape plantings.

Future energy options will need to be considered, planned, and adopted. Fuel alternatives like bio-diesel exist and flex-fuel vehicles are available that can use traditional gas and an ethanol mix (E85). They will become more popular as fueling stations become more widely distributed.

Hybrid vehicles (electric and gas combinations) have limited availability at the time of this writing. I purchased a gas-electric hybrid Chevrolet pickup truck in 2006, but it was very difficult to find one to purchase. Although it gets only a few more miles per gallon than a conventional gas-only truck, it is a step in the right direction. For me, it is one more step in the conversion of our company into a leading Eco-Friendly firm.

In the future, electric and fuel cell vehicles will become available, reducing our dependency of fossil fuels. Equipment we use in our business–lawn mowers, leaf blowers, and weed whackers–will also move toward electric, quiet, and eco-friendly models. Those companies that use these alternate vehicles and equipment will not only help the environment but have a distinct marketing advantage over their competition.

2. <u>The Looming Water Crisis</u>

Although planet Earth is 97% water, only 1% is fresh water available to meet our needs–agricultural, industrial, and personal. Water is truly our most valuable natural resource. Our livelihoods and lifestyles are completely dependent on fresh water, especially those of us in horticultural businesses.

All of the potential resource shortages will impact our horticultural industry, but water scarcity could have a crippling effect on our profession. Today, 33% of the world's population is living without access to adequate fresh water. By 2025, 66% may be facing significant water shortages, including over 33% of cities in the U.S. Areas of the U.S. are already experiencing severe droughts, including Texas and southeast regions from Florida to the Carolinas. Western states are facing water shortages–the farm belt in the mid-west is draining the huge underground aquifer 14 times faster than nature can replenish it[2].

The water crisis is exacerbated by several factors. Climate change is altering precipitation patterns, which affects fresh water sources like glaciers and snow pack. We are diverting and polluting surface waters, over-mining groundwater, deforesting watersheds, and paving over our essential natural systems.

Of the water we use in the U.S., 46% goes to industrial uses, 41% agricultural needs, and 13% personal and municipal use. The average person in the U.S. uses 150 gallons of water per day. It takes 600 gallons of water to grow the amount of corn to produce a 1/3 lb. hamburger and 74 gallons to produce 1 cup of coffee[3].

How can we solve the water crisis? And, more specifically for our horticultural industry, what steps can we take to help ameliorate the effect of looming what shortages?

As with oil, we have passed the point of cheap, clean water. Solving the water crisis will not be easy, but adopting conservation measures is a necessary first step. Managing water resources better will be essential. Reducing waste in our delivery system, particularly in irrigation use for agriculture and industrial use, is also important. Increasing water recycling and protecting our valuable fresh water sources from pollution and contamination is critical. We all will need to fully understand the true cost of water and learn to value it as the extremely valuable resource that it is.

In our horticultural profession water is indispensable. Faced with water shortages during droughts and experiencing summer water bans with some of our customers, it is important for us to have a game plan to deal with lack of water. I have listed a few steps you can take to help overcome water shortages:

a. Incorporate rain-barrels and underground cisterns to collect run-off water to be re-used. At WRE's landscape design center, we collect the run-off water from our walkways in two 2,000 gallon underground cisterns, from which we can re-use the water on the design center plantings.

b. Increase efficiency of your irrigation systems: check for leaks, reduce watering frequency, and where practical, install drip irrigation systems.

c. Prepare properties before the summer drought season with appropriate mulching of plant beds, addition of compost, application of compost tea, and ensuring that plants are properly fertilized (if needed).

d. Choose plants (perennials, annuals, shrubs, and trees) that are appropriate for the landscape with minimal water needs. Sustainability is very important for plants to survive and flourish in challenging environments. Natives tend to perform well, but judiciously incorporating some non-natives can contribute to a diverse, successful, sustainable landscape. Be careful to avoid invasive plants, which can be found listed on your state's website.

e. Adopting xeriscaping principles can improve the success of plants and lawns during stressful periods, especially droughts. Organizing plants in garden beds according to water needs will help in the maintenance of the landscape during periods of water shortages.

3. <u>Sustainability and Organic Approaches to Horticulture</u>

With concerns about shortages of water and the effect of pesticides on our environment, and the desire to install plants with minimal care, the concept of sustainability and organic techniques to maintain landscapes has grown in importance. These techniques are not new; organic methods of composting, raising crops, improving soil health, efficiently using water, and choosing appropriate plants for sustainability have been known and used for hundreds of years. One organization that has promulgated the organic principles is the Northeast Organic Farming Association (NOFA).

One of the founders of the NOFA Organic Land Care Program, Kimberly Stoner, Ph. D., succinctly describes the primary mission, philosophy, and goals of the program in "The NOFA Organic Lawn and Turf Handbook," excerpts from which are outlined below[4].

The mission of the NOFA Organic Land Care Program is to extend the vision and principles of organic agriculture to the landscapes where people spend their daily lives. The primary goals of the NOFA Organic Land Care Program are:

- Maintain soil health
- Eliminate the use of synthetic pesticides and synthetic fertilizers
- Increase landscape diversity
- Improve the health and well being of the people and web of life in our core

Additional points in the NOFA organic program are:

- No synthetic pesticides, including insecticides, fungicides, and herbicides
- No genetically engineered organisms
- Build healthy soil that can support diverse soil life
- Use good cultural practices to encourage the growth of sustainable plants and reduce the need for irrigation and other inputs.
- Increase the diversity of plantings, making sure the right plant is designated for the right spot.

Concerns about pesticides' effects on human health and the environment have spurred the movement to adopt organic methods. Pesticides may be needed in certain situations to protect against the spread of human pathogens or invasive species. However, evidence of harmful effects of pesticides on human health and the environment has increased steadily since the first concerns were raised by Rachel Carson's "Silent Spring" in 1962. As the evidence has accumulated, some pesticides that were once widely used have been restricted or banned. There is considerable scientific evidence that associate birth defects, hormonal disruptions and neurological effects with pesticides still being used today (Ontario College of Family Physicians. 2004 "Pesticide Literature Review: Systematic Review of Pesticide Human Health Effects").

In organic land care it has been the philosophy to avoid the use of pesticides as much as possible through management of the entire ecological system, and through using cultural methods like planting insect- and disease resistant varieties of plants, avoiding monocultures, building healthy soil and altering growing conditions to reduce susceptibility to pests and disease.

In both organic agriculture and organic land care some pesticides are allowed. The main principle used in deciding which pesticides to allow is their being based on natural products, not synthetic chemicals. Certain natural products which are known to be highly toxic are not allowed, however. Examples of acceptable pesticides are *Bacillus thuringiensis*

(Bt), Spinosad, Milky Spore®, pyrethrin, neem, hot pepper wax, clove oil, horticultural oil, and insecticidal soaps.

All pesticides, including those allowed in organic land care, involve some risk. Non-chemical alternatives should be considered before using any pesticide. Pesticide applicator licenses are needed for anyone applying pesticides for hire and all State and Federal laws and guidelines need to be followed.

Specifically, for landscape professionals looking to become organic and provide sustainable plants for customers there are several guidelines to follow:

- Choose plants that are disease resistant, appropriate for the location, and not invasive
- Follow organic landscape management methods
- Devise a watering program that deep waters plants and lawns infrequently
- Compost yard wastes onsite or at a compost facility
- Use natural mulches (no dyed products) at the appropriate depth (2-3") and not up against the trunks of trees or shrubs
- Conduct soil tests before planting or installing a lawn
- Use organic fertilizers, compost, compost tea, over seeding, and aerating to build up the soil for healthy lawns.
- Choose the least toxic approach for plant health care including cultural methods and those pesticides approved by NOFA

Sustainability and organic approaches are not a fad–they are here to stay. Focusing on healthy soil, the organic approach will result in sustainable, healthy landscapes which will enhance our environment.

4. Climate Change

Greenhouse gases (CO_2, methane, water vapor, nitrous oxide, and others) surround Earth, letting sunlight in but retaining reflected warmth. With the increased amount of greenhouse gases in our atmosphere (mainly CO_2), too much long-wave energy is trapped, warming the planet. Although the result has been only a 1-degree C average global temperature increase, that degree can have significant results[5]:

- Glaciers will melt
- Oceans will heat up causing stronger hurricanes
- Animals and plants might go extinct because they cannot adapt to change in temperature

The overwhelming scientific consensus is that the biggest contributor to the increase in greenhouse gases is the burning of fossil fuels. The carbon released from the burning combines with oxygen to form CO_2, which is released into the atmosphere. New cleaner technologies will help improve the situation, but ultimately using alternate energy sources such as solar, wind, and fuel cells will make the biggest improvement.

We can measure the amount of CO_2 pollution that is emitted from the energy we use–it is called our carbon footprint. Annually, the average American adult emits 20 tons of CO_2. All of your daily activities; using your computer, driving your car, taking a shower, washing and drying clothes, and turning on lights use energy, contributing to your carbon footprint. It is extremely important to conserve energy and offset our daily CO_2 emissions[6].

Forests and oceans help us by absorbing CO_2 and thus acting as a carbon sink. Unfortunately, the forests and the oceans are also warming up, making it more difficult for them to absorb CO_2[7].

There are steps we horticultural businesses can take to reduce our carbon footprint:

- Reduce our home and office energy use
- Investigate alternate sources of energy for our trucks, homes, and offices (bio-diesel, gas-electric hybrids, flex fuel, ethanol, solar, wind, and geothermal)
- Recycle and re-use paper products, plastic pots, used lumber, metal tree cages, twine, etc.
- Compost yard wastes (clippings, weeds, sod, leaves, wood chips, etc.)
- Plant more trees and shrubs to increase action of CO_2 absorption.
- Explore the use of new electric mowers, vehicles, and equipment as they become available

We certainly cannot solve the climate change crisis on our own, but we can take very positive steps to lower the carbon footprints of our horticultural businesses and ourselves.

5. Permaculture

Bill Mollison coined the term "permaculture" in 1974. Permaculture is defined as a design system for creating sustainable human environments. Permaculture deals with plants, animals, buildings, the land, and infrastructures, and the relationships that can be created by the way they are placed in the landscape. The aim is to create systems that are ecologically sound and economically viable. They are also sustainable, self-sufficient, and non-polluting. Permaculture is based on the observation of natural systems, traditional farming systems, and modern scientific and technological knowledge[8].

We all can start by decreasing our energy consumption, re-fitting our houses for energy efficiency, cutting vehicle use, saving water run-off, recycling grey water, and starting some form of food production. In all sustainable cultures, the energy needs of the system are provided by that system. Unfortunately, modern agriculture is totally dependent on external energy. Conventional farming is mined of its fertility to produce grains and vegetables, non-renewable resources are used to support yields, the land is eroded through over-stocking of animals and frequent plowing, and the land and water are polluted by chemicals.

Permaculture embraces three ethics regarding the care of the earth, care of people, and the dispersal of surplus time, money, and materials towards those ends[9]:

- Care of the earth means care for soils, species and their varieties, the atmosphere, forests, animals, and waters.

- Care of the earth also implies care of people so that basic needs for food, shelter, education, and employment are taken care of.

- The third component is the contribution of surplus time, money and energy to achieve the aims of earth and people care.

The permaculture system also has a basic life ethic, recognizing the intrinsic worth of every living thing. The permaculture ethic pervades all aspects of the environmental, community, economic and social system.

As we move forward in exploring alternatives to our energy-dependent world, adoption of sustainable systems like permaculture will increase. On a horticultural level, we can design landscapes which offer small food-producing gardens along with plant selections that offer multiple uses (like blueberries and cedar trees). Areas for composting can be established, as well as water-collecting cisterns that can capture and re-use the water for landscape and food plants. The important point is to consider all aspects of the property: the plants, the buildings, the people, and the overall sustainability of the landscape. Taking into account these permaculture principles will help create less energy-dependent, more sustainable, and more ecologically balanced landscapes. Combining solar and wind or other alternative power sources a property can move away from energy dependence to an energy independent, sustainable existence.

These five future changes and challenges are presented to stimulate thought, consideration, and possible action. The future for horticultural businesses will be anything but predictable. Changes, new technologies, crises, unexpected major disruptions, and unplanned situations will abound. Being aware of change, ready to react, and willing to adapt your business to an uncertain future will be the hallmark of operating a horticultural firm in the future. Obviously I cannot predict the future, but I will share a scenario of what I believe designing and installing a landscape project might look like in the year 2025…for your consideration!

Landscape Project Scenario: The year 2025

A new client, Mr. George Smith, contacted our company through our website to have our company design and install a landscape for his new summer home in Charlestown, RI. He sent a video stream of his property with several detailed pages of his requirements. Our Landscape Architect completed a 3-dimensional plan and emailed the plan back to George for his comments. Once the final plan was accepted, a detailed estimate, timetable, and contract were emailed the same day. The customer confirmed the order with a special code number which directly put the requested deposit in my bank account–checks and credit cards are rarely used in our profession anymore.

All of the plants were chosen from a New England sustainable list available on an extensive virtual nursery plant availability site, including of all the major nurseries in our area. After inserting our plant list, all of the needed plants were assembled from the availability list, picked out from the nurseries based on virtual plant lists showing size, color, and shape, and scheduled for direct shipment to the site within several days.

Two days later, the plants arrived on fuel cell powered trucks and were unloaded with electric lifts charged using electricity from renewable sources. Our foreman arrived at the site with a hand-held computer with a 3-D plan showing the locations, specific plants, and special planting instructions for each plant.

Because of global warming the plant selection had expanded to include plants from as far away as Georgia (formerly zone 9), although just 15 years ago southern New England was planting zone 6.

The installation included special southern New England, regionally-made compost and manufactured loam. No chemical fertilizers or pesticides have been allowed in landscaping since 2015, when an "organic only" ordinance was passed in our region. Because of water shortages, drip irrigation, rain barrels, and underground cisterns are mandatory in all landscapes. Outdoor water-use bans are in effect from May through September, and any water used for outdoor landscape use costs $5/gallon, making it critical to minimize the water used. Xeriscaping (landscaping for water conservation) has been in effect for 15 years, since the groundwater was contaminated with salt water infiltration from the nearby ocean and weather patterns had created a drop in annual rainfall from 46 inches to 10 inches per year.

After the plants were installed using quiet, efficient, electric portable backhoes, the foreman reported into his hand-held device all of the daily activities, plants, materials, trucking, and labor to our office program. At the office, the actual job cost is automatically calculated and an updated bill is emailed to the client. Once he approves the bill, he authorizes a password and code number to instantaneously deposit the final payment owed for the project into our business account!

Sound far-fetched? In reality, much of the technology for and trends toward this scenario already exist. My timing may be off–it could be here before you know it! It is a valuable exercise to look into the future and consider possible scenarios. With alternate possibilities you can develop strategies to address even the least likely scenarios and not be caught ill prepared.

Future Horticultural Plans

I firmly believe that horticulture, in all of its forms, will continue to expand and increase in importance to our customers. With the demonstrated health benefits of gardening and the huge numbers of baby boomers ready to retire, I see gardening–including design, growing plants, maintenance services, and providing supplies–as a sure bet for the future. I also see organics increasing in our field; some by local and state mandates, and more by customer demand. Organic lawn care and planting materials, plant health care, sustainable plant selection, water conservation, recycling, and composting will increase substantially in the future.

A plan for the future of a horticultural business might include many of the following:

- Conversion to organic methods of planting, maintaining properties, and lawn care.

- Composting on site, along with compost tea production, as a valuable resource.

- Recycling of plastic pots, office supplies, and construction debris.

- Use of rain barrels and in-ground cisterns to collect run-off water for watering plants in nurseries, garden centers, and residential/commercial properties.

- Making sustainable gardens the norm for designers and landscape installers.

- No pesticides except for those allowed by NOFA standards to be used on clients' properties.

- Use of renewable sources of energy (solar, wind, etc.) to help supply the electricity for office buildings, to recharge electric vehicles and equipment, and to heat greenhouses.

- Purchasing of alternative-fuel vehicles and equipment. In addition to hybrid pickup trucks, vehicles purchased in the future may include flex fuel (E-85) and biodiesel for larger trucks. When commercial-grade electric mowers, leaf blowers, and weed whackers become available, they will be featured in many horticultural businesses.

In Conclusion

All of us in the horticultural field have experienced adversities such as poor weather, non-productive employees, financial crises, customer frustrations, and personal difficulties, but we continue to move ahead, revising our plans and strategies, finding new markets, establishing successful niches, and finding success–one client at a time. In his book <u>Failing Forward</u>, John C.

Maxwell, says: "To achieve your dreams, you must embrace adversity and make failure a regular part of your life. If you're not failing, you're probably not really moving forward.[10]"

I can honestly say that the adversities I have faced have helped to shape my business, my philosophy, and my personal life.

As we move through our daily lives, we try to keep all our experiences in perspective, maintain an even keel, never getting too high or too low. Maintain a clear vision for the future. Pursue your dreams with confidence, persistence, and determination. Learn from your mistakes, and enjoy your journey.

I hope you find the information in this handbook valuable to you and your business. Feel free to copy and adapt any of the forms included here to your business. I wish you present and future success!

"The purpose of life is not to win. The purpose of life is to grow and share. When you come to look back on all that you have done in life, you will get more satisfaction from the pleasure you have brought to other people's lives than you will from the times that you out did and defeated them." (Rabbi Harold Kushner)[11].

Chapter 19: EPILOGUE

I have spent over two years researching, writing, and editing this handbook…a compilation of years of accomplishments, experiences, business successes and some failures. With each bump in the road I have tried to learn from my missteps, recalibrate my vision, and move ahead with a revised and improved plan for my business's future. In past recessions (1989-1991 and 2003), the adaptations and corrections I made seemed to work – until the most recent downturn in the economy (2008-2011). Of the ten business challenges that were listed in the introduction (Chapter 1), WRE encountered eight in a relatively short period of time. Even with careful planning, meetings with our accountant and business lawyer to develop an economic plan, significantly reducing the size of our company, reducing overhead, increasing marketing efforts, fine-tuning our estimating and job costing system, offering discounts to clients, and putting my savings into the business, WRE was unable to weather the perfect storm of financial events, leaving me no option but to permanently close the company on October 1, 2010. The closing was sudden, but the process leading up to the closure was not. Being an optimistic person, I always hoped that the next season would be better economically; unfortunately, this was not the case in 2008, 2009, or 2010.

What happened? The accumulation of factors which contributed to the necessity of closing Wood River Evergreens includes the following:

1. A 70% gross sales drop from 2007 through 2010.
2. Increasing insurance and benefit costs. Health insurance for our employees had increased an average of 15% per year for the past four years.
3. Stiffer competition, especially from firms willing to bid extremely low for landscape projects.
4. A severe economic recession which affected our clientele (including many high-end coastal property owners) to the point that for the last 2½ months leading up to our closing date we were unable to finalize a single landscape project.
5. Local banks unwilling to loan money to small businesses and eliminating credit lines…a valuable source of funds especially during the slow winter months.
6. My reluctance to lay off employees sooner because of my loyalty to them and their families…even though it ultimately hurt the entire business.
7. Carrying a heavy debt load on the property, in addition to several business loans taken on to help WRE get through the winter months.
8. Offering discounts on projects to attract customers even though it severely affected the ultimate profit margin.

9. One of the final blows was the extreme damage we suffered in the historic flood that struck Rhode Island in the spring of 2010. Severe flooding of the Wood River, which runs adjacent to WRE, caused over $93,000 worth of damage to our property and two story design center building. The 500-year flood event was overwhelming and not covered by insurance; a disaster loan we applied for through the Federal Government (SBA) was not approved.

In all my years running WRE, I never expected it to end this way. As I am going through this difficult series of events and completing this handbook, I cannot help but feel that having a resource like this book years ago might have helped me to better prepare for this situation; however, sometimes outside forces can overtake you and your business even if you are doing many things right. I certainly bear the brunt of responsibility for my company's closing, although I realize the severe recession of 2008-2011 was a significant factor in its demise.

After getting through the initial shock and emotions of the closing process, I have begun to look back at WRE's accomplishments and assemble a list of lessons that I will share with readers of this handbook. Certainly the essential points contained in this book would be extremely helpful to re-read and implement. Here are twelve lessons I can share:

1. As my accountant Terry Malaghan stated in his article: <u>Business = Risk</u>. A business's survival and longevity is not guaranteed. Every business has a finite lifespan, even if you are doing many things correctly to operate your firm.

2. Loyalty to your employees is important to build trust and dedication, but not to the point of jeopardizing your company's survival. Ultimately, this benefits no one.

3. Look ahead and try to anticipate future economic conditions so that you can make decisions before it becomes life or death for your company.

4. To the best of your ability, keep your debt load manageable. A high debt load made it impossible for our business to succeed when sales decreased significantly.

5. Communicate with your staff, bankers, accountants, and advisors on a regular basis so that everyone is aware of changing conditions in the business and the potential for significant changes that may be needed in the future.

6. Create and fund a separate buffer savings account to help you during disasters: floods, hurricanes, droughts, winter storms, etc.

7. Be aware of your competition and fine tune your estimating system so that if discounts are needed you know your revised profit margins…and then decide if you can live with the lower profit margin.

8. Draw a line in the sand regarding your willingness to use personal funds to keep the business going, and do not cross over that line. Unfortunately, I know this is much easier said than done – this should have been one of my first steps as sales began to seriously decline.

9. When you are maxed-out financially and banks are declining loan requests, turning to family members and friends may not be a good option. You run the risk of severely damaging relationships if you borrow money from someone close to you and the business fails. Count on your life partner, family, and close friends for love, support, and encouragement…not funding.

10. Do not be hesitant to seek advice from professionals: accountants, bankers, lawyers, consultants, and those who have experienced similar business problems. Listen to your trusted advisors, even when what they say is not what you want to hear. It took me two years to fully comprehend the severity of my financial situation. My fiancée, Elise, was instrumental in getting me to see the big picture and has provided love and understanding throughout this difficult process. Sometimes we cannot see the forest for the trees, especially when we are in it.

11. Pay close attention to your own relationships–your life partner, family, and friends– who will help you through this difficult process…if you embrace them and let them in. You do not have to go through this alone! Thankfully, my fiancée has been steadfast in her love, support, and assistance even when I was still in denial about my financial situation. Without her help (for which I am eternally grateful), I would not have been able to successfully deal with the closing of WRE, the business receivership, and personal bankruptcy.

12. Throughout difficult times do not ignore your physical and emotional health. I have found that counseling, regular exercise, regular meditation sessions, and tai chi kept me healthy, moving forward, and in a healthy enough mental state to deal with the stresses of going through this traumatic experience.

Although I am extremely disappointed with seeing my long-term business close, I do look back with pride at all of the wonderful, award-winning landscapes WRE designed, installed, and maintained in southern New England. I treasure the talented, dedicated employees who made all of these successful projects possible. I was very fortunate to work for fantastic clients, many of whom are my long-term friends. I believe we have left the southern New England landscape in better shape than when I first began WRE in 1972.

I have my life partner, family, close friends, good health, and numerous opportunities ahead of me. I plan on moving forward with ideas, interests, and goals I have wanted to pursue for years, including helping small horticultural businesses succeed so that they will not have to go through what I have had to experience. Using this book, consultations, teaching, seminars, and speaking engagements, I plan to dedicate myself to sharing my lessons with others with the goal of helping to improve the performance and success of other small businesses.

"Sometimes it takes losing everything to gain everything."

\- Frank Crandall

Bibliography

Aaker, David A. 1996. Building Strong Brands. New York, NY: The Free Press.

Abrams, Rhonda. 2005. Business Plan in a Day: Get it Done Right, Get it Done Fast™. Palo Alto, CA: The Planning Shop™.

Abrams, Rhonda. 2005. The Owner's Manual for Small Business. Palo Alto, CA: The Planning Shop™.

Adams, Bob, M.B.A. 1996. Adams Streetwise Small Business Start-Up. Avon, MA: Adams Media, an F & W Publications Company.

Axelrod, Alan. 2009. Winston Churchill, CEO. New York, NY: Sterling Publishing Co., Inc.

Bain, Dwight. 2003. Destination Success: A Map for Living Out Your Dreams. Grand Rapids, MI: Fleming H. Revell, a division of Baker Book House Company.

Blanchard, Ken. 2004. Leadership Smarts—Inspiration and Wisdom from the Heart of a Leader. Colorado Springs, CO: Honor Books.

Blanchard, Ken. 2004. The On-Time, On-Target Manager: How "Last Minute Manager" Conquered Procrastination. New York, NY: Harper Collins Publishers, Inc.

Blanchard, Ken, Bill Hybels, and Phil Hodges. 1999. Leadership by the Book: Tools to Transform Your Workplace. New York, NY: William Morrow and Company, Inc.

Blanchard, Ken, Dana Robinson, and Jim Robinson. 2002. Zap the Gaps! Target Higher Performance and Achieve It! New York, NY: Harper Collins Publishers, Inc.

Blanchard, Ken, Patricia Zigarmi, and Drea Zigarmi. 1985. Leadership and The One Minute Manager: Increasing Effectiveness through Situational Leadership. New York, NY: William Morrow and Company, Inc.

Blanchard, Kenneth and Sheldon M. Bowles. 1993. Raving Fans – A Revolutionary Approach to Customer Service. New York, NY: William Morrow and Company, Inc.

Bruce, Anne and James S. Pepitone. 1999. Motivating Employees. New York, NY: McGraw Hill.

Caplan, Suzanne. 2000. Streetwise® Finance and Accounting. Avon, MA: Adams Media, an F & W Publications Company.

Cappelli, Peter, adviser. 2002. Hiring and Keeping the Best People. Boston, MA: Harvard Business School Press.

Canfield, Jack, Mark Victor Hansen, and Les Hewitt. 2000. The Power of Focus. Deerfield Beach, FL: Health Communications, Inc.

Carlson, Richard. Ph.D. 1998. Don't Sweat the Small Stuff at Work – Simple Ways to Minimize Stress and Conflict While Bringing Out the Best in Yourself and Others. New York, NY: Hyperion.

Carlson, Richard. Ph.D. 2005. Easier than You Think…Because Life Doesn't Have to be So Hard! New York, NY: Harper San Francisco.

Carnegie, Dale. 1981. How to Win Friends and Influence People. New York, NY: Pocket Books.

Carter, David E. 1997. Logos of American Restaurants. Dusseldorf, Germany: Nippon Shuppan Hanbai Deutschland GmbH.

Chase, Cochrane and Kenneth L. Barasch. 1977. The Marketing Problem Solver. Radnor, PA: Chilton Book Company.

Christians, Nick and Michael L. Agnew. 2000. The Mathematics of Turfgrass Maintenance. Hoboken, NJ: John Wiley & Sons, Inc.

Collins, Jim. 2001. Good to Great: How Some Companies Make the Leap…and Others Don't. New York, NY: HarperCollins Publishers, Inc.

Collins, Jim. 2009. How the Mighty Fall: And Why Some Companies Never Give In. New York, NY: HarperCollins Publishers, Inc.

Connellan, Thomas K. Ph.D. 2003. Bringing Out the Best in Others! Three Keys for Business Leaders, Educators, Coaches, and Parents. Austin, TX: Bard Press.

Covey, Stephen R. 1999. Living the 7 Habits – Stories of Courage and Inspiration. New York, NY: City: Simon & Schuster.

Crandall, Frank H., III. 2005. Lessons from the Landscape: My Path to Business Success and Personal Fulfillment. Hope Valley, RI: Wood River Productions.

DarConte, Lorraine A., ed. 2001. Lessons for Success. New York, NY: Barnes & Noble Books.

David, Laurie and Cambria Gordon. 2007. The Down-to-Earth Guide to Global Warming. New York, NY: Orchard Books, an Imprint of Scholastic, Inc.

DiGiacomo, Gigi, Robert King, and Dale Nordquist. 2003. Building a Sustainable Business: A Guide to Developing a Business Plan for Farms and Rural Businesses. St. Paul, MN: Minnesota Institute for Sustainable Agriculture and Sustainable Agriculture Network.

Gillman, Joan with Sarah White. 2001. Business Plans that Work. Avon, MA: Adams Media, a F & W Publications Company.

Gitomer, Jeffrey H. 1994. The Sales Bible. New York, NY: William Morrow and Company, Inc.

Hayward, Steven F. 1997. Churchill on Leadership--Executive Success in the Face of Adversity. Rocklin, CA: Prima Publishing.

Jennings, Ken and John Stahl-Wert. 2003. The Serving Leader—5 Powerful Actions that Will Transform Your Team, Your Business, and Your Community. San Francisco, CA: Berrett-Koehler Publishers, Inc.

Johnson, Spencer. M.D. 2003. The Present – The Gift that Makes You Happier and More Successful at Work and in Life, Today! New York, NY: Doubleday.

Johnson, Spencer. M.D. 2009. Peaks and Valleys: Making Good and Bad Times Work for You at Work and in Life. New York, NY: Atria Books, a division of Simon & Schuster, Inc.

Kaatz, Ron. 1995. Advertising and Marketing Checklists: 107 Proven Checklists to Save Time and Boost Advertising and Marketing Effectiveness, 2nd ed. Lincolnwood, IL: NTC Business Books.

Kabat-Zinn, Jon. 1994. Wherever You Go, There You Are—Mindfulness Meditation in Everyday Life. New York, NY: Hyperion.

Lasher, William. 1994. The Perfect Business Plan Made Simple. New York, NY: Doubleday.

Levine, Stuart R. 2004. The Six Fundamentals of Success – The Rules for Getting It Right for Yourself and Your Organization. New York, NY: Currency Doubleday.

Lohan, Tara, Editor. Water Consciousness: How We All Have to Change to Protect Our Most Critical Resource. 2008. San Francisco, CA: Alter Net Books.

Lyons, John. 1987. Guts: Advertising from the Inside Out. New York, NY: Amacom.

Manchester, William. 1983. The Last Lion: Winston Spencer Churchill; Visions of Glory: 1874-1932. Boston, MA: Little, Brown and Company.

Manchester, William. 1988. The Last Lion: Winston Spencer Churchill; Alone: 1932-1940. Boston, MA: Little, Brown and Company.

Mars, Ross and Jenny. 2007. Getting Started in Permaculture. White River Junction, VT: Chelsea Green Publishing Company.

Maxwell, John C. 1999. The 21 Indispensable Qualities of a Leader – Becoming the Person Others Will Want to Follow. Nashville, TN: Thomas Nelson, Inc.

Maxwell, John C. 2000. Failing Forward – Turning Mistakes Into Stepping Stones for Success. Nashville, TN: Nelson Books.

Maxwell, John C. 2001. The 17 Indisputable Laws of Teamwork – Embrace Them and Empower Your Team. Nashville, TN: Thomas Nelson Publishers.

Maxwell, John C. 2002. Leadership 101. Nashville, TN: Thomas Nelson Publishers.

Maxwell, John C. 2002. The 17 Essential Qualities of a Team Player. Nashville, TN: Thomas Nelson, Inc.

Michaels, Nancy and Debbi J. Karpowicz. 2000. Off the Wall Marketing Ideas. Avon, MA: Adams Media, an F & W Publication Company.

Mollison, Bill with Reny Mia Slay. 2004. Introduction to Permaculture. Tasmania, Australia: A Tagari Publication.

O'Neil, William J. (Introduction). 2004. Business Leaders and Success. New York, NY: McGraw-Hill.

Ogilvy, David. 1983. Ogilvy on Advertising. New York, NY: Random House.

Organic Land Care Committee of the Northeast Organic Farming Association (NOFA), Connecticut and Massachusetts Chapters. 2007. Stevenson, CT: Organic Land Care Committee of the Northeast Organic Farming Association, Connecticut and Massachusetts Chapters.

Real, Terrence. 1997. I Don't Want to Talk About It – Overcoming the Secret Legacy of Male Depression. New York, NY: Scribner.

Ruiz, Don Miguel. 2000. The Four Agreements Companion Book. San Rafael, CA: Amber-Allen Publishing.

Rye, David. 2002. Attracting and Rewarding Outstanding Employees. Newburgh, NY: Entrepreneur Press.

Sandys, Celia and Jonathan Littman. 2003. We Shall Not Fail – The Inspiring Leadership of Winston Churchill. London, England: Penguin Group.

Schwartz, Peter. 1991. The Art of the Long View. New York, NY: Currency Doubleday.

Tolle, Eckhart. 1999. The Power of Now – A Guide to Spiritual Enlightenment. Novato, CA:
    Namaste Publishing and New World Library.

Vander Kooi, Charles. 1996-1998. Trouble-Shooting Your Contracting Business to Cause
    Success. Littleton, CO: Blue Willow, Inc.

Vander Kooi, Charles. 2005. The Complete Business Manual for Contractors. Littleton, CO:
    Vander Kooi and Associates, Inc.

White, Frank, Jon Belber, and Ted Hirsch. A Growing Relationship: The School Garden,
    Classroom and Organic Farm. Cohasset: Friends of Holly Hill Farm, Inc.

Appendix A: Websites with Additional Information

I) <u>Horticultural Licenses, Regulations, and Certifications</u>

A. <u>Pesticide License Information and Regulations</u>
- RI: http://www.dem.ri.gov/programs/bnatres/agricult/faqs.htm
- CT: http://www.ct.gov/dep/cwp/view.asp?a=2709&q=324224&depNav_GID=1643
- MA: http://www.mass.gov/agr/pesticides/, http://www.umassgreeninfo.org/
- NH: http://www.nh.gov/agric/divisions/plant_industry/
- VT: http://www.vermontagriculture.com/
- ME: http://www.maine.gov/agriculture/pesticides/cert/questions.htm
- NY: http://www.dec.ny.gov/permits/209.html
- NJ: http://www.state.nj.us/dep/enforcement/pcp/

B. <u>Aborist License/Certification</u>
- RI: http://www.dem.ri.gov/pubs/regs/regs/forest/arborist.pdf
- CT: http://www.ct.gov/dep/cwp/view.asp?a=2710&q=324234
- MA: http://www.massarbor.org/
- NH: http://www.nharborists.org/id16.html
- VT: http://www.newenglandisa.org/certification.html
- ME: http://www.maine.gov/agriculture/pi/arborist/licensing.htm, http://www.mainearborist.org/
- NY: http://www.nysarborists.com/certify.htm
- NJ: http://www.njarboristsisa.com/

C. <u>Nursery License, Inspection Information</u>
- RI: http://www.dem.ri.gov/programs/bnatres/agricult/nursery.htm
- CT: http://www.ct.gov/caes/cwp/view.asp?a=2821&q=377486
- MA: http://www.mass.gov/agr/farmproducts/plants/index.htm
- NH: http://www.nh.gov/agric/divisions/plant_industry/index.htm
- VT: http://www.vermontagriculture.com/regulations.htm
- ME: http://www.maine.gov/agriculture/pi/horticulture/index.htm
- NY: http://www.agmkt.state.ny.us/nurseryDealers.html
- NJ: http://www.nj.gov/agriculture/divisions/pi/

D. <u>Home Improvement, Contractor License Requirements</u>
- RI: http://www.crb.ri.gov/
- CT: http://www.ct.gov/dcp/site/default.asp

- MA: http://www.contractors-license.org/ma/ma.htm
- NH: http://www.sos.nh.gov/
- VT: http://www.sec.state.vt.us/
- ME: http://www.maine.gov/dep/index.shtml
- NY: http://www.nyc.gov/html/dca/html/licenses/100.shtml
- NJ: http://www.state.nj.us/lps/ca/HIC/

E. Employment Regulations
- RI: http://www.dlt.ri.gov/
- CT: http://www.ctdol.state.ct.us/
- MA: http://www.mass.gov/?pageID=elwdhomepage&L=1&L0=Home&sid=Elwd
- NH: http://www.nh.gov/nhes/
- VT: http://www.labor.vermont.gov/
- ME: http://www.maine.gov/portal/employment/
- NY: http://www.labor.ny.gov/home
- NJ: http://www.state.nj.us/nj/gov/njgov/alphaserv.html

F. Sales Tax Information
- RI: https://www.ri.gov/taxation/business/index.php
- CT: http://www.ct.gov/drs/site/default.asp
- MA: http://www.mass.gov/
- NH: New Hampshire does not have a general sales tax
- VT: http://www.state.vt.us/tax/index.shtml
- ME: http://www.maine.gov/revenue/salesuse/homepage.html
- NY: http://www.tax.ny.gov/
- NJ: http://www.state.nj.us/treasury/taxation/su.shtml

G. Commercial Drivers Licenses
- RI: http://www.dmv.ri.gov/licenses/commercial/index.php
- CT: http://www.ct.gov/dmv/site/default.asp
- MA: http://www.mass.gov/rmv/license/8cdl.htm
- NH: http://www.nh.gov/safety/divisions/dmv/driverlic/
- VT: http://dmv.vermont.gov/licenses/commercial/cdl
- ME: http://www.maine.gov/sos/bmv/licenses/getlicense.html
- NY: http://www.nydmv.state.ny.us/cdl.htm
- NJ: http://www.state.nj.us/mvc/Commercial/index.htm

II) Horticultural and Organic Resources

A. College Horticultural Programs
   - Cornell University Department of Horticulture: http://www.gardening.cornell.edu/
   - Cornell University of Agricultural and Life Sciences: http://www.cals.cornell.edu/
   - University of Connecticut Horticulture Program:
     http://www.plantscience.uconn.edu/horticulture.html
   - University of Rhode Island Horticulture Program: http://cels.uri.edu/pls/,
     http://www.uri.edu/cels/ceoc/
   - University of Massachusetts Extension: http://www.extension.umass.edu/agriculture/
   - United State Department of Agriculture (USDA):
     http://www.usda.gov/wps/portal/usda/usdahome
   - University of Vermont Horticultural Research Center:
     http://www.uvm.edu/pss/dept/hort_farm/
   - University of New Hampshire Horticulture Program:
     http://www.envhorticulture.unh.edu/
   - University of New Hampshire Extension Program:
     http://extension.unh.edu/agric/agbmgmt.htm
   - University of Maine Horticulture Program: http://www.umaine.edu/lhc/

B. Organic Horticulture Information
   - Northeast Organic Farming Association (NOFA): http://www.organiclandcare.net/,
     http://www.ctnofa.org/ (CT), http://www.nofamass.org/ (MA), http://nofari.org/ (RI),
     https://www.nofany.org/ (NY), http://nofanh.org/ (NH), http://nofavt.org/ (VT),
     http://nofanj.org/ (NJ), http://mofga.org/ (ME)
   - Pennsylvania Certified Organic: http://www.paorganic.org/
   - Rodale Institute: http://www.rodaleinstitute.org/

III) Design Associations
   - American Society of Landscape Architects: http://www.asla.org/,
     http://www.riasla.org/ (RI), http://www.ctasla.org/ (CT), http://www.bslaweb.org/
     (MA), http://www.njasla.net/ (NJ), http://www.nyasla.org/index.php (NY),
     http://www.nyuasla.org/ (Upstate NY), http://www.vtasla.org/ (VT)
   - Association of Professional Landscape Designers: http://www.apld.com/,
     http://www.apldne.org/ (New England Chapter)

IV) New England Horticultural Associations

- Cape Cod Landscape Association, Inc.: http://www.capecodlandscape.org
- Connecticut Nursery and Landscape Association: http://www.flowersplantsinCT.com
- Ecological Landscaping Association: http://www.ecolandscaping.org
- Maine Landscape and Nursery Association: http://www.melna.org
- Massachusetts Flower Growers' Association: http://www.massflowergrowers.com
- Massachusetts Horticultural Association: http://www.masshort.org
- New England Grows: http://www.newenglandgrows.org/
- New England Wild Flower Society: http://www.newenglandwild.org
- New Hampshire Landscape Association: http://www.nhlaonline.org
- New Hampshire Plant Growers Association: http://www.nhpga.org
- The Rhode Island Nursery and Landscape Association: http://www.rinla.org
- Vermont Nursery and Landscape Association: http://www.vaph.org
- Arnold Arboretum of Harvard University: http://www.arboretum.harvard.edu
- Blithewold Mansion, Gardens, and Arboretum: http://www.blithewold.org/
- Tower Hill Botanic Garden: http://www.towerhillbg.com
- Dig Safe System, Inc.: http://www.digsafe.com
- Irrigation Association of New England: http://www.IrrigationAssociationNE.org
- Professional Landscape Network (PLANET): http://www.landcarenetwork.org
- The Underground: http://www.theunderground.pbwiki.com

V) Invasive Plant Information

- RI: http://www.ririvers.org/wsp/class_7/invasiveplantlist.htm
- CT: http://www.hort.uconn.edu/cipwg/
- MA: http://www.massnature.com/Plants/Invasives/invasiveplants.htm
- NH: http://www.nhfgc.org/invasive.htm
- VT: http://www.vtinvasiveplants.org/
- ME: http://umaine.edu/publications/2500e/
- NY: http://nyis.info/
- NJ: http://www.nj.nrcs.usda.gov/technical/agriculture/invasives_exotics.html
- New England: http://nbii-nin.ciesin.columbia.edu/ipane/

VI) <u>Business Resources</u>
- Angel Capital Association: http://www.angelcapitalassociation.org/
- National Association of Small Business Investment Companies: http://www.nasbic.org/
- Better Business Bureaus: http://www.bbb.org/
- National Association of Women Business Owners: http://www.nawbo.org/
- QuickenBooks Business Software: http://quickbooks.intuit.com/
- Service Corps of Retired Executives (SCORE): http://www.score.org
- Small Business Administration of the US Government (SBA): http://www.sba.gov/

A. <u>Business Plans</u>
- Business Plans: http://www.Bplans.com
- Rhonda Abrams Online: http://www.rhondaonline.com/
- The Planning Shop Books and Tools for Entrepreneurs: http://www.planningshop.com/

B. <u>Branding</u>
- Entrepreneur: http://www.entrepreneur.com/
- The Write Market: http://www.thewritemarket.com/
- A Home-Based Business Online: http://www.ahbbo.com/

C. <u>Marketing Plans for Small Businesses</u>
- Smart Marketing Basics for your Small-Medium Business: http://www.smbmarketer.com/
- Simple, Effective and Affordable Small Business Marketing: http://www.ducttapemarketing.com/
- Microsoft Business for Small & Midsize Companies: http://www.microsoft.com/business/en-us/

D. <u>Company – Legal Entities</u>
- Wikipedia: http://en.wikipedia.org/wiki/Corporation
- IRS – Small Business: http://www.irs.gov/businesses/small/

E. <u>Hiring and Firing Employees</u>
- Bloomberg Businessweek: http://www.businessweek.com/managing/team/hiring_firing/
- TTG Consultants, Human Resources Consultants: http://www.ttgconsultants.com/articles/hiringAndFiring.html
- About.com, Small Business Information: http://sbinformation.about.com/od/hiringfiring/

F. Employee Evaluations
- http://business.lovetoknow.com/wiki/Sample_Completed_Employee_Evaluations

G. Leadership
- Free career help, business training, and organizational development:
  http://www.businessballs.com/leadership.htm
- Free Management Library™: http://managementhelp.org/ldr_dev/ldr_dev.htm
- Winston Churchill Leadership: http://www.winston-churchill-leadership.com/

Appendix B: Measurement, Conversion, and Equivalent Tables for Horticulturalists

I. Area Measurements

1. Rectangle: area = length x width (a = l x w)
2. Triangle: area = base x height ÷ 2 (a = b x h ÷ 2)
3. Circle: area = π (3.14) x radius squared (a = 3.14 x r²)
4. Oval: area = length x width x 0.8 (a = l x w x 0.8)
5. Irregular shape area (offset method)[1]:
    a) Determine the center line (longest axis of area); label the ends A and B.
    b) Mark offset lines at a 90° angle to the center line. Determine the number of offset lines needed to divide the center line into equal segments (for example, segments of 5', 10', 20', etc.).
    c) Measure the length of each offset line.
    d) Add up all of the lengths of the offset lines and multiply that total by the distance between offset lines. The result is the approximate square footage of the shape to be measured (within 5% or so).

    Example: Find the area of an irregular landscape bed.

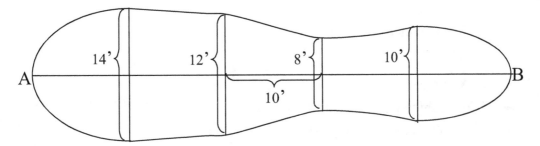

Answer:
1. Measure the center line distance: A to B = 50'.
2. Establish offset lines at regular intervals: in this example, every 10'.
3. Measure the offset lines and add them: 14' + 12' + 8' + 10' = 44'.
4. Multiply the offset line total length (44') by the interval distance (10'). The result is the area of the irregular bed in square feet: 44' x 10' = 440 sq. ft.

II.   Dry and Liquid Measures

    1.   Dry Measure
- 3 level teaspoons = 1 tablespoon (0.5 oz.)
- 16 level tablespoons = 1 cup (8 oz.)
- 2 cups = 1 pint (16 oz.)
- 2 pints = 1 quart (32 oz.)
- 8 quarts = 1 peck (256 oz.)
- 4 pecks = 1 bushel (1,024 oz.)

    2.   Liquid Measure
- 50-60 drops = 1 level teaspoon
- 3 level teaspoons = 1 level tablespoon
- 2 level tablespoons = 1 fluid ounce
- 8 fluid ounces = 1 cup
- 2 cups = 1 pint
- 2 pints = 1 quart
- 4 quarts = 1 gallon
- 31.5 gallons = 1 barrel

    3.   Square Measure
- 144 square inches = 1 square foot
- 9 square feet = 1 square yard

    4.   Cubic Measure
- 1,728 cubic inches = 1 cubic foot
- 27 cubic feet = 1 cubic yard

III. Material Coverage Table

Use this table to figure out the volume, in cubic yards, of material (loam, mulch, compost, etc.) needed to cover areas at various depths.

Table 11: Material Coverage Table

Depth of Material	Sq. Ft. Volume Factor	Cu. Ft. ÷ 27 = Cubic Yards
0.5"	Sq. ft. ÷ 24 = cu. ft.	
1"	Sq. ft. ÷ 12 = cu. ft.	
2"	Sq. ft. ÷ 6 = cu. ft.	
3"	Sq. ft. ÷ 4 = cu. ft.	
4"	Sq. ft. ÷ 3 = cu. ft.	
5"	Sq. ft. ÷ 2.4 = cu. ft.	
6"	Sq. ft. ÷ 6 = cu. ft.	For all cubic footages: cu. ft. ÷ 27 = cu. yds.
7"	Sq. ft. ÷ 1.71 = cu. ft.	
8"	Sq. ft. ÷ 1.5 = cu. ft.	
9"	Sq. ft. ÷ 1.33 = cu. ft.	
10"	Sq. ft. ÷ 1.2 = cu. ft.	
11"	Sq. ft. ÷ 1.09 = cu. ft.	
12"	Sq. ft. ÷ 1 = cu. ft.	

Example: How many cubic yards of compost would be needed to cover an 8' x 30' perennial bed to a depth of 3 inches?

Answer:
1. (l x w = sq. ft.): 8 ft. x 30 ft. = 240 sq. ft.
2. (sq. ft./ depth factor = cu. ft.): 240 sq. ft./ 4 = 60 cu. ft.
3. (cu. ft./ 27 = cu. yds.): 60 cu. ft./ 27 = 2.22 cu. yds.

IV.   Weight Conversion Table

Table 12: Weight Conversion Table

Unit	Multiply Factor	Result
ounces (oz.)	0.0625	pounds (lbs.)
pounds (lbs.)	16	ounces (oz.)
pounds (lbs.)	0.0005	tons
tons	2,000	pounds (lbs.)

Examples:

You have 2.5 lbs. of insecticidal soap to apply–how many ounces is this?
Answer: 2.5 lbs. x 16 oz. = 40 oz.

10.7 tons of crushed stone are being delivered–how many pounds is this delivery?
Answer: 10.7 tons x 2,000 lbs./tons = 21,400 lbs.

V.   Materials Weight Table*

Table 13: Materials Weight Table

Material	Lb./cu. ft.	Lb./ cu. yd.	Cu. yd./ton	Ton/cu. yd.
Loam (dry, compacted)	95 lbs.	2,565 lbs.	0.78	1.28
Gravel	125 lbs.	3,375 lbs.	0.59	1.69
Sand (dry)	100 lbs.	2,700 lbs.	0.74	1.35
Clay (dry)	100 lbs.	2,700 lbs.	0.74	1.35

* Weights are approximate; exact weight will depend on the specific material and whether the materials are wet, dry, or mixed ingredients.

Examples:

How many tons of sand are in a 10 cu. yd. truck load?
Answer: 10 cu. yd. ÷ 0.74 = 13.50 tons

If you order 30 tons of loam, how many cubic yards would the delivery be?
Answer: 30 tons ÷ 1.28 = 23.4 cu. yds.

VI.   Volume Conversion Table

Table 14: Volume Conversion Table

Unit	Multiplier Factor	Result
sq. ft.	x 3	cu. ft.
cu. ft.	÷ 3	sq. ft.
cu. ft.	x 0.037	cu. yds.
cu. yds.	x 27	cu. ft.
cu. ft.	÷ 27	cu. yds.

Examples:

How many cubic yards are there in 300 cubic feet of mulch?

Answer: 300 cu. ft. / 27 = 11.11 cu. yds.

How many cubic feet are there in 22 cubic yards?

Answer: 22 cu. yds. x 27 = 594 cu. ft.

VII.   Liquid Equivalent Table

This table can be used to determine the quantity of concentrated chemical to dilute with water when using less than the 100 gallon volume for a specific application.

Table 15: Liquid Equivalent Table

	Amount (Volume) of Water			
	100 gallons	25 gallons	5 gallons	1 gallons
Amount of Concentrated Chemical to Mix with Water	2 gal.	2 qt.	12.87 oz.	2.5 oz.
	1 gal.	1 qt.	6.33 oz.	1.25 oz.
	2 qt.	1 pt.	3.25 oz.	0.62 oz.
	1 qt.	0.5 pt.	1.56 oz.	0.31 oz.
	1.5 pt.	6 oz.	1.2 oz.	0.25 oz.
	1 pt.	4 oz.	0.87 oz.	1 tsp.
	8 oz.	2 oz.	0.44 oz.	0.5 tsp.
	4oz.	1 oz.	0.20 oz.	0.25 tsp.

Example: If you were applying 3 gallons of a spray application at the 1 gallon/100 gallons dilution rate, how many ounces of chemical concentrate would you need to dilute with water?

Answer: a) To make 1 gallon of a spray that is diluted at a rate of 1 gallon/100 gallons, use 1.25 oz./gal. (last column of table, second row)

b) 1.25 oz. x 3 gallons = 3.75 ounces concentrated chemical needed

VIII.   The Difference between Markup and Margin

1. Markup is the percentage added to the cost of goods or a service to arrive at a selling price.

Example: A 5'-6' blue spruce costs $100; to get the selling price, add a 50% markup ($50): $100 + $50 = $150 (the selling price).

2. Gross Profit Margin is the selling price of an item or service minus the cost, then divided by the selling price.

Example: The blue spruce selling price ($150) minus the cost ($100), then divided by the selling price ($150), gives the Gross Profit Margin: $150 – $100 = $50; $50 ÷ $150 = 0.33. Multiplying 0.33 by 100 gives a 33% Gross Profit Margin. In this example, a 50% markup results in a 33% Gross Profit Margin.

3. Markups are generally used to set the price of a good or service. Margins are useful to analyze sales and expenses to find the appropriate percentage to meet expenses and a desired profit. Gross profit margins are useful to compare with the previous year's markups used with plants, materials, and services to see where markup percentages may need to be adjusted to ensure the profit desired.

Table 16: Markup vs. Gross Profit Margin

Markup vs. Gross Profit Margin Table		
Markup %	Margin %	Multiplier % x cost to achieve margin
15%	13%	115% (multiply by 1.15)
20%	16.7%	120% (multiply by 1.2)
25%	20%	125% (multiply by 1.25)
33%	25%	133% (multiply by 1.33)
40%	28.6%	140% (multiply by 1.4)
50%	33%	150% (multiply by 1.5)
75%	42.9%	175% (multiply by 1.75)
100%	50%	200% (multiply by 2)
150%	60%	250% (multiply by 2.5)
200%	67.3%	300% (multiply by 3)

Example: 1 yard of compost cost $45. I want a 33% gross profit margin–by what number do I multiply the cost to determine my selling price?

Answer: Find 33% in the "Margin %" column; the corresponding markup is 50% and the multiplier is 150% (multiply by 1.5).
Compost cost is $45 x 1.5 = $67.50 (selling price).
Gross Profit Margin = $67.50 (selling price) –$45 (cost) = $22.50 (profit).
Gross Profit Margin % = $22.50 (profit) ÷ $67.50 (selling price) = 33%.

Endnotes

Chapter 5

[1] Rhonda Abrams, Business Plan in a Day: Get it Done Right, Get it Done Fast™ (Palo Alto, CA: The Planning Shop™, 2005), bk.

Chapter 8

[1] Bob Adams, MBA, Adams Streetwise Small Business Start-Up (Avon, MA: Adams Media, an F & W Publications Company, 1996), 333.
[2] Wikipedia
[3] Wikipedia
[4] Wikipedia

Chapter 11

[1] Management 2000 LLC, Providence, RI 02903.
[2] Charles Vander Kooi, The Complete Business Manual for Contractors (Littleton, CO: Vander Kooi & Associates, Inc., 2005), 36.
[3] Ibid, 49-55.

Chapter 12

[1] Charles Vander Kooi, The Complete Business Manual for Contractors (Littleton, CO: Vander Kooi & Associates, Inc., 2005), 49-55.

Chapter 14

[1] Jeffrey H. Gitomer, The Sales Bible: The Ultimate Sales Resource (New York: William Morrow and Company, Inc., 1994), 182.
[2] Kenneth Blanchard and Sheldon M. Bowles, Raving Fans: A Revolutionary Approach to Customer Service (New York, NY: William Morrow and Company, Inc., 1993), 40.
[3] Jeffrey H. Gitomer, The Sales Bible: The Ultimate Sales Resource (New York: William Morrow and Company, Inc., 1994), 68-70.

Chapter 15

[1] Susan Ward, http://sbinfocanada.about.com/od/leadership/g/leadership.htm

[2] Ian Chamberlin, http://www.winston-churchill-leadership.com/drucker-definition.html

[3] Ian Chamberlin, http://www.winston-churchill-leadership.com/adair-definition.html

[4] http://www.businessdictionary.com/definition/leadership.html

[5] John C. Maxwell, The 21 Indispensable Qualities of a Leader: Becoming the Person Others Will Want to Follow, (Nashville, TN: Thomas Nelson, Inc., 1999), bk.

[6] Ibid, bk.

[7] Ken Blanchard, Patricia Zigarini, and Drea Zigarini, Leadership and the One Minute Manager: Increasing Effectiveness through Situational Leadership (New York, NY: William Morrow and Company, Inc., 1985), bk.

[8] www.goodreads.com/author/quotes/1655.Mark_Twain (November 2010).

[9] Ken Jennings and John Stahl-Wert, The Serving Leader: Powerful Actions that will Transform Your Team, Your Business, and Your Community (San Francisco, CA: Berrett-Koehler Publishers, Inc., 2003), chap. 18.

[10] Stuart R. Levine, The Six Fundamentals of Success (New York, NY: Currency Doubleday, 2004), bk.

Chapter 16

[1] Ken Mazur, personal communication, September 2004.

Chapter 17

[1] Spencer Johnson, M.D., Peaks and Valleys (New York, NY: Atria Books, a Division of Simon & Schuster, Inc., 2009), 65.

[2] Ken Blanchard, The Heart of a Leader (Tulsa: Honor Books, 1999), 18.

[3] Spencer Johnson, M.D., Peaks and Valleys (New York, NY: Atria Books, a Division of Simon & Schuster, Inc., 2009), bk.

[4] John C. Maxwell, The 17 Essential Qualities of a Team Player (Nashville, TN: Thomas Nelson, Inc., 2002), 130.

[5] Spencer Johnson, M.D., Who Moved My Cheese? (New York, NY: G.P. Putnam and Sons, 1998), bk.

Chapter 18

[1] Peter Schwartz, The Art of the Long View (New York, NY: Currency Doubleday, 1991), bk.

[2] Eleanor Sterling and Erin Vintinner, "How much is left? An overview of the crisis," in Water Consciousness, Tara Lohan, ed. (San Francisco, CA: Alter Net Books, 2008), Chap. 1.

[3] Ibid, Chap. 1.

[4] Kimberly Stoner, Ph.D., "Why Organic?" in The NOFA Organic Lawn and Turf Handbook (Stevenson, CT: Organic Land Care Committee of the Northeast Organic Farming Association, Connecticut and Massachusetts Chapters, 2007), Chap. 1.

[5] Laurie David and Cambria Gordon, The Down-to-Earth Guide to Global Warming (New York, NY: Orchard Books, an Imprint of Scholastic, Inc., 2007), bk.

[6] Ibid, 26-27.

[7] Ibid, 24-25.

[8] Bill Mollison, with Reny Mia Slay, Introduction to Permaculture (Tasmania, Australia: A Tagari Publication, 2004), bk.

[9] Ross and Jenny Mars, Getting Started in Permaculture (White River Jct., VT: Chelsea Green Publishing Company, 2007), 1-2.

[10] John C. Maxwell, Failing Forward: Turning Mistakes into Stepping Stones for Success (Nashville, TN: Thomas Nelson Publishers, 2000), 115.

[11] Rabbi Harold Kushner, Life Quotes (http://www.about-personal-growth.com/life-quotes.html).

Appendix B

[1] Nick Christians, Michael L. Agnew, The Mathematics of Turfgrass Maintenance (Hoboken, New Jersey: John Wiley & Sons, Inc., 2000), 7-9.

<u>Books Available by Frank H. Crandall III</u>

<u>Lessons from the Landscape: My Path to Business Success and Personal Fulfillment</u> (2005)
$19.95 + Shipping and Handling

<u>The *Essential* Horticultural Business Handbook: Proven Techniques, Forms, and Resources to Make Your Small Business More Focused, Organized…and Profitable!</u> (2011)
$29.95 + Shipping and Handling

<u>Speaking Engagements</u>

Frank is a popular speaker who has addressed audiences at green industry trade shows, conferences, and seminars throughout New England and the U.S. Topics like the future of horticulture in New England, transitioning your landscape business from traditional to organic land care, and improving your business estimating and job costing, have entertained, educated, and improved small business owners for over 25 years.

<u>Business Consultations</u>

One of Frank's goals in life is to assist horticultural businesses to become more organized, focused, and profitable. Using his 38 years of small business experiences (successes *and* failures), he will share the valuable lessons learned to help your company reach its true potential!

<u>G.E.M. (Growth, Effectiveness, and Management) Seminars</u>

Annually, Frank hosts a highly acclaimed, in-depth seminar covering such topics as estimating and job costing; hiring, retaining, and firing employees; and management tips for success. These comprehensive, day-long seminars have been well received throughout the industry for over seven years.

<u>Contact Information</u>

Mailing: Frank Crandall
P.O. Box 132
Wood River Junction, RI 02894

Email: <u>FrankCrandall3@gmail.com</u>

CPSIA information can be obtained
at www.ICGtesting.com
Printed in the USA
LVHW051911120123
737043LV00006B/441